D0908128

Understanding
A Tale of Two Cities

A caricature satirizing the inequality of taxation in France before the Revolution:
an elderly peasant carries on his back a bishop and a nobleman.

UNDERSTANDING

A Tale of Two Cities

A STUDENT CASEBOOK TO ISSUES, SOURCES, AND HISTORICAL DOCUMENTS

George Newlin

The Greenwood Press
"Literature in Context" Series
Claudia Durst Johnson, Series Editor

GREENWOOD PRESS
Westport, Connecticut • London

Library of Congress Cataloging-in-Publication Data

Newlin, George, 1931–
    Understanding A tale of two cities : a student casebook to issues,
    sources, and historical documents / George Newlin.
        p.   cm. — (The Greenwood Press "Literature in context" series;
    ISSN 1074–598X)
    Includes bibliographical references and index.
    ISBN 0–313–29939–0 (alk. paper)
    1. Dickens, Charles, 1812–1870.   Tale of two cities.   2. Dickens,
Charles, 1812–1870.   Tale of two cities—Sources.   3. France—
History—Revolution, 1789–1799—Literature and the revolution.
I. Title.   II. Series.
PR4571.N49   1998
823'.8—DC21   98–4803

British Library Cataloguing in Publication Data is available.

Library of Congress Catalog Card Number: 98–4803
ISBN: 0–313–29939–0
ISSN: 1074–598X

First published in 1998

Greenwood Press, 88 Post Road West, Westport, CT 06881
An imprint of Greenwood Publishing Group, Inc.

Printed in the United States of America

The paper used in this book complies with the
Permanent Paper Standard issued by the National
Information Standards Organization (Z39.48–1984).

10 9 8 7 6 5 4 3 2 1

To Sandy and Fred Rose
from a grateful user of the
New York Public Library

Contents

Introduction

A Tale of Two Cities is one of the most successful, if not *the* most successful, historical novels ever written. One of Charles Dickens's shortest works, it does not waste a word in telling a humanly touching, suspenseful tale against the background of one of the most bizarre and bloody events in history: the French Revolution of 1789 and its aftermath, culminating in the Terror of 1793–94.

There is no way to estimate the number of copies of the novel that have been sold since its publication in 1859, but it is probably greater than for any other work of Dickens—and that means for any other novel written in the nineteenth century.

A Tale of Two Cities has been translated into virtually every language and is read in schools and colleges all over the world, for it combines two things teachers and students value: the stature and endurability of a classic, and the page-turning grip of a masterful plot with a completely satisfying closure. The plot is regarded by Sir John Shuckburgh as "beyond comparison, better constructed, more elaborate, and of more sustained interest than that of any of Dickens's other books."

The novel contains some of Dickens's most famous literary passages as well as ideas about the nature of the Self and other matters which seem as advanced and timely today as they were when they were written.

A study of the novel by itself, without reference to its historical context, would naturally be devoted primarily to consideration of its literary elements, discussed in Chapter 1. But to understand what Dickens accomplished, and what he did *not* attempt, it is necessary to broaden our scope. The special case of this novel provides the opportunity to consider carefully the book that inspired it: Thomas Carlyle's *The French Revolution* (1837).

Chapters 3 and 4 report on the contents of the Carlyle work. Their length need not intimidate the reader: they can be regarded as reference guides—not to be read straight through, though teachers not recently exposed to the historical aspects may find them valuable refreshers. Chapter 3 gives the sequence of events, first presented in a schematic Chronology, including the incidents of the novel italicized to distinguish them as fictional, and then as told in Carlyle. Chapter 3 also identifies the principal figures of the Revolution; many are referred to elsewhere in quoted texts.

Chapter 5 is designed to permit comparative analysis of Carlyle and Dickens and exploration of some aspects of the fiction-making process. By looking at a number of major and minor elements in *The French Revolution* and noticing those Dickens chose to use and those he did not, those he transformed and those he emphasized (or de-emphasized), we can learn a good deal about how fiction is created—at least, when Dickens is doing it.

Besides its literary importance, and its significance as an influence on Dickens, Carlyle's work is useful to us because, once written, it became the principal, authoritative lens through which Englishmen viewed the Revolution. One of the things to bear in mind in studying *A Tale of Two Cities* is that at the time of the Revolution and for decades afterward the English were mightily concerned about the possibility of its "happening here." After the Napoleonic Wars ended in 1815, the movement for economic and political reform in England grew and grew, but there was a great deal of resistance to it from elements in the upper classes.

Would this slow, inexorable upheaval be contained and permitted to work itself out peacefully? Or might catastrophe strike in London as it had in Paris? Dickens himself, with his strong social concerns for the poor, for their education, sanitation, recreation, and general happiness, often warned his public that if steps to improve conditions were not quickly taken, there could be a rising (see Chapter 8). In thinking about *A Tale of Two Cities* it is as well to remember that fiction can be (and often has been) written to influence opinion as well as to entertain.

AN ASSIGNMENT FOR A GOOD READER

Anatole France wrote a relatively brief novel about life in Paris during the days of the Revolution called *Les Dieux ont soif (The Gods Are Athirst*, 1912), which is apparently not read in schools here. Many consider it his finest work, and it is an excellent way to see the Terror from a French point of view.

SOURCE REFERENCES

Of the works cited, three are particularly suitable for secondary school library reference. One is a recent, very readable history of the French Revolution, *Citizens*, by Simon Schama (1989), which is valuable for its analysis of conditions *before* the conflagration and the ways in which France was already making great forward progress, more interrupted than accelerated by the events of 1789–94. History students will find this generously illustrated work a pleasure as well as an important learning tool. Also valuable is *The Age of Napoleon*, by Will and Ariel Durant (1975), a well-written, popular history of the period from 1789 to Napoleon's fall in 1815.

A fresh, detailed, and absorbing book is Christopher Hibbert's *The Days of the French Revolution* (1980). It is for the general reader for whom the subject may be new. It carries the story to Napoleon's *coup* of 18th Brumaire, 1799. There is a rich illustrations section.

Locations of material in *A Tale of Two Cities* refer to book (small Roman) and chapter (Arabic number), e.g., *TTC* iii 15 (the final soliloquy). The present work omits page numbers because editions vary, and many different versions are used in schools. Citations from Carlyle's *The French Revolution* are to Part (large Roman), Book (small Roman), and chapter (Arabic), e.g., II iii 5. Other works by Dickens (also one by Anthony Trollope) quoted herein are cited by abbreviation and chapter (*not* page, for the reason given above). Works by others are cited by author abbreviation (e.g., SS for Schama, DD for Durant) and page number and will be found in the Suggested Readings and Works Cited at the end of chapters.

GLOSSARY

There are words, phrases, and references in *A Tale of Two Cities*, *The French Revolution*, and other texts quoted that may be obscure to today's readers. Many of these are listed in the Glossary, with definitions or explanations. Do not overlook this aid.

1 ———————————

A Literary Analysis of *A Tale of Two Cities*

No literary work, no matter how immense, covers everything within its potential scope. Aside from the sheer impracticability of the task, anything approaching such a result would be unreadable. The art of fiction, particularly when it is historical, is the art of selection: of themes; of the attributes to be exemplified in the characters; of pace, tone, language, point of view, time sequence, and myriad other elements, of which the story is only one. And of course there is technique: the use of certain literary devices to achieve effects.

THEMES

The success of *A Tale of Two Cities*, one of the most popular, universally read novels of the last two hundred years, can be attributed to Dickens's artful setting of a touching human story against the background of the world-shaking events of the French Revolution, and to its powerful, universal themes. Among these themes, the greatest seems to be that of Sacrifice, for a cause greater than oneself, as the road to self-fulfillment. A counter-theme is Retribution: the inexorable devastation wrought by a people wronged past all enduring. And underlying these is Human Loyalty—benign and sympathetic in the case of the Manettes, father and daughter, and Miss Pross; appalling though understandable in the case of Madame Defarge, who can never forget what the Evrémondes did to her family.

The unifying idea of Resurrection, discussed in the last paragraph of this chapter, is both a theme and a literary device.

Another theme, particular rather than universal, is the resemblances and parallels Dickens wants us to see between London and Paris. Though they will be greatly overshadowed by the Paris tumbrils, Dickens cites first the London carts and coaches, in which "pale travellers set out continually on a violent passage into the other world" from the criminal court and prison of Old Bailey (*TTC* ii 2). Later, before he depicts the mob in Paris, he gives us a London crowd, which "in those times stopped at nothing, and was a monster much dreaded" (*TTC* ii 14).

CHARACTERS

Readers of Dickens have often noticed that his most memorable characters tend to be the eccentrics, the odd-balls in his works. In *A Tale of Two Cities* there are few of these: Miss Pross and Jerry Cruncher are the two most notable. The pushing, shouldering Stryver is there as a foil; he is not really entertaining. Probably Dickens felt that, with the suspenseful plot he had contrived, he had no need to hold the reader's interest with personal peculiarities. So, Sydney Carton, Charles Darnay, Lucie Manette, the good Doctor Manette, and Jarvis Lorry all seem relatively normal people, who in other circumstances would not be very interesting.

The same might even be true of the Defarges, husband and wife. Had they not had a revolution to fight, their lives might have been routine, humdrum, and not worth investigating.

But in this novel, the force which moves and shakes is an *impersonal* one. Its impact on character is felt most strongly when we consider the two principal antagonists: Sydney Carton and Madame Defarge. In the former case, we seem to have a spoiled man who has somehow lost his nerve and his self-respect and bitterly knows it. He gets the chance to do a noble thing and, in doing it, redeems his wasted life. But, had there been no such opportunity, we must suspect that he would have gone on in his downward track, drinking more and enjoying it less, and at some not too distant point being cast off by the now affluent Stryver—the man who has used him to his own great benefit—when he needs him no longer.

Madame Defarge is cut altogether from other cloth. She has never lacked for backbone, and we feel that she would have made her powerful way in the world regardless of circumstances. In her fate, Dickens teaches the lesson that relentless implacability, unrelieved by any sense of proportion, let alone mercy, will meet the end expressed in the old saying about those who live by the sword. But she is truly an

Renée Bordereau (called Langevin), who fought *against* the Revolution in the Vendée region of western France, could have been Dickens's inspiration for Madame Defarge (from the French *Bibliothèque Nationale*).

actor on the stage Dickens provides: all the others by comparison seem like *re*actors.

PACE

It is fascinating to take an overview of *A Tale of Two Cities* in terms of narrative pace. The opening scene of the Dover mail lumbering painfully up a long hill starts us off at an agonizingly slow rate, set by the exhausted horses surrounded by fog and darkness. At the end of the book, on the other hand, we are whirled along at breathtaking speed—in a horse-drawn coach once more—but no matter how fast we move it seems not enough, for the occupants' fear of pursuit grips the reader as surely as it grips them.

In between, Dickens contrives a very gradual acceleration, broken by pauses for breath, which comes to the final, protracted climax introduced by our sight of Madame Defarge taking her determined way through the Paris streets, heading for the apartment the reader knows is no longer occupied by her prey.

The final soliloquy, however, seems to have no pace at all, for the narrative is over: we are spending a moment in someone's mind. We are endowed, for an instant, with a godlike ability to see the future. We achieve, with Carton, the "peace which passeth all understanding." The sudden shock of release Dickens gives the reader in this, the most famous epilogue in fiction, is almost *too* much: emotions well up, often tears are shed—for Carton, for the happy family he has saved, for innocence victimized.

TONE

Tone is achieved by language, chosen to achieve certain kinds of psychological effects. For example, there is the blood-chilling sarcasm of the first chapter's early warning Dickens gives of blood to come:

> Under the guidance of her Christian pastors, [France] entertained herself, besides, with such humane achievements as sentencing a youth to have his hands cut off, his tongue torn out with pincers, and his body burned alive, because he had not kneeled down in the rain to do honour to a dirty procession of monks which passed within his view, at a distance of some fifty or sixty yards. (*TTC* i 1)

Dickens was an absolute master at establishing tone and used different tones to suit different psychological situations. The famous "coffin-chase," for example, takes a horrific situation (a son watching his very own father digging up a coffin containing a recently buried dead human being) and applies an overlay of macabre humor. "Curiosity kills a cat": in this case a naughty boy's chances for a good night's sleep. The reader doesn't know whether to shudder or laugh, and probably does both.

LANGUAGE

Is there a more famous passage in literature than the first paragraph of this novel? "It was the best of times, it was the worst of times, it was the age of wisdom, it was the age of foolishness, it was the epoch of belief, it was the epoch of incredulity, it was the season of Light, it was the season of Darkness." "Times," "age," "epoch," "season"—we are thrust at once into the Dickensian rhythm, our ears already tingling to the sonorousness of the language even as we are lulled by its simplicity and the variation of the phrases as the crescendo builds. And then, suddenly, just as we think we are entering orbit, we are jolted back to earth: "in short, the period was so far like the present" and a complex, almost clumsy finish which takes a little thinking about before we get it.

Here is Dickens warning us that we are going to experience an absorbing drama—violent, disruptive, earth-shaking, and deeply moving—even as he tells us that things are not all that different *right now*: that this is not escapist fiction but rather a story with lessons for us to learn and apply in our lives.

One of the finest passages in all of Dickens's works comes at the beginning of Chapter 3 of Book 1. It comments on the isolation in which, in the last analysis, every individual spends his entire life—family, friends, and loved ones to the contrary notwithstanding. This, he says, is man's "natural and not to be alienated [removed, or escaped from] inheritance" and thus sets a boundary which no man can pass. It is profound, philosophical, beautiful; and it is here, so very early in the book, without explanation or any real context. It is stated in the first person: "My friend is dead, my neighbour is dead, my love, the darling of my soul, is dead." Yet the book's denouement might suggest that the boundary can be passed after all if the circumstances are extraordinary enough.

Another case of what seems like language for its own sake is the remarkable allusion to what today's occultists call Akashic Records:

> Château and hut, stone face and dangling figure, the red stain on the stone floor, and the pure water in the village well—thousands of acres of land—a whole province of France—all France itself—lay under the night sky, concentrated into a faint hair-breadth line. So does a whole world, with all its greatnesses and littlenesses, lie in a twinkling star. And as mere human knowledge can split a ray of light and analyse the manner of its composition, so, sublimer intelligences may read in the feeble shining of this earth of ours, every thought and act, every vice and virtue, of every responsible creature on it. (*TTC* ii 15)

POINT OF VIEW

An author can decide to tell a story from the point of view of a principal character, through whose eyes the reader sees all the action. Sometimes, this even takes the form of narration in the first person. Dickens's great novel, *David Copperfield*, is a supreme example. At the other extreme is the omniscient narrator, the impersonal storyteller who knows everyone's motives and what is happening everywhere.

In between is the style which alternates between objective depiction from the outside and subjective observation from within. And there is another way, exemplified in the early passage on the Self we have mentioned above, where the first person is used, as though philosophically, by the writer himself.

A fine example of the subjective approach is Jarvis Lorry's meditation in the coach as he rides toward Dover, when he seems to see Doctor Manette (and we know instinctively that we are seeing him as he is and has been). The Carton soliloquy at the end is another.

TIME SEQUENCE

At first blush, *A Tale of Two Cities* seems to move along in strict, and extremely explicit, chronological order, with time gaps between plateaus of action. It begins, "It was the year of Our Lord one thousand seven hundred and seventy-five." Chapter 1 of the second book, called "Five Years Later," narrates Charles Darnay's trial for treason, and Chapter 6 tells us immediately that "the waves of four months had rolled over" that trial. Chapter 10's first words are, "More months, to the number of twelve, have come and gone." Succeeding chapters tell us the month, sometimes the day.

Then the sequence is told in the human terms of courtship, marriage, and the arrival of children, and in Chapter 21 we are brought to July 1789 and to the fall of the Bastille. In Chapter 24, we jump to August 1792, when Charles Darnay receives a letter (dated July 21) from his former servant Gabelle and decides to go to France to help him. Book The Third, "The Track of a Storm," gives us the headlong action Darnay has precipitated, describes the massacre of September 1792 in "The Grindstone," and tells of Lucie's long, long wait for her husband's trial. Suddenly, we are in the Terror of 1793–94. And suddenly we are not: it is December 1767, and Doctor Manette is telling us how he came to be immured in prison ten years before. We have almost a feeling of vertigo as we are plunged into the despotic, frozen, seemingly immutable world of the *lettre de cachet*, the infamous means aristocrats could use to

jail their enemies without trial or accusation, indefinitely or forever, out of time, out of contact, out of any hope.

And then the present re-erupts, and Dickens whirls us on to the
finish and, wonder of wonders, on into the future of a "beautiful
city and a brilliant people rising from this abyss." Dickens's use of
time is breathtakingly adroit: the high-wire act of a master.

TECHNIQUE

Dickens is the supreme humorist of the English language. He is
irrepressible, even in the gloomiest circumstances. One way he
uses his gift is for *comic relief*: the device every reader of *Macbeth*
remembers, exemplified by the "porter scene" directly following
Duncan's murder. A fine example in *A Tale of Two Cities* is the
coffin-chase, when little Jerry Cruncher thinks the coffin he has
just spied his father digging up is racing him home to bed (*TTC* ii
14).

Dickens is an expert at *foreshadowing*, hinting now at what is
to come. A humorous example occurs after Jerry Cruncher hears
the password: "Recalled to life." He says to himself, " 'You'd be
in a Blazing bad way, if recalling to life was to come into fashion,
Jerry!' " (*TTC* i 2). It's a long time before we can begin to guess
what he means, and one wonders whether the reader will remember this moment. Another instance is Miss Pross's laying "a brawny
hand" on Lorry's chest and sending him flying. "('I really think
this must be a man!' was Mr Lorry's breathless reflection)" (*TTC* i
5), and the alert reader will find her success in the struggle with
Madame Defarge (*TTC* iii 14) less surprising.

Of course, there cannot be Dickens without *humor* even in so
serious and tragic a story as *A Tale of Two Cities*. See, for instance,
his description of the bank clerks at Tellson's: "When they took a
young man into Tellson's London house, they hid him somewhere
till he was old. They kept him in a dark place, like a cheese, until
he had the full Tellson flavour and blue-mould upon him" (*TTC* ii
1). It is worthwhile noticing how he lightens a dark and gloomy
story with asides like this, and even with full-blown episodes like
the coffin-chase. Another way Dickens works in humor is by using
many words where few would do, as: "His surname was Cruncher,
and on the youthful occasion of his renouncing by proxy the works
of darkness, in the easterly parish church of Houndsditch, he had

received the added appellation of Jerry" (*TTC* ii 1). Much more fun than "He was christened Jerry."

Hyperbole, extreme exaggeration for effect, is a useful device, particularly when a humorous effect is intended. A nice example is Dickens's description of the Dover atmosphere: "The air among the houses was of so strong a piscatory flavour that one might have supposed sick fish went up to be dipped in it, as sick people went down to be dipped in the sea" (*TTC* i 4).

One of the most common and most powerful devices in writing is the *metaphor*, the transferring, to one word, of the sense of another without the use of "like" or "as." The great passage on the isolation of the Self (*TTC* i 3), with the "book" and the "water" and the "light playing on its surface," uses metaphors to compress vast meaning into a little space. It might take several pages of explanation, or a good ten minutes' thought, to get at its full meaning.

Charles Dickens used *personification* a great deal. He often increased the vividness of his writing by attributing to inanimate things human feelings and motivations. He would do this even with human facial features, as when he describes Jerry Cruncher's eyes as "much too near together—as if they were afraid of being found out in something, singly, if they kept too far apart" (*TTC* i 3).

Another device Dickens uses when a certain kind of atmosphere is needed is *repetition*. When Jarvis Lorry dreams in the Dover coach, he sees Doctor Manette in prison and asks, " 'Buried how long?' 'Almost eighteen years.' " and this exchange is repeated and repeated, driving home to the reader the appalling fact that a man has been " 'buried alive for eighteen years!' " This device is used in a profoundly moving way later, when the words of Jesus Christ come again and again like a mantra in the book's closing chapters: "I am the Resurrection and the Life, saith the Lord: he that believeth in me, though he were dead, yet shall he live" (*TTC* iii 9 ff.). As the tension builds, and this refrain recurs, some readers find it almost unbearable and cannot read the work without being overwhelmed by emotion. It is an intensification of the effect achieved in Lorry's dream.

Dickens often used *simile*, where one thing is likened to another, dissimilar, thing by the use of "like" or "as." He was adept at tailoring it to the situation to add flavor, as when he describes

Jerry Cruncher's "old cocked-hat like a three-cornered spittoon" (*TTC* i 3).

Another technique is *symbolism*, the representation of a thing by the use of symbols. It is a huge subject, great fun to rummage about in, and often in the eye of the beholder. There is Carton's action in pouring his brandy "slowly out upon the hearth" and watching it as it falls (*TTC* iii 8). Brandy is a kind of wine. Remember the Last Supper, when Jesus gives his disciples wine to drink, saying, "This is my blood, which is given for thee." Christian doctrine teaches that Christ knew at that moment that he was going to give his life for mankind, and in *A Tale of Two Cities* it appears that Carton may well be planning to sacrifice himself for Darnay. Careful readers of Dickens can often find surprising things hidden just below the surface of a rattling good tale.

A Tale of Two Cities contains a splendid example of the *unifying device*: an idea or theme carried through a work, although manifested in different forms. In the novel, this device is the idea of Resurrection. It is worked out on three levels. As the title of the first book, "Recalled to Life," reminds us, the plot hinges on the return of a man from a living death in prison. In the second book, the principal comic character, Jerry Cruncher, is a "Resurrection Man" who removes corpses from their graves for commercial purposes. The third book tells how the final hours of Sydney Carton are inspired by his memory of Christ's words, "I am the Resurrection and the Life."

TOPICS FOR WRITTEN AND ORAL DISCUSSION

1. We have noted some ways in which Dickens seeks to draw parallels between London and Paris. Is he successful? Is he reaching a little to justify his title? Is his title in fact well chosen? Can you think of a better one? (An annotated bibliography of writings on the novel lists 672 entries. Only eight are indexed to "London.")

2. Pick a scene from the book and consider its *pace*: does it hurry us on? allow us a moment to breathe? Try charting the chapters in terms of "miles per hour."

3. As you read the novel, notice your own state of mind. Are you, at a given moment, amused, diverted, horrified, tense, afraid, sad? Is this feeling enhanced by the words you are reading, independent of the events they describe? If you can spot examples of this, you are discovering something about *tone*.

4. We discussed *point of view* above. You might find it interesting to chart the shifts Dickens makes in the way the events in the book are perceived. Ask yourself, "through whose eyes am I looking now?"

5. Reread the passage on the Self, as slowly and attentively as you can. Can you identify the *metaphors* used? Are they "right on," or do any seem strained? Do you find they help you to understand what is being said?

6. As you read the novel, try to spot examples of *personification*. When you see them, take a moment to think about them and decide how effective they are.

7. In the example of *simile*, Dickens compares Jerry Cruncher's hat to a spittoon, which is a container intended to hold human spit, usually expectorations of tobacco juice. Can you imagine Dickens describing the *banker's* hat—even if old and three-cornered—in that way? If not, why not?

8. It is suggested that Sydney Carton's brandy, which he pours out "slowly upon the hearth" instead of drinking it, is a *symbol* of sacrifice. Does this seem valid to you? Study the plot sequence to test this interpretation. Can you identify other elements in the story which seem to have symbolic significance? Remember, there is no "right" or "wrong" in answering this kind of question: this is an opportunity to both stretch and deepen your own imagination and to have fun with fiction. Try things out, and defend your choices in an essay.

9. Can you spot things in the novel, in addition to those mentioned above, which exemplify the *unifying device* of Resurrection? Don't

be too literal about it: think of "rising from the dead" as a *metaphor*. Does Carton himself, for example, have some kind of resurrection? And what about France?

10. In a letter to his friend John Forster (August 25, 1859), Dickens remarks, "I set myself the little task of making a *picturesque* story, rising in every chapter with characters true to nature but whom the story itself should express, more than they should express themselves, by dialogue. I mean, in other words, that I fancied a story of incident might be written, pounding the characters out in its own mortar, and beating their own interests out of them." Discuss this metaphor and relate it to the points about the characters made above in this section.

2

Before the Deluge

INTRODUCTION

The French Revolution was, in its time, the most frightening, inspiring, threatening, exhilarating, volcanic, horrific, uplifting, unimaginable, portentous, appalling, implausible, imponderable event in the remembered history of the world. It played itself out in the largest, most populous (in the West), potentially most powerful country on the globe. Its neighbors were aghast and fascinated, intoxicated and terrified. It was indeed both the best of times and the worst.

The dynamics of the Revolution are still under debate, but a few elements can be listed as likely always to be considered important factors. One was the feudal system of French governance: an absolute monarchy perpetuated the status quo by granting valuable privileges and exemptions (as from taxation) to the church and the nobility (the first two Estates), while burdening the rest of the nation (the Third Estate) with financial obligations it was the least able of the three to discharge. A grievance we find hard to credit today was the *lettre de cachet*, under which a nobleman could imprison an enemy or a recalcitrant family member on his whim without proving anything against him. (We do not take it seriously because it seems incredible—like something out of Dumas *père*—but see pages 183 ff.)

Another element was the bankruptcy of the government. It had fought the Seven Years' War (in North America, the French and Indian War) and lost. It then was seduced, out of a yearning for revenge, to spend heavily to support the American colonies against the enemy which had humiliated it. The American Revolution not only drained France financially but exported radical ideas of human equality and freedom not likely to be easily absorbed in the French body politic. Soaring inflation, disastrous weather, and inefficient distribution led to food shortages which hit the Third Estate, and particularly the people of Paris, especially hard. Successive ministers of finance, some of them both honest and brilliant, fought to put the State on a proper fiscal footing, but King Louis XVI, abetted by his more intelligent but reactionary brothers, and his charming and (it turned out) courageous but arrogant and mercurial queen, Marie Antoinette, slighted their advice, or heeded it only fitfully and when it was too late.

Frustration and resentment were building in the upper echelons of the Third Estate: the rising mercantile interests, the professions, the small proprietors of land and businesses. They bore more than their share of the burden of supporting the government and enduring its deficiencies, but they were given little or no share in it.

An imponderable but major influence on events was the Enlightenment—the philosophico-literary movement led in France by François-Marie Arouet (Voltaire), Jean-Jacques Rousseau, and the Baron de Montesquieu. They looked at democratic forms of government emerging in England and at its religious independence of Rome and made eloquent and invidious comparisons with native institutions.

Important "secondary" works of scholarship by historians and scholars like the Durants, Schama, and others are less valuable in a work of this nature than "primary" materials: documents created at the time by participants, direct observers, and official recorders. They are essential grist for scholars, and they have an immediacy and an authenticity which make them invaluable for the study of "context."

YOUNG'S ENLIGHTENING TRAVEL REPORTS

We are fortunate that an energetic human camera from England visited France in the years just before the fall of the Bastille and reported his observations, comments, and conclusions to his countrymen. Arthur Young (1741–1820) traveled extensively in France in the years 1787 through 1790. The younger son of a Suffolk squire, he had farmed unsuccessfully (he was an enthusiastic but improvident experimenter), but he became a prolific recorder of the evolution of agriculture as a science. His *Annals of Agriculture* went through forty-six volumes from 1785–1815. The work popularized improved techniques of agriculture and animal husbandry and enormously influenced English farming methods.

Young's biggest hit, however, was *Travels in France* (1790). It included descriptions, mostly at first-hand, of the circumstances of the daily life in France as well as the early political events of the Revolution. This made it of huge interest in England, and it sold like hotcakes. Its bulk is a detailed, systematic daily diary, with depictions of the countryside, public works, buildings both elegant and humble, dress, conduct, manners, and especially observations of French agriculture (and lack of it), often with comparisons to English methods. (Remember that the price and availability of bread were critical issues for the French.) Young discusses politics, the arts, taxation, government regulation, and extreme contrasts of affluence and wretched poverty. His work is thorough, objective, and, above all of course, contemporaneous. We have taken several extracts from it and provided captions for ready reference. In a few places italics highlight passages of particular interest to readers of *A Tale of Two Cities*.

Page references to the 1892 imprint of the 1790 edition are given at the end of each passage. Pages 1–110 cover 1787; pages 111–148, 1788; pages 149–285, 1789. Young concludes with a long chapter "On the Revolution of France" which ably summarizes his view of its causes (and it is a view which has found wide acceptance then and since), but we have omitted the discussion here because of its essentially "secondary" nature. Students of the French Revolution as such should not fail to consult it. An abridged version of *Travels* was published in 1929, edited by Constantia Maxwell.

FROM ARTHUR YOUNG, *TRAVELS IN FRANCE DURING THE YEARS 1787, 1788, 1789* (1790)
Matilda Betham-Edwards, ed.
4th ed. corr. and rev. London: G. Bell, 1892
[*captions and italicized emphases added*]

Country Life

Agriculture. To Nonant-le-Fuzelier, a strange mixture of sand and water. Much inclosed, and the houses and cottages of wood filled between the studs with clay or bricks, and covered not with slate but tile, with some barns boarded like those in Suffolk—rows of pollards in some of the hedges; an excellent road of sand; the general features of a woodland country; all combined to give a strong resemblance to many parts of England; but the husbandry is so little like that of England that the least attention to it destroyed every notion of similarity.

The same wretched country continues to La Loge; *the fields are scenes of pitiable management, as the houses are of misery. Yet all this country highly improveable, if they knew what to do with it: the property, perhaps, of some of those glittering beings, who figured in the procession the other day at Versailles. Heaven grant me patience while I see a country thus neglected*—and forgive me the oaths I swear at the absence and ignorance of the possessors (19).

At Harvest. The vintage itself can hardly be such a scene of activity and animation as this universal one of treading out the corn, with which all the towns and villages in Languedoc are now alive. The corn is all roughly stacked around a dry firm spot, where great numbers of mules and horses are driven on a trot round a centre, a woman holding the reins, and another, or a girl or two, with whips drive; the men supply and clear the floor; other parties are dressing, by throwing the corn into the air for the wind to blow away the chaff. Every soul is employed, and with such an air of cheerfulness, that the people seem as well pleased with their labour, as the farmer himself with his great heaps of wheat. The scene is uncommonly animated and joyous. I stopped and alighted often to see their method; I was always very civilly treated, and my wishes for a good price for the farmer, and not too good a one for the poor, well received. This method, which entirely saves barns, depends absolutely on climate . . . there has been nothing like rain; but one unvarying clear bright sky and burning sun, yet not at all suffocating, or to me even unpleasant (45–46).

City Life

A Local Town. [Limoges] is ill built, with narrow and crooked streets, the houses high and disagreeable. They are raised of granite, or wood with lath and plaister, which saves lime, an expensive article here, being brought from a distance of twelve leagues; the roofs are of pantiles, with projecting eaves, and almost flat; a sure proof we have quitted the region of heavy snows. The best of their public works is a noble fountain, the water conducted three quarters of a league by an arched aqueduct brought under the bed of a rock 60 feet deep to the highest spot in the town, where it falls into a bason 15 feet diameter, cut out of one piece of granite; thence the water is let into reservoirs, closed by sluices, which are opened for watering the streets, or in cases of fires.

The cathedral is ancient, and the roof of stone; there are some arabesque ornaments cut in stone, as light, airy, and elegant as any modern house can boast (22).

Paris. This great city appears to be in many respects the most ineligible and inconvenient for the residence of a person of small fortune of any that I have seen; and vastly inferior to London. The streets are very narrow, and many of them crouded, nine tenths dirty, and all without foot-pavements. Walking, which in London is so pleasant and so clean, that ladies do it every day, is here a toil and a fatigue to a man, and an impossibility to a well dressed woman. The coaches are numerous, and, what are much worse, there are an infinity of one-horse cabriolets, which are driven by young men of fashion and their imitators, alike fools, with such rapidity as to be real nuisances, and render the streets exceedingly dangerous, without an incessant caution. *I saw a poor child run over and probably killed*, and have been myself many times blackened with the mud of the kennels. This beggarly practice, of driving a one-horse booby hutch about the streets of a great capital, flows either from poverty or wretched and despicable œconomy; nor is it possible to speak of it with too much severity. If young noblemen at London were to drive their chaises in streets without foot-ways, as their brethren do at Paris, they would speedily and justly get very well threshed, or rolled in the kennel (103–4).

Intellectual Leadership. It is to be regretted that Paris should have these disadvantages, for in other respects I take it to be a most eligible residence for such as prefer a great city. The society for a man of letters, or who has any scientific pursuit, cannot be exceeded. The intercourse between such men and the great, which, if it is not upon an equal footing, ought never to exist at all, is respectable. Persons of the highest rank pay an attention to science and literature, and emulate the character they confer. I should pity the man who expected, without other advantages of a very different nature, to be well received in a brilliant circle at London, because he was a fellow of the Royal Society. But this would not be the case with a member of the Academy of Sciences at Paris; he is sure of a good reception every where. Perhaps this contrast depends in a great measure on the difference of the governments of the two countries (104).

A Contrast. Come to an improvement in the midst of these deserts, four good houses of stone and slate, and a few acres run to wretched grass, which have been tilled, but all savage, and become almost as rough as the rest. . . . I demanded how it had been done? Pare and burn, and sow wheat, then rye, and then oats. *Thus it is for ever and ever! the same follies, the same blundering, the same ignorance; and then all the fools in the country said, as they do now, that these wastes are good for nothing.* To my amazement [I] find the incredible circumstance, that they reach within three miles of the great commercial city of Nantes! . . . Arrive—go to the theatre, new built of fine white stone, and has a magnificent portico front of eight elegant Corinthian pillars, and four others within, to part the portico from a grant vestibule. Within all is gold and painting, and *a coup d'œil* at entering, that struck me forcibly. It is, I believe, twice as large as Drury-Lane, and five times as magnificent. It was Sunday, and therefore full. *Mon Dieu!* cried I to myself, do all the wastes, the deserts, the heath, ling, furz, broom, and bog, that I have passed for 300 miles lead to this spectacle? *What a miracle that all this splendour and wealth of the cities in France should be so unconnected with the country! There are no gentle transitions from ease to comfort, from comfort to wealth: you pass at once from beggary to profusion,*—from misery in mud cabins to Mademoiselle St Huberti, in splendid spectacles at 500 liv. a night. . . . The country deserted, or if a gentleman in it, you find him in some wretched hole, to save that money which is lavished with profusion in the luxuries of a capital (132).

Inns and Travel

Eating and Sleeping. Having now crossed the kingdom, and been in many French inns, I shall in general observe, that they are on an average better in two respects, and worse in all the rest, than those in England. We have lived better in point of eating and drinking beyond a question, than we should have done in going from London to the Highlands of Scotland, at double the expence. But if in England the best of every thing is ordered, without any attention to the expence, we should for double the money have lived better than we have done in France; the common cookery of the French gives great advantage. It is true, they roast every thing to a chip, if they are not cautioned: but they give such a number and variety of dishes, that if you do not like some, there are others to please your palate. The desert [*sic*] at a French inn has no rival at an

English one; nor are the liqueurs to be despised.—We sometimes have met with bad wine, but upon the whole, far better than such port as English inns give. Beds are better in France; in England they are good only at good inns; and we have none of that torment, which is so perplexing in England, to have the sheets aired; for we never trouble our heads about them, doubtless on account of the climate. After these two points, all is a blank (35).

At St Geronds [I] go to the Croix Blanche, the most execrable receptacle of filth, vermin, impudence and imposition that ever exercised the patience, or wounded the feelings of a traveller. A withered hag, the dæmon of beastliness, presides there. I laid, not rested, in a chamber over a stable, whose effluviæ through the broken floor were the least offensive of the perfumes afforded by this hideous place. . . . Spain brought nothing to my eyes that equalled this sink, from which an English hog would turn with disgust. But the inns all the way from Nismes are wretched. . . . St Geronds must have, from its appearance, four or five thousand people. Pamiers near twice that number. *What can be the circulating connection between such masses of people and other towns and countries, that can be held together and supported by such inns?* There have been writers who look upon such observations as rising merely from the petulance of travellers, but it shews their extreme ignorance. Such circumstances are political data. We cannot demand all the books of France to be opened in order to explain the amount of circulation in that kingdom: a politician must therefore collect it from such circumstances as he can ascertain; and among these, traffic on the great roads, and the convenience of the houses prepared for the reception of travellers, tell us both the number and the condition of those travellers; by which term I chiefly allude to the natives, who move on business or pleasure from place to place; for if they are not considerable enough to cause good inns, those who come from a distance will not . . . go in England to towns that contain 1500, 2000, or 3000 people, in situations absolutely cut off from all dependence, or almost the expectation of what are properly called travellers, yet you will meet with neat inns, well dressed and clean people keeping them, good furniture, and a refreshing civility; your senses may not be gratified, but they will not be offended; and if you demand a post chaise and a pair of horses . . . it will be ready to carry you, whither you please. *Are no political conclusions to be drawn from this amazing contrast?* It proves that such a population in England have connections with other places to the amount of supporting such houses. The friendly clubs of the inhabitants, the visits of friends and relations, the parties of pleasure, the resort of farmers, the intercourse with the capital and with other towns, from the support of good inns; and in a country where they are not to be found, it is a proof that there is not the same quantity of motion; or that it moves by means of less wealth, less consumption, and less enjoyment (57–58).

Public Roads and Works. There is a bridge of a single arch, and a causeway to it, truly magnificent; we have not an idea of what such a road is in England. The traffic of the way, however, demands no such exertions; one-third of the breadth beaten, one-third rough, and one-third covered with weeds. In 36 miles, I have met one cabriolet, half a dozen carts, and some old women with asses. For what all this waste of treasure?—in Languedoc, it is true, these works are not done by corvées [levies of labor]; but there is an injustice in levying the amount not far short of them. The money is raised by tailles, and, in *making the assessment, lands held by a noble tenure are so much eased, and others by a base one so burthened*, that 120 arpents [1.25 acres] in this neighbourhood held by the former, pay 90 liv[res] and 400 possessed by a plebeian right, which ought proportionally to pay 300 liv. is, instead of that, assessed at 1400 liv.

Women without stockings, and many without shoes; but if their feet are poorly clad they have a *superb* [Young's italic] consolation in walking upon magnificent causeways; the new road is 50 feet wide, and 50 more digged away or destroyed to make it (45).

In this journey through Languedoc, I have passed an incredible number of splendid bridges, and many superb causeways. But *this only proves the absurdity and oppression of government*. Bridges that cost 70 or 80,000 l[iv] and immense causeways to connect towns, that have no better inns than such as I have described, appear to be gross absurdities. They cannot be made for the mere use of the inhabitants, because one-fourth of the expense would answer the purpose of real utility. They are therefore objects of public magnificence, and consequently for the eye of travellers. But what traveller, with his person surrounded by the beggarly filth of an inn, and with all his senses offended, will not condemn such inconsistencies as folly, and will not wish for more comfort and less appearance of splendour (p. 58). [Young seems to miss the fact that the roads enabled the nobility to commute rapidly to and from Versailles and the royal court.]

A Success. The canal of Languedoc [created under Louis XIV by Riquet, it links the Mediterranean and the Atlantic] is the capital feature of all this country. The mountain through which it pierces is isolated, in the midst of an extended valley, and only half a mile from the road. It is a noble and stupendous work, goes through the hill about the breadth of three toises [fathoms; each about 6 feet]; and was digged without shafts.

Leave the road, and crossing the canal, follow it to Beziers; nine sluice-gates let the water down the hill to join the river at the town.—A noble work! The port is broad enough for four large vessels to lie abreast; the

greatest of them carries from 90 to 100 tons. Many of them were at the
quay, some in motion, and every sign of an animated business. This is
the best sight I have seen in France. Here Lewis XIV thou art truly great!—
Here, with a generous and benignant hand, thou dispensest ease and
wealth to thy people!—*Si sic omnia* [had it been thus in everything], thy
name would indeed have been revered. To effect this noble work, of
uniting the two seas, less money was expended than to besiege Turin, or
to seize Strasbourg like a robber. Such an employment of the revenues
of a great kingdom is the only laudable way of a monarch's acquiring
immortality; all other means make their names survive with those only
of the incendiaries, robbers, and violators of mankind (46).

The Nobility

Philanthropy. Nearer to the chateau the duchess of Liancourt has built a
menagerie and dairy in a pleasing taste. The cabinet and anti-room are
very pretty; the saloon elegant, and the dairy entirely constructed of marble. At a village near Liancourt, the duke has established a manufacture
of linen and stuffs mixed with thread and cotton, which promises to be
of considerable utility; there are 25 looms employed, and preparations
making for more. As the spinning for these looms is also established, it
gives employment to great numbers of hands who were idle, for they
have no sort of manufacture in the country though it is populous. Such
efforts merit great praise. Connected with this is the execution of an
excellent plan of the duke's for establishing habits of industry in the
rising generation. The daughters of the poor people are received into an
institution to be educated to useful industry: they are instructed in their
religion, taught to write and read, and to spin cotton: are kept till
marriageable, and then a regulated proportion of their earnings given
them as a marriage portion. There is another establishment of which I
am not so good a judge; it is for training the orphans of soldiers to be
soldiers themselves. . . . There are at present 120 boys, all dressed in uniform.—My ideas have all taken a turn which I am too old to change: I
should have been better pleased to see 120 lads educated to the plough,
in habits of culture superior to the present; but certainly the establishment is humane, and the conduct of it excellent (83).

Husbandry. The nobility in France have no more idea of practising
agriculture, and making it an object of conversation, except on the mere
theory, as they would speak of a loom or a bowsprit, than of any other
object the most remote from their habits and pursuits. I do not so much
blame them for this neglect, as I do that herd of visionary and absurd
writers on agriculture, who, from their chambers in cities, have, with an
impertinence almost incredible, deluged France with nonsense and theory, enough to disgust and ruin the whole nobility of the kingdom (146).

The Poor

Their Shoes. Pass Payrac, and meet many beggars, which we had not done before. All the country, girls and women, are without shoes or stockings; and the ploughmen at their work have neither sabots nor feet to their stockings. *This is a poverty, that strikes at the root of national prosperity; a large consumption among the poor being of more consequence than among the rich: the wealth of a nation lies in its circulation and consumption;* and the case of poor people abstaining from the use of manufactures of leather and wool ought to be considered as an evil of the first magnitude. It reminded me of the misery of Ireland (27).

Their Clothes. To Montauban. The poor people seem poor indeed; the children terribly ragged, if possible worse clad than if with no cloaths at all; as to shoes and stockings they are luxuries. A beautiful girl of six or seven years playing with a stick, and smiling under such a bundle of rags as made my heart ache to see her: they did not beg, and when I gave them any thing seemed more surprized than obliged. One third of what I have seen of this province seems uncultivated, and nearly all of it in misery. *What have kings, and ministers, and parliaments, and states, to answer for their prejudices, seeing millions of hands that would be industrious, idle and starving, through the execrable maxims of despotism, or the equally detestable prejudices of a feudal nobility* (125).

Their Women. Walking up a long hill, to ease my mare [on July 12, 1789], I was joined by a poor woman, who complained of the times, and said that it was a sad country; demanding her reasons, she said her husband had but a morsel of land, one cow, and a poor little horse, yet they had a *franchar* (42 lb.) of wheat, and three chickens, to pay as a quit-rent to one Seigneur; and four *franchar* of oats, one chicken and 1f to pay to another, besides very heavy tailles [tax from which the nobility was exempt] and other taxes. She had seven children, and the cow's milk helped to make the soup. But why, instead of a horse, do not you keep another cow? Oh, her husband could not carry his produce so well without a horse; and asses are little used in the country. It was said, at present, that *something was to be done by some great folks for such poor ones, but she did not know who nor how* [Young's italic], but God send us better *car les tailles & les droits nous ecrasent* [the taxes and imposts crush us].—*This woman, at no great distance, might have been taken for sixty or seventy, her figure was so bent, and her face so furrowed and hardened by labour,—but she said she was only twenty-eight.* An Englishman who has not travelled, cannot imagine the figure made by infinitely the greater part of the countrywomen in France; it speaks, at the first sight, hard and severe labour: I am inclined to think, that they work harder than the men, and this, united with the more miserable labour of bringing a new race of slaves into the world, destroys absolutely all symmetry of person and every feminine appearance. To what are we to attribute this difference in the manners of the lower people in the two kingdoms? TO GOVERNMENT (198).

Politics

Apprehensions. Dined to-day with a party, whose conversation was entirely political. . . . Both [Calonne and Loménie de Brienne] were condemned on all hands in the lump; as being absolutely unequal to the difficulties of so arduous a period. One opinion pervaded the whole company, that they are on the eve of some great revolution in the government: that every thing points to it: the confusion in the finances great; with a *deficit* impossible to provide for without the states-general of the kingdom, yet no ideas formed of what would be the consequence of their meeting: no minister existing, or to be looked to in or out of power, with such decisive talents as to promise any other remedy than palliative ones: *a prince on the throne, with excellent dispositions, but without the resources of a mind* that could govern in such a moment without ministers: *a court buried in pleasure and dissipation*; and adding to the distress, instead of endeavouring to be placed in a more independent situation: a great ferment amongst all ranks of men, who are eager for some change, without knowing what to look to, or to hope for: and *a strong leaven of liberty, increasing ever since the American revolution*; altogether form a combination of circumstances that promise e'er long to ferment into motion, if some master hand, of very superior talents, and inflexible courage, is not found at the helm to guide events, instead of being driven by them. It is very remarkable, that such conversation never occurs, but bankruptcy is a topic: the curious question on which is, *would a bankruptcy occasion a civil war, and a total overthrow of the government?* [Young's emphasis]. The answers that I have received to this question, appear to be just: such a measure, conducted by a man of abilities, vigour, and firmness, would certainly not occasion either one or the other. But the same measure, attempted by a man of a different character, might possibly do both. *All agree, that the states of the kingdom cannot assemble without more liberty being the consequence; but I meet with so few men that have any just ideas of freedom, that I question much the species of this new liberty that is to arise.* They know not how to value the privileges of THE PEOPLE: as to the nobility and the clergy, if a revolution added any thing to their scale, I think it would do more mischief than good (98).

Nantes is as *enflammé* in the cause of liberty, as any town in France can be; the conversations I witnessed here, prove how great a change is effected in the minds of the French, nor do I believe it will be possible for the present government to last half a century longer, unless the clearest and most decided talents are at the helm. The American revolution has laid the foundation of another in France, if government does not take care of itself (134).

The Press. The business going forward at present [June 1789] in the pamphlet shops of Paris is incredible. I went to the Palais Royal to see what new things were published, and to procure a catalogue of all. Every hour produces something new. Thirteen came out to-day, sixteen yesterday, and ninety-two last week. We think sometimes that Debrett's or Stockdale's shops at London are crouded, but they are mere deserts, compared to Desein's, and some others here, in which one can scarcely squeeze from the door to the counter. The price of printing two years ago was from 27 liv. to 30 liv. per sheet, but now it is from 60 liv. to 80 liv. This spirit of reading political tracts, they say, spreads into the provinces, so that all the presses of France are equally employed. *Nineteen-twentieths of these productions are in favour of liberty, and commonly violent against the clergy and nobility*; I have to-day bespoke many of this description, that have reputation; but enquiring for such as had appeared on the other side of the question, to my astonishment I find there are but two or three that have merit enough to be known. *Is it not wonderful, that while the press teems with the most levelling and even seditious principles, that if put in execution would overturn the monarchy, nothing in reply appears, and not the least step is taken by the court to restrain this extreme licentiousness of publication.* It is easy to conceive the spirit that must thus be raised among the people (153).

Agitation. But the coffee-houses in the Palais Royal present yet more singular and astonishing spectacles; they are not only crouded within, but other expectant crouds are at the doors and windows, listening [open-mouthed] to certain orators, who from chairs or tables harangue each his little audience: the eagerness with which they are heard, and the thunder of applause they receive for every sentiment of more than common hardiness or violence against the present government, cannot easily be imagined. I am all amazement at the ministry permitting such nests and hotbeds of sedition and revolt, which disseminate amongst the people, every hour, principles that by and by must be opposed with vigour, and therefore it seems little short of madness to allow the propagation at present (153–54).

Crisis. Every thing conspires to render the present period in France critical: the want of bread is terrible: accounts arrive every moment from the provinces of riots and disturbances, and calling in the military, to preserve the peace of the markets. The prices . . . for the common sort, eaten by the poor . . . are beyond their faculties, and occasion great misery. At Meudon, the police, that is to say the intendant, ordered that no wheat should be sold on the market without the person taking at the same time an equal quantity of barley. What a stupid and ridiculous regulation, to lay obstacles on the supply, in order to be better supplied; and to shew the people the fears and apprehensions of government, creating thereby an alarm, and raising the price at the very moment they wish to sink it (154).

Hope. This [June 15, 1789] has been a rich day, and such an one as ten years ago none could believe would ever arrive in France; a very important debate being expected on what, in our house of commons, would be termed the state of the nation. . . . The spectacle of the representatives of twenty-five millions of people, just emerging from the evils of 200 years of arbitrary power, and rising to the blessings of a freer constitution, assembled with open doors under the eye of the public, was framed to call into animated feelings every latent spark, every emotion of a liberal bosom. To banish whatever ideas might intrude of their being a people too often hostile to my own country,—and to dwell with pleasure on the glorious idea of happiness to a great nation—of felicity to millions yet unborn (163).

Ill omen. In regard to their general method of proceeding, there are two circumstances in which they are very deficient: the spectators in the galleries are allowed to interfere in the debates by clapping their hands, and other noisy expressions of approbation: this is grossly indecent; it is also dangerous; for, if they are permitted to express approbation, they are, by parity of reason, allowed expressions of dissent; and they may hiss as well as clap; which it is said, they have sometimes done:—this would be, to overrule the debate and influence the deliberations. Another circumstance, is the want of order among themselves; more than once to-day there were an hundred members on their legs at a time (165).

A prophet. A gentleman of an excellent understanding, and apparently of consideration, from the attention paid him, with whom I had some conversation on the subject [in Metz on July 14, 1789], lamented in the most pathetic terms, the situation of his country; he considers a civil war as impossible to be avoided. There is not, he added, a doubt but the court, finding it impossible to bring the National Assembly to terms, will get rid of them; a bankruptcy at the same moment is inevitable; the union of such confusion must be a civil war; and it is now only by torrents of blood that we have any hope of establishing a freer constitution: yet it must be established; for the old government is rivetted to abuses that are insupportable. . . . *As to a war, Heaven knows the event; and if we have success, success itself may ruin us; France may have a Cromwell in its bosom, as well as England* [Young's italics] (199–200).

TOPICS FOR WRITTEN AND ORAL DISCUSSION

1. Reading these extracts, look for examples of conditions which might have caused deep anger and resentment among the Third Estate of France—the people, rich and poor, who were neither noble nor clerical. What, for instance, would you say was the state of education for the peasants?

2. What does the extract "At Harvest" suggest about conditions outside Paris?

3. The first passage on Paris lets us see what one Englishman thought of the "Two Cities." Do you think his comments on London are unbiased?

4. How do you think the magnificent theater at Nantes was paid for?

5. What political conclusions would you draw from the misery of French roadside inns as compared with those in England?

6. Do you think poorly shod people were consoled by the magnificence of the roads, as Young seems to say? Why does he say it the way he does?

7. Discuss Young's remarks under "A Success" about the best way a monarch can spend money. Do you agree? Did it apply in France before the Revolution? Has it since, there or in other countries?

8. The nobility's "Husbandry" seems to suffer from as bad an education as that of the common people. What do you think the effects of this deficiency were for the health of France and its political system?

9. The material captioned "The Poor" probably comes closest of any of Young's observations to the concerns addressed by Charles Dickens, both generally and in *A Tale of Two Cities*. Discuss.

10. Camille Desmoulins was a coffee-house orator. His exhortations led directly to the storming of the Bastille. Discuss Young's remarks under "Agitation" in light of this fact.

11. What does the French observer in the very last selection mean by saying that "France may have a Cromwell in its bosom"? Was he right? What happened?

SUGGESTED READINGS

DD/RR   Durant, Will and Ariel. *Rousseau and Revolution*. New York: Simon and Schuster, 1967.

SS   Schama, Simon. *Citizens: A Chronicle of the French Revolution*. New York: Alfred A. Knopf, 1989.

3

The Events of the French Revolution

INTRODUCTION

On August 8, 1788, the Estates-General, which had last met in 1614, was convoked by the troubled King Louis XVI to meet on May 1, 1789 and resolve the financial crisis. During the intervening months, the cities and regions to be represented were to reflect on and compile lists of their grievances and concerns. At first, the people were grateful for the chance to be heard, but over time, as might have been expected, their reflections on what was the matter began to generate both resentments and rising expectations—which were to become demands.

The course of events thereafter was like an accelerating slide into an abyss. In this chapter, they are presented in two ways: first schematically and then in a narrative tracing Thomas Carlyle's version as he gives it in his great work *The French Revolution*, first published in 1837.

In the Chronology, events of *A Tale of Two Cities* are interpolated in italics.

CHRONOLOGY

1756–63	Seven Years' War (from 1754, the French and Indian War in North America): England defeats France and substantially expels it from the New World
Dec. 1757	*Doctor Manette is engaged by the Evrémondes and subsequently imprisoned in the Bastille under a* lettre de cachet
1759	Quebec falls to the English, Montreal the next year
1763	Treaty of Paris: almost all French Canada now British
Dec. 31, 1767	*Doctor Manette conceals his manifesto, cursing the Evrémonde family to all generations, in the chimney of his cell*
Dec. 16, 1773	The Boston Tea Party
May 10, 1774	Death of King Louis XV of France: his grandson succeeds
Aug. 1774	Louis XVI appoints Turgot finance minister: France is near bankruptcy
June 17, 1775	American Revolution against England begins at Bunker Hill
Nov. 1775	*Jarvis Lorry and Lucie Manette meet at Dover to go to Paris to find her father, just released from the Bastille*
May 1776	Turgot dismissed, Necker appointed: deficits worsen
Oct. 17, 1777	Americans defeat British at Saratoga, gain credibility in Europe
Feb. 6, 1778	France formally allies with America: England declares war
Mar. 1780–July 1780	*Charles Darnay is tried in England for treasonous collaboration with the Americans: he is acquitted; later, he visits his uncle in France and renounces his inheritance; the Marquis is murdered*
May 1781	Necker is dismissed: deficits go on getting worse
Summer 1781	*Darnay speaks to Doctor Manette of his love for Lucie; some time later they marry; little Lucie, then little Charles, are born*
Jan. 20, 1783	Treaty of Versailles: America acknowledged as an independent nation by England

Nov. 1783	Calonne becomes finance minister
Feb.–May 1787	First Convocation of Notables: the aristocracy and the church decline to be taxed
Apr. 1787	Calonne is dismissed, succeeded by Loménie de Brienne
July 13, 1788	Devastating hailstorm hits wide agricultural area around Paris; famine in the city will follow
Aug. 1788	Necker is recalled: will convene Estates-General
Nov. 6, 1788	The Notables reconvene, debate, and do not conclude; they adjourn forever
Jan. 1789	French elections are held for the Estates-General
May 4, 1789	"Baptism day" of the Revolution: Estates-General meet and attend church service; stalemate ensues as the Third Estate holds out for power; on June 13 the clergy begins to join them
June 20, 1789	The Third Estate is locked out: the Oath at the Tennis-Court
July 12, 1789	Hearing news that Necker has been dismissed again, Paris is aflame, inspired by Desmoulins
July 14, 1789	The fall of the Bastille: its commandant is cut down in the street *and is decapitated by Madame Defarge; Ernest Defarge, a leader in the siege, enters the prison, finds and searches Doctor Manette's former cell*
Summer 1789	Burnings and lootings of châteaux throughout France: *the château of the Evrémondes is burned*
Aug. 4, 1789	An all-night session of the Estates abolishes tithes, seignorial dues, excises, "feudalism root and branch"
Aug. 27, 1789	Declaration of the Rights of Man and of Citizens
Sept. 23, Oct. 1, 1789	Inflammatory Royalist banquets of the military at Versailles
Oct. 5–6, 1789	Insurrection of Women: they march on Versailles, bring the king and queen back to Paris; the king withdraws his opposition to Lafayette's Declaration of the Rights of Man
Feb. 4, 1790	The king visits the Constituent Assembly; National Oath

Aug. 31, 1790	A mutiny of unpaid soldiers is put down at Nancy with much loss of life; riotous mobs at the funeral of the slain
Jan. 21, 1791	The king signs a decree ejecting dissident clergy who object to being put under civil authority
Apr. 2, 1791	Death of Mirabeau: the last chance to guide the Revolution toward moderation is gone
June 20–25, 1791	The royal family's flight to Varennes; their capture and ignominious return
July 17, 1791	People's rally demanding the king be deposed is dispersed by musketry at Mayor Bailly's direction
Aug. 25–27, 1791	Convention at Pillnitz: Austrian and Prussian monarchs meet with French emigrant princes to deplore events in France; agree to "interfere by effectual methods," much to the indignation of the French people
Sept. 14, 1791	Constitution is finished and accepted by the king
Oct. 1, 1791– Sept. 21, 1792	France's first legislative assembly meets and bogs down immediately, the Court's inertia contributing; 264 conservative *Feuillants* sit on the *right*; 136 *Jacobins* and *Cordeliers* on the *left*; 355 nonaligned delegates (the "Plain") in the *center* (and so political shades of view are characterized ever since)
Feb. 7, 1792	Treaty of mutual defense between Austria and Prussia
Mar. 15–23, 1792	The king appoints Patriots Dumouriez, Servan, and Roland ministers
Apr. 20, 1792	French Assembly declares war on Austria, later on Prussia
June 13, 1792	The king dismisses his Patriot ministers, appointing a more conservative group; the people are agitated
June 20, 1792	Parisian populace, hungry and exasperated by legislative inaction, invade the Tuileries and force an audience with the king; his calm is disarming, but it is the beginning of the end
June 28, 1792	After futile efforts to restore order and his authority, "gossamer colossus" Lafayette withdraws, his influence gone
July 11, 1792	The Assembly calls for conscription of all able-bodied Frenchmen

July 24, 27, 1792	Prussia declares war: Brunswick's Coblenz Manifesto threatens "military execution" against France if its king is interfered with: French fury
Aug. 10, 1792	The people of Paris rise in the "Commune," invade the Tuileries, massacre the Swiss Guard; the Assembly is forced to acknowledge their authority and, dissolving, calls for election of a parliament with supreme powers
Aug. 13, 1792	King, Queen, and Dauphin, who had taken refuge in the hall of the Assembly, are arrested and imprisoned in the Temple
Aug. 14, 1792	A decree for the confiscation of the property of emigrants
The same day	*Charles Darnay leaves for France to help his servant Gabelle; he is imprisoned in Paris when he arrives*
Aug. 19, Sept. 2, 1792	The Prussians take the border fortresses of Longuy and Verdun, fueling widespread panic
Sept. 2–7, 1792	Marat's Committee of Public Surveillance instigates September Massacre of 1,400 prisoners as Roland, minister of the interior, and Danton avert their eyes: *"The Grindstone"*
Sept. 3, 1792	*Lorry is in Paris; Lucie and her family arrive in search of the imprisoned Darnay*
Sept. 20–22, 1792	Dumouriez repulses the Prussians at Valmy: the king's hope of a foreign rescue is gone; Goethe remarks, "From this place and this time forth commences a new era in world history."
Sept. 22, 1792	The newly convened parliament deposes the king and institutes a revolutionary calendar; though it is in majority Girondist, the Jacobins come to dominate, led by their elite *Montagnards* Robespierre, Danton, and Marat, seated on the highest bench
Nov. 6, 1792	Dumouriez defeats the Austrians at Jemappes in Belgium; the Convention receives a report on crimes of the king, considers trying him
Dec. 22, 1792– Jan. 16, 1793	The Convention tries the king for treason and finds him guilty; each delegate must vote publicly for or against the death penalty: it prevails by 901 to 848
Jan. 21, 1793	Louis XVI is guillotined; England breaks with France

Feb. 1, 1793	France declares war on England and Holland; invades latter
Feb. 25, 1793	Starving Parisians rise up, confiscate and distribute grocers' inventories
Mar. 7, 1793	France declares war on Spain
Mar. 10, 13, 1793	The mortal struggle of Girondists and Jacobins begins; Danton sets up the Revolutionary Tribunal; Vergniaud warns that "the Revolution, like Saturn, successively devouring its children, will engender, finally, only despotism with the calamities that accompany it."
Apr. 1–3, 1793	Girondists break with Danton; after a defeat, Dumouriez goes over to the Austrians to avoid losing his head
Apr. 6, 1793	Danton leads the Committee of Public Safety toward absolute power; the Girondists excluded, later expelled from the Convention
May 20 and Sept. 29, 1793	The Law of the Maximum, fixing retail prices on commodities
May 31–June 2, 1793	Insurrectionary magistrates led by Henriot envelop the Convention and break power of the Girondists; leaders arrested
July 13, 1793	Charlotte Corday, Girondist sympathizer, slays Marat in his bath; resultant searches of her associates' papers produce incriminating material fatal to the arrested Girondists
Aug. 22, 1793	English siege at Dunkirk, Jacobins attack Girondists at Lyons
Sept. 5–17, 1793	Anarchic Revolutionary Army; the Law of Suspect
Oct. 9, 1793	Lyons surrenders; Gorsas, a Girondist deputy, is guillotined
Oct. 16, 1793	After a trial on trumped-up charges, the Queen goes to the guillotine; that day the English are repulsed at Dunkirk
Oct. 31, 1793	Many Girondists are guillotined; Roland, escaping, will commit suicide on hearing his wife has been executed
Nov. 6, 8, 10, 1793	Philippe Egalité is guillotined; then Mme. Roland, and former Mayor Bailly: the Terror has begun

Nov.–Dec., 1793	Sieges of Girondist towns; atrocities throughout France; Toulon falls when the British fleet becomes exposed to artillery fire through a brilliant exploit of young Napoléon Bonaparte
Dec. 1793	*Lucie watches Parisians dance the Carmagnole*
Dec. 1793–Jan. 1794	*Charles Darnay is tried, acquitted, and rearrested; Sydney Carton replaces him and dies in his stead*
Mar. 24, 1794	Hébert and eighteen followers are guillotined
Apr. 3, 1794	Convicted of conspiracy, Danton and followers are executed
July 28, 1794	The *Montagnards* turn on Robespierre, and he and followers go to their deaths, unexpectedly ending nine months of the Terror in which many died (estimates vary from 18,000 to 260,000)
Oct. 6, 1794	Victorious French armies enter Cologne
Nov. 10–12, 1794	Paris reaction against Robespierre's Terror: the Jacobin Club stormed and closed
Dec. 1794	French army overruns Holland
Dec. 24, 1794	The Law of the Maximum is abolished
Jan. 1795	French success in Spain; they nearly reach Madrid
Feb.–May 1795	Death throes of sansculottism: two uprisings ("12 Germinal" and "1 Prairial") fail
Apr. 5, 1795	Prussia makes peace with France, with Spain three months later
May 8, 1795	Fouquier-Tinville, Jacobin prosecutor, guillotined
May–June 1795	The "White Terror": Reactionaries massacre hundreds of Jacobins in the provinces
July 15–20, 1795	Emigrant invasion in English ships demolished at Quiberon
Oct. 5, 1795	Last insurrection ("13 Vendémiaire") is quelled by grapeshot fired on orders of Napoléon Bonaparte

PRINCIPAL FIGURES

The Royal Family

Louis XV (1710–74)—Became king at five years of age; presided over a disastrous war, financial decline: bequeathed to grandson a crippled France

Louis XVI (1754–93)—Only twenty when he became king; vacillated, obstructed, intrigued; tried unsuccessfully to flee; refused to accept constitutional status; died on the guillotine January 21, 1793, at 38 years of age

Queen Marie Antoinette (1755–93)—Daughter of the Austrian monarch Francis I and wife of Louis XVI; capricious, superficial, uncooperative; helped alienate the monarchy from the people; guillotined October 16, 1793

Charles-Philippe, comte d'Artois—The king's younger brother, he led emigrant forces rallied at Coblenz and threatening invasion of France, leading to reprisals in Paris against the aristocrats

Louis Philippe Joseph, duc d'Orléans (known as Philippe Egalité; 1747–93)—The king's cousin; sympathizer with the people, voted for the king's death; later guillotined

Controllers-General of Finance

Anne Robert Jacques Turgot (1727–81)—Former administrator of Limoges: August 1774–May 1776

Jacques Necker (1732–1804)—Swiss who became a rich Paris banker: May 1776–May 1781

Charles-Alexandre de Calonne (1734–1802): November 1783–April 1787

Archbishop Etienne Charles Loménie de Brienne (1727–94): April 1787–August 1788

Necker again: August 1788–July 1789—His dismissal led to a rising in Paris and the fall of the Bastille

Constitutional Leaders

Bailly, Jean Silvain (1736–93)—Astronomer and politican; president of the National Assembly, mayor of Paris; lost influence when he allowed the Guard to fire on the crowds and was guillotined November 10, 1793

Barnave, Antoine (1761–93)—Grenoble native and *feuillant* revolutionary; escorted the royal family back to Paris from Varennes but subsequently developed Royalist inclinations; advocated a constitutional monarchy: guillotined on November 29, 1793

Lafayette, Marie Joseph, marquis de (1757–1834)—Hero of the American Revolution and for a while revered leader in the French new order; drafted the Declaration of the Rights of Man, inspired by John Locke, Rousseau, and the American Bill of Rights; saved the king and his family in the Insurrection of Women; lost influence and retired; hated by extremists for his moderation, he rode over the frontier to an Austrian prison in mid-August 1792

Mirabeau, Honoré Gabriel Riqueti, comte de (1749–91)—Politician and orator who advocated a constitutional monarchy but failed to persuade Louis XVI; lost influence as the Revolution progressed; made President of the Assembly in 1791 but died soon after

Sieyès, Emmanuel Joseph, comte de (Abbé Sieyès; 1748–1836)—Political theorist and clergyman; principal draftsman of the new constitution; became member (1795) of the Committee of Public Safety

Revolutionary Leaders

Brissot, Jacques Pierre (1754–93)—Lawyer and journalist imprisoned for four months on false charge of pamphleteering against the queen; elected to the National Assembly from Paris; became important early leader of the Revolution; the leader of the Girondists, who lost out to the more ruthless Jacobins, he was guillotined with Vergniaud and others October 31, 1793

Danton, Georges Jacques (1759–94)—Lawyer practicing in Paris in 1789; formed the Cordelier's Club of revolutionary extremists and became minister of justice in 1792; voted to execute the king and was an original member of the Committee of Public Safety but, a relative moderate, lost leadership to Robespierre: arrested for conspiracy, he defended himself eloquently but was guillotined April 3, 1794

Desmoulins, Camille (1760–94)—Journalist and influential pamphleteer from Guise; his oratory made him a leader in storming the Bastille; a founder of the Cordelier's Club, he voted for the death of the king; a fierce opponent of the Girondists, he came to urge moderation as the Terror progressed and was guillotined with Danton April 3, 1794

Hébert, Jacques René (1757–94)—Political journalist ("Père

Duchesne") and member of both the Cordeliers and Jacobins; joined the Revolutionary Council and played a leading part in the September massacres of 1793; denounced the Committee of Public Safety for failure to aid the poor; guillotined with seventeen followers March 24, 1794

Marat, Jean Paul (1743–93)—Born in Switzerland, he studied medicine; joined Danton in the Cordelier's Club; elected to the National Convention, he advocated radical reforms as a *Montagnard* and fiercely opposed the Girondins; Charlotte Corday, Girondist, murdered him in his bath July 13, 1793; thereafter briefly hailed as a martyr

Robespierre, Maximilien François Marie Isidore de (1758–94)—Lawyer, born in Arras; elected to the Estates General and gained influence for incorruptibility; founder of the Jacobins and a leader of the extremist *Montagnards*, he defeated and destroyed the Gironde and in 1793 became a member of the Committee of Public Safety, which he dominated; instituted the Terror; its excesses led to his fall and execution July 28, 1794

Roland de la Platière, Jean Marie (1734–93)—Industrial scientist, husband of Marie-Jeanne Philipon, whose influence gained him the ministry of the interior; dismissed three months later by Louis XVI, he was reinstated after the latter's overthrow; a Girondist, he had to flee Robespierre, but his wife was guillotined November 8, 1793, and he committed suicide

Saint-Just, Louis Antoine Léon de (1767–94)—Studied law, wrote poetry and essays, notably *L'Esprit de la Révolution* (1791); Robespierre cohort; as member of the Committee of Public Safety helped destroy Danton and Hébert; president of the Convention in 1794 but fell with Robespierre and died with him on the guillotine July 28

Vergniaud, Pierre Victurien (1753–93)—Advocate from Bordeaux, he was elected to the National Assembly and became a spokesman for the Girondists; argued for sparing the king, but then voted for his death; defeated in the struggle with the *Montagnards*, he was guillotined October 31, 1793

Military Leaders

Bonaparte, Napoléon (1769–1821)—As officer of artillery devised the stratagem which dislodged the British fleet from Toulon (December 1793) and led to the city's surrender to the French revolutionary army; his decisiveness in suppressing the third and last sans-culotte uprising of 13 Vendémiaire (October 4, 1795) is considered to have marked the end of the French Revolution.

Brunswick-Lüneburg, Karl Wilhelm Ferdinand, Duke of (1753–1806)—Nephew of Frederick the Great, father of England's Queen Caroline; Prussian general whose invasion of France precipitated massacres of aristocrats; his disastrous failures in the Ardennes and at Valmy and subsequent withdrawal from France were a decisive setback for revolutionary France's enemies

Dumouriez, Charles François (1739–1823)—Born at Cambrai, he defeated the Prussians at Valmy and the Austrians at Jemappes, saving the Revolution; suspected of monarchical leanings, he was denounced and, to keep his head, went over to the Austrians in 1793; his desertion embarrassed the Girondists and led to their defeat by the Jacobins

Jourdan, Jean-Baptiste, comte (1762–1833)—Defeated Austrians in Holland at Wattignies (1793) and importantly at Fleurus (1794); drove Austrians across the Rhine, took Luxembourg and besieged Mainz; later met defeats, but Napoléon made him marshal and governor of Naples; in 1814 went over to Louix XVIII who ennobled him

Kellermann, François-Christophe (1735–1820)—With Dumouriez, led the French in the critical defeat of Brunswick in the Ardennes and at Valmy

Kléber, Jean-Baptiste (1753–1800)—Led the army which crushed the Vendée revolt at Savenay, December 23, 1793; later career in Egypt with Napoléon

Pichegru, Charles (1761–1804)—French general who had great success in the war in the Netherlands, thereby contributing decisively to the survival of the Revolution

In 1857, an edition of Carlyle's collected works was published, including *The French Revolution*. (See Chapter 4 for a discussion of this work.) His devoted secretary, Henry Larkin, is believed to have been the "Philo" who created a sequential summary of the work, which was printed with it. It is a convenient way to get an overall grasp of the flow of events as Carlyle narrates them. Following is an abridged, slightly simplified version. Interpolations by the author are italicized and bracketed.

ADAPTED FROM "PHILO" SUMMARIZES *THE FRENCH REVOLUTION* (1857) BY THOMAS CARLYLE

I: The Bastille (May 10th, 1774–October 5th, 1789)

1774

Louis XV dies at Versailles, May 10th, at age 64 of small-pox in the 59th year of his nominal "reign" (he had become king at the age of five in 1715). The Boston Tea Party has taken place December 16, 1773.

[Louis XV (1710–74), king of France 1715–74, had succeeded his great-grandfather, Louis XIV. Cardinal Fleury served as Louis XV's educator and advisor from 1723 until he died in 1743, when the king decided he would run the nation personally and did so with calamitous results. Bored by court life, he was also bored by the details of administration. He had a succession of mistresses, notably the Duchess of Châteauroux, Mme. de Pompadour, and Mme. du Barry. Consequent intrigues at court offended the powerful clergy.

The Seven Years' War (1756–63) led to the loss of much of France's colonial empire, notably French Canada, and nearly bankrupted the nation. Louis tried to reform the Parliament in 1771 in order to tax the aristocracy. The new Maupeou Parliament, named for his chancellor, reflected his attempts to diminish aristocratic privilege (Louis XVI restored the old Parliament). But his reign was a series of disasters— financial, military, and political.

A Parliament was more of a judicial than a legislative body, but it had a veto power which it could exercise by declining to "register" laws promulgated by the executive.]

Louis XVI, the grandson of Louis XV, was almost twenty years old at his accession. His Queen was Marie-Antoinette, daughter (8th daughter, 12th child) of Austria's Francis I and Empress Maria-Theresa. Married four years before, they felt they were "too young to reign."

Their first child, a daughter (the Duchess d'Angoulême), was born in 1778. Two sons followed, successively called "Dauphin"; but both died, the second (Louis XVII) at age ten in 1795 in prison. Their last child, a daughter (1786) lived eleven months.

1774–1783

Change of Administration: The Comte de Maurepas (1701–81), now 73 and a man of great levity and wit, is appointed Prime Minister. The Comte de Vergennes (1717–87), favorably known for correct habits and for his embassies in Turkey and Sweden, gets the Department of Foreign Affairs.

The "Parlement Maupeou," which had been invented for getting edicts, particularly tax-edicts, "registered," and made available in law, is dismissed. Turgot is made Controller-General of Finances in August 1774, giving rise to high hopes, as he is already known as a man of much intelligence, speculative and practical, of noble patriotic intentions, and of a probity beyond question.

There are many changes, but one steady fact of supreme significance: continued Deficit of Revenue. That is the only history of the period. Noblesse and Clergy are exempt from direct imposts, and no tax that can be devised, on such principles, will yield due ways and means. Turgot tries in vain to institute juster principles. The domestic corn trade is "made free," and there are many improvements and much high intention, with great discontent at Court in consequence. But famine-riots occur, and starving protesters are hanged. Turgot's attempts to tax the nobility and the clergy provoke a tempest of astonishment and indignation, and he is dismissed in May 1776. Necker, who had become rich as a Paris banker and was supported by the Philosophes (thinkers favoring the Enlightenment and emphasizing rationalism, toleration and secularization), is appointed Controller.

The Deficit of Revenue continues. Necker's plans for dealing with it are opposed, hardly examined. Frugality is of slow operation, curtailment of expenses occasions numerous dismissals, and there is much discontent among the nobility and the clergy. If their privileges are touched, what is to be hoped?

The American Revolution (the Battle of Bunker Hill occurred June 7, 1775), leads to the arrival of Benjamin Franklin and other American agents in Paris, where their cause is in high favor. There is extensive official smuggling of supplies to the Americans, in which the playwright Beaumarchais is much concerned, and a treaty is signed with the revolutionists February 6, 1778.

[More attuned to politics than to finance, Necker's reports disguised the extent of the deficit to facilitate aid to the Americans. Simon Schama feels that "For France, without any question, the Revolution began in America" (SS).]

The Marquis de Lafayette leads French "volunteer" Auxiliaries to America. These "volunteers" are not sanctioned but countenanced and furthered, the public clamor being strong that way. The British, in consequence, declare war. Rochambeau leads official Auxiliaries to America.

Continued Deficit of Revenue. Necker's plans meet intensified opposition from nobility and clergy. In January 1781 he publishes an "Account Rendered," of which 200,000 copies are sold. He is dismissed in May and returns to Switzerland to write. Maurepas dies in November.

[France in 1780 was the most populous and prosperous nation in Europe, with 25 million inhabitants (Russia had 24 million, Great Britain, only 9 million, Italy 17, Spain 10, Prussia 8.6, Austria 7.9, Ireland 4, Switzerland 1.4 million). Paris, with 650,000, was the largest city and its people were "the best-educated and most excitable" in Europe (DD/AN3).]

France and Spain unite in 1782 in a siege of Gibraltar, hopeless since the day (September 13th) of the red-hot balls, which set fire to attacking ships. American Independence is recognized in the Peace of Versailles, January 20, 1783. Lafayette returns in triumph.

1783–1787

Ever-increasing Deficit of Revenue. Worse, not better, since Necker's dismissal. After one or two transient Controllers, who can do nothing, Calonne, a memorable one, is nominated in November 1783. He continues, with lavish expenditure raised by loans, contenting all the world by his liberality, "quenching fire by oil thrown on it" for three years and more. "All the world was holding out its hand, I held out my hat." Ominous, scandalous affair of the Diamond Necklace compromises the name of the Queen, who has no vestige of concern with it, and leads to a notorious trial in 1785, with penal sentences and immense rumor and conjecture from all mankind.

Calonne, his borrowing resources exhausted, convokes the Notables for the first time in February 1787 to sanction his new tax plans. They will not hear of them or him, and he is dismissed and "exiled" in April. The First Convocation of Notables treats not of this thing only, but of all manner of public things, the Estates-General among others. It sits from February 22 to May 25, 1787.

[The Estates-General was a representative body, not convened since 1614, of delegates from each of three Estates. The First Estate was the clergy (about 130,000 people); the Second, the nobility (about 400,000); and the Third, all the rest: the "people," led by merchants, tradesmen, and other sectors of a France in some respects emerging late from feudalism.]

Loménie de Brienne, who has long been ambitious of the post, succeeds Calonne. A man of sixty, dissolute, worthless, he devises tax edicts, including a stamp tax and others, with "successive loans," and the like; which the Parlement, greatly to the joy of the Public, will not register.

Ominous condition of the public, all virtually in opposition. Parlements, at Paris and elsewhere, have a cheap method of becoming glorious: obstruction. Contests of Loménie and Parlement. The latter is "exiled" to the provinces on August 15, 1787 and returns under constraints, September 20. Increasing ferment. Loménie helps himself by temporary shifts while secretly preparing to wrestle down the rebellious Paris Parlement.

1788

Spring: there is a grand scheme of dismissing the Parlement altogether, and nominating instead a "Plenary Court" which shall be obedient in "registering" the unpopular tax edicts and in other points. The scheme for this *coup d'état* from the top is discovered before quite ripe, and Parlement goes into permanent session. An all-night harangue (May 3) is accompanied by applause from idle crowds inundating the outer courts. D'Espréménil and Goeslard de Monsabert, Parlement leaders, are seized by the military at dawn and whirled off to distant prison. The Parlement is exiled again.

There is an attempt to govern (that is, to raise revenues) by royal edict, the "Plenary Court" having expired at birth. Provincial Parlements rebel, the idle public more and more noisily approving and applauding. A July 13 hailstorm, devastating to crops around Paris, will have a portentous anniversary. On August 8, a royal edict convokes the Estates-General to meet in May. A proclamation that "Treasury Payments be henceforth three-fifths in cash, two-fifths in paper" announces *de facto* insolvency, and Loménie is immediately dismissed. An immense explosion of popular rejoicing, more riotous than usual.

[Besides the great hail storm, which devastated a swathe of usually fertile land 180 miles long, from Normandy to Champagne, a severe drought had already stunted crops, and the 1788–89 winter was the worst in eighty years. In the spring, there were disastrous floods, and by summer famine was everywhere. Few actually died of starvation, but many came close, and St.-Antoine alone had 30,000 paupers to care for. Cheap imports under a new trade treaty put many out of work— 80,000 in Paris alone. Despite the impression Dickens gives, state, church, and private charities did try to alleviate the suffering, but it was still immense. These facts must be kept in mind if we are to understand the frenzy and desperation of the Paris mob in the following years.]

Necker, favorite of all the world, is immediately recalled from Switzerland to be "Saviour of France." There is a Second Convocation of Notables, called by Necker to settle how the Estates-General shall be held. Are the three Estates (Nobility, Clergy, People) to meet as one body? As three? Two? Above all, what is to be the relative force, in the decision-making process, of the Third Estate, or Commonalty? The Notables, as other less formal assemblages have done and do, depart without settling any of the points in question, most especially the question of the relative power of the Third Estate.

1789

Elections begin everywhere in January. France's troubles seem now to be about to become France's revolution. The commencement of the "French Revolution," henceforth a phenomenon absorbing all others for mankind, is commonly dated here [says Philo: today it is considered to be the fall of the Bastille the following July 14].

[Besides electing deputies, the people set down their grievances and hopes for the future in cahiers. *"The subsequent events of the Revolution are so dramatic that they distract attention from the magnitude of the experiment that took place across the whole of the country from February to April 1789. Nothing like it had ever been attempted, not in France or anywhere else—certainly not in that paragon of constitutional excellence, the Kingdom of Great Britain. Twenty-five thousand* cahiers *were drawn up in a simultaneous act of consultation and representation that was unprecedented in its completeness" (SS 60).*

The voters were taxpayers of twenty-five or over. The electorate was about six million people, much the largest ever in the history of the world to that time.

There was a problem, however: while outside Paris a man who paid any tax could vote, in Paris the franchise extended only to those who paid a high poll tax. This left about 500,000 Parisians out of the electoral process. These sans-culottes *(literally, those who did not wear aristocratic knee-breeches: the lower classes) were "led to feel that only through the violent force of their number could they express their aliquot [proportional] part of the general will. They would be heard from, they would be avenged. In 1789 they would take the Bastille; in 1792 they would dethrone the King; in 1793 they would be the government of France" (DD/AN 12).]*

The Estates-General assemble at Versailles in May, with a procession to the Church of St Louis on the 4th. The Third Estate has the nation behind it and wishes to be a main element in the business. It hopes and, led by Mirabeau and other able heads, decides, that it must be the main element of all, and will continue "inert" and do nothing until the other Estates join with it, in which conjunct state it can outvote them and may become what it wishes. Its "inertia" consists of harangues and adroit formalities (filibusters), persevered in for seven weeks, much to France's hope and the alarm of Necker and the Court.

[On June 13, three clerics from Poitou join the Third Estate to acclamation; more follow. On June 17, by a vote of 490 to 90, the group names itself the National Assembly. Politically, the Revolution has begun. By June 19, more than one hundred have moved over, and the First Estate, 149 to 137, votes to merge with the Third. The Church hierarchy joins with the nobility to protest to the king.]

The crown intervenes, and on Saturday, June 20, the Versailles assembly hall is padlocked. The Third Estate deputies adjourn to a neighboring tennis court, where they take an oath of solidarity "to God and the *Patrie* [our homeland] never to be separated until we have formed a solid and equitable Constitution as our constituents have asked us to." The king's speech is presented on Monday, with an open intimation of much significance: "If you Three Estates cannot agree, I the King will myself achieve the happiness of my People." The nobility and clergy leave the hall following the king, and the Third Estate remains, pondering this statement.

Enter the supreme Usher, de Brézé, to command their departure. Mirabeau defies him in fulminant words and he retreats, fruitless and worse, "amid seas of angry people." All France is on the edge of blazing out, and the Court recoils: the Third Estate, the other two now joining it, triumphs, successful in every particular. The Estates-General are henceforth the "National Assembly," called to make the Constitution, a perfect Constitution, under which the French People might realize their Millennium.

Great hope, great excitement, great suspicion. The Court, terrified, turns to Maréchal Broglie, the son and grandson of marshals of France. On Sunday, July 12, there is news that Necker is dismissed again and gone homewards overnight. Panic terror in Paris kindles to hot frenzy and ends in the siege of the Bastille, which is taken, chiefly by infinite noise, the *Gardes Françaises* mutely assisting in the rear. The prison falls, "like the City of Jericho, by sound," on Tuesday July 14th, 1789, in the "fire-baptism" of the Revolution, which is henceforth insuppressible and beyond hope of suppression.

[The fourteenth-century Bastille had been primarily a political prison and as such a symbol of monarchical tyranny. In 1789 it was practically

empty (only seven prisoners, including two lunatics and four forgers, were there to be released). The garrison had a two-day food supply but no source of water. The crowd's actual aim was not to destroy the Bastille but to seize its powder magazine.

Commandant Marshal de Launay, having raised a flag of truce, ordered firing, killing forty besiegers (ninety-eight died in all). Carlyle hints at this, but Dickens omits it. Enraged, the mob stormed the prison and, after a summary trial, took de Launay into custody. He was slaughtered in the street, his head paraded on a pike.]

All France, "as National Guards, to suppress Brigands and enemies to the making of the Constitution," takes arms. Lafayette and astronomer Bailly are central figures. Hope, terror, suspicion, excitement, rising ever more, towards the transcendental pitch. There is a continued scarcity of grain.

The Régiment de Flandre (a portion of the army which has been stationed in the Low Countries) arrives at Versailles on September 23. The officers have a banquet on October 3, with much demonstration and gesticulative foolery, of an anti-constitutional and monarchic character. Paris, semi-delirious, hears of it the next day, with endless emotion, and on October 5, ten thousand women (men would have been summarily arrested and worse) march on Versailles, followed by endless miscellaneous multitudes and finally by Lafayette and the National Guard. They bring the royal family and the National Assembly home with them to Paris, thereafter centre of the Revolution.

The First Emigration of certain higher nobility and princes of the blood begins, and it continues more or less through the ensuing years, and at length on an altogether profuse scale. Much legal inquiring and procedure as to Philippe Egalité, who sides with the Third Estate, and his alleged involvement in the Insurrection of Women. He prudently retires to England for a while.

II: The Constitution (January 1790–August 12, 1792)

1790

Constitution-building and its difficulties and accompaniments. Clubs, Journalisms; advent of anarchic souls from every quarter of the world. The King visits the Constituent Assembly; emotion thereupon and National Oath, which flies over France. General "Federation," or mutual Oath of all Frenchmen, on the "Feast of Pikes" (July 14th).

General disorganization of the Army, and attempts to mend it. Mutiny of unpaid troops at Nancy put down in the "Massacre of Nancy." Mutinous Swiss sent to the Galleys at Brest; solemn Funeral-service for the slain at Nancy (September 20) and riotous menaces and mobs in conse-

quence. Steady progress of disorganization, of anarchy spiritual and practical. Mirabeau, desperate of Constitution-building under such accompaniments, has interviews with the Queen, and foresees great things.

1791

The death of Mirabeau on April 2 ends the last chance of guiding or
controlling this Revolution. The Royal Family still hopes to control it and
means to get away from Paris as the first step. They are suspected of this
intention, and their visit to St Cloud is violently prevented by the populace (April 19). Their flight to Varennes (June 20) and misadventures
there lead to their ignominious return in captivity to Paris in a frightfully
worsened position (June 25). The "Republic" is mentioned in Placards
during the King's flight, which is generally reprobated. Barnave escorts
royalty, feeling some sympathy. A throne held up, as if "set on its vertex,"
to be held there by hand. Should not this runaway King be deposed?
Immense assemblage, petitioning at Altar of Fatherland to that effect
(Sunday June 17), is dispersed by musketry, from Lafayette and Mayor
Bailly, with extensive shrieks following, and leaving remembrances of a
very bitter kind.

Foreign governments, who had long looked with disapproval on the
French Revolution, now set about preparing for actual interference. Convention of Pillnitz (August 25–27): Austria's Emperor Leopold II, Fried-
rich Wilhelm II, King of Prussia, with certain less important Potentates,
and Emigrant Princes of the Blood, assembling at a country-house near
Dresden, express their sorrow and concern at the impossible posture of
the French king, which they think calls upon regular Governments to
interfere and mend. They themselves, prepared at present to "resist
French aggression" on their own territories, will cooperate with each
other in "interfering by effectual methods." This Document rouses violent indignations in France, blazing up higher and higher and not
quenched for twenty-five years after.

The Constitution is finished and accepted by the King (September 14).
The constituent assembly proclaims (September 30) that its sessions are
ended and goes its ways amid "illuminations." It rules (led by Robespierre, who has conspiracy in mind) that its members are ineligible for
the Legislative Assembly, leaving the latter bereft of experience and leadership.

The Legislative Assembly, elected according to the Constitution, the first
and also the last assembly of that character, sits October 1, 1791 till September 21, 1792. More republican than its predecessor; inferior in talent;
destitute, like it, of parliamentary experience. Its debates, futilities, staggering parliamentary procedure lead to little accomplishment. The Court,
"pretending to be dead," does not help to implement the Constitution.

A revolutionary's murder in a church at Avignon results in ghastly massacre. The people's suspicions of their King, and of each other; anxieties about foreign attack, and whether they are in a right condition to meet it; painful questionings of Ministers, continual changes of Ministry—occupy France and its Legislature with sad debates, growing ever more desperate and stormy in the coming months. Narbonne made war-minister: he survives six months; Servan, three months, Dumouriez five days: the "Ghosts of ministries."

1792

Terror of rural France (February–March); royalist camp at Jalès in the Cevennes mountains; copious emigration. The Emperor and the Prussian king make a treaty to keep down disturbance and if attacked to assist one another. Sardinia, Naples, Spain, and even Russia and the Pope, are understood to be in the rear of these two. The French Assembly declares war against Austria April 20. This is the first declaration of war, to be followed by others like pieces of a great Firework blazing out now here, now there. That against Prussia, some months after, is the immediately important one.

In the presence of these alarming phenomena, the government cannot act: the people say it will not. The King vetos and obstructs. Fearing foreign invasion, Clubs, Journalists and the Paris populace grow ever more violent and desperate. On June 20, anniversary of the Oath of the Tennis-Court, a vast procession marches through the streets of Paris "to quicken the Executive." Peaceable but dangerous, it finds the Tuileries gates closed. It squeezes, crushes, and is squeezed, crushed against the gates and doors till they give way. The admission to the King, and the dialogue with him and behavior in his house, are of an utterly chaotic kind, dangerous and scandalous, though peaceable, giving rise to much angry commentary in France and over Europe.

General Lafayette suddenly appears in the Assembly, without invitation; he makes fruitless attempts to reinstate his authority in Paris (June 28) and then withdraws, his influence exhausted.

A reconciliation in the Assembly. Question of establishing a nucleus of force near Paris, which the Court opposes. A patriot writes to Marseilles for "500 men who know how to die," who accordingly start for Paris, to the beat of a new marching song. The Assembly proclaims that the "Country is in danger."

Prussia declares war. The Duke of Brunswick's Manifesto, issued at Coblentz in the name of the Emperor and the Prussian King, threatens France "with military execution" if its Royalty are meddled with. The Duke, nephew of Frederick the Great, is to command. (The proclamation, which awakes endless indignation in France and much criticism elsewhere, is understood to have been prepared by French emigrant elements, who are with the Duke in force, and to have been signed reluctantly by him.) The Prussians, and Austrians from the Netherlands, advance. Marseilles marchers "who know how to die" arrive in Paris.

Indignation waxes desperate at Paris, and France is boiling with ability and will, tied up from defending itself by "an inactive government," fatally unable to act. Secret conclaves, consultations of municipality and clubs; Danton understood to be the presiding genius there. Assembly members plot and participate, having no other course. On August 10, there is a universal insurrection of the armed population of Paris: the Tuileries are forced and the Swiss Guard cut to pieces. The King, anticipating the violence, with his family seeks shelter in the Assembly Hall and remain there, listening to the debates, in a reporter's box. They are conducted thence to the Temple, "as hostages," and do not get out again except to die.

The Assembly has its Decree ready: that the state of the crisis requires calling a National Convention, with a Parliament with absolute powers to be elected. After which the Legislative only waits till it be fulfilled.

III: The Guillotine (August 10, 1792–October 4, 1795)

1792

The Legislative sits, pending completion of the Election. The enemy advances, led by emigrants, and takes Longuy almost without resistance, then moves on Verdun, which falls. The Austrians besiege Thionville. Dumouriez seizes and blocks all ways through the forest of the Argonne. Great agitation in Paris leads to the September Massacre of suspected "royalists."

[Of 162 persons killed at Bicêtre prison, forty-three were delinquent boys under eighteen. Many in other prisons were common criminals, beggars, and prostitutes. About half of all the prisoners in Paris died, in some prisons 80 percent of the occupants. The total is reported to have been 1,089, including 202 priests, mostly executed after brief trials held right in the prisons. These atrocities horrified all Europe and indelibly stained the Revolution, which had previously been admired by many.]

Dumouriez, famine and rain delay the Prussians in the Argonne and, to the surprise of the world, the French hold at Valmy.

The Convention meets September 22 and decrees a Republic. The Austrians, renouncing Thionville, attack Lille unsuccessfully. The Prussians, drenched deep in mud, dysentery and famine, are obliged to retreat: the total failure of the Brunswick Enterprise.

The Convention tries the King for treason (Tuesday December 11 through Sunday December 16).

1793

The Convention holds three votes (January 15–17) and convicts; the sentence by a narrow margin is death, each member obliged to record his vote publicly. The King is guillotined at about 10:00 o'clock in the morning of January 21, and the English ambassador quits Paris. War between France and England is imminent.

Dumouriez, in rear of retreating Austrians, has seized and holds the Austrian Netherlands. France declares war against England and Holland. England reciprocates and Dumouriez invades Holland. The English, led by the Duke of York, give aid. The Committee of *Salut Public* ("Public Safety") is the supreme governance in France.

The Girondist and Jacobin parties struggle for dominance. War with Spain. Three epochs in the political struggle; the Girondins fear they will be massacred by the anarchic Paris population. Danton gains establishment of the Revolutionary Tribunal. (Dumouriez is badly defeated at Neerwinden and withdraws homewards faster and faster.) The Girondists break with Danton. Dumouriez, exasperated with the Convention but unable to get his forces to follow him to Paris, goes over to the Austrians. His defection embarrasses the Girondists. The Jacobins seize their chance. Twenty-two Girondist leaders are put under house arrest, never to come out again.

Revolts in the departments, Girondist in temper, come to nothing, and end in "a mutual shriek" (at Vernon in Normandy, July 15). Girondist sympathizer Charlotte Corday's assassination of Marat leads to great vengeances: deputies Barbaroux, Pétion, Louvet, Gaudet and others wander ruined, disguised, over France; the imprisoned twenty-two, including Brissot and Vergniaud, await trial. Lyons and other Girondin localities are to be signally punished. Valenciennes, besieged by the English, surrenders July 26.

The Mountain (Jacobin leadership), victorious, rests on the "Forty-four thousand Jacobin Clubs and Municipalities"; its severe summary procedure rapidly develops into a "Reign of Terror." Austrians force the lines of Weissembourg and penetrate into France from the East; Dunkirk is besieged by the Duke of York. Lyons is bombarded by Dubois-Crancé of the Mountain, and its powder magazine explodes. Barère's Proclamation of Levy: "France risen against tyrants": the anarchic Revolutionary Army and the Law of the Suspect. Lyons, after frightful sufferings, surrenders "To be razed from the earth."

Gorsas, a Girondin deputy, is captured after being declared "outside the law" and is immediately guillotined, the first deputy to die in this fashion. The Queen is executed October 16 after a trial on trumped-up charges of immorality, and the twenty-two Girondists are executed after a lengthy trial. The Duke of York has been repulsed from Dunkirk, and

General Jourdan drives Cobourg and the Austrians over the Sambre again.

The Reign of Terror commences in November. Terror is the Order of the Day. Philippe Egalité is executed November 6, Mme Roland two days later, Mayor Bailly two days after that. The Goddess of Reason (the first of them) sails into the Convention. The churches are plundered.

[One historian, at least, feels that in terms of carnage The Terror differed only in degree from what had happened earlier:

"The assumption that there was a direct relationship between blood and freedom—indeed between blood and bread—is usually thought of as the standard language of punitive Jacobinism, of the Terror. But it was the invention of 1789, not 1793. The Terror was merely 1789 with a higher body count. From the first year it was apparent that violence was not just an unfortunate side effect from which enlightened Patriots could selectively avert their eyes; it was the Revolution's source of collective energy. It was what made the Revolution revolutionary" (SS 447).]

The war with Spain, neglected and not successful, may become important. Toulon is dangerously Girondin in a dangerous vicinity. Hood and the English, even "Louis XVIII" is there. A siege. Toulon falls to the French (Napoleon Bonaparte serving in the artillery). Carrier at Nantes: *Noyadings* (mass drownings) by night, the second of them December 14, become the "Marriages of the Loire" and other horrors. "Death poured out in great floods." Weissembourg is retaken by St Just at the end of the year.

1794

"The Revolution is eating its own children." Hébert and followers die in March, Danton and his in April. The armies succeed in the Netherlands against the Austrians and in Spain. England's Admiral Howe wins a sea-victory, but Jourdan defeats the Austrians at Fleurus in Holland. Tallien, other *Montagnards* conspire against Robespierre to save themselves, and he is guillotined with his allies July 28: which, unexpectedly, ends the Terror.

Victorious French armies enter Cologne, Spain, the Netherlands. In the reaction against the Terror the mob assaults the Jacobins and their club is shut. Pichegru and his army of 70,000 overrun Holland.

1795

Holland's Stadtholder flees to England; Rosas in Spain falls to the French, followed by other strongholds; Madrid is almost in sight. Continued downfall of Sansculottism. Effervescence of luxury; La Cabarrus; Greek

The cell of Queen Marie Antoinette at the Conciergerie prison.

The cell where the moderate Girondins were held before execution.

Costumes; *La Jeunesse Dorée*; balls in flesh-colored drawers. Sansculotte insurrection of 12 Germinal (April 2) fails.

Prussia and Spain make peace, as French armies are everywhere successful. There is famine among the lower classes, but their second Insurrection of 1 Prairial (May 20) is suppressed. An emigrant invasion, in English ships, lands at Quiberon and is blown to pieces. La Vendée, which had before been three years in Revolt, rises again and struggles for eight months.

Reactionary "Companies of Jesus" and "Companies of the Sun" hunt down and kill Jacobins in the Rhone region. A new Constitution is instituted, establishing a Directory and Consuls, with two-thirds of the Convention to be reelected. There are objections and some rebellion. The last Sansculotte Insurrection, 13 Vendémiaire (October 4), is quelled by grapeshot on orders of the decisive Napoleon Bonaparte, at which point the Revolution (as Carlyle defines it) ends: Anarchic Government, if still anarchic, will proceed by softer methods than that of continued insurrection.

TOPICS FOR WRITTEN AND ORAL DISCUSSION

1. A case might be made that the Revolution would never have happened as it did if the great hailstorm of 1788 had not occurred. What were its near-term consequences? What were long-term effects?

2. How important do you think the American Revolution was in fomenting unrest and ultimate upheaval in France?

3. Carefully review the Chronology of the Revolution in Chapter 3, noting the italicized entries, which reflect the events of *A Tale of Two Cities*. Try to visualize these occurrences in the context of the larger story. Do you think Dickens has managed the sequence of his events adroitly? Does anything in his story seem too far-fetched or coincidental to be readily accepted while reading the novel?

4. Communications at the end of the eighteenth century were usually slow (some sophisticates used carrier pigeons), and when Darnay left London to go to his servant's aid he could have had no idea of the changes that had just been taking place in Paris. What were these changes? If he had known of them, would he have gone? Did he take seriously enough his responsibilities to his family? Was there an element of pride, or fear of criticism, in his decision?

5. As might be suggested in Chapter 7 in the discussion of "devoted family retainers," Darnay's concern for Gabelle, in light of the Evrémonde property interests in France, might have seemed to revolutionists not a sign of goodness and loyalty, but part of a scheme to avoid the consequences of punitive laws aimed at emigrants. Discuss.

6. Looking ahead to the chapter on Revolution as such, reflect on the extraordinary events of 1789–94 in France. Have they had any impact on your life? Can you identify elements heaved up by the French convulsion and/or its aftermath that are still visible today?

SUGGESTED READINGS AND WORKS CITED

Doyle, William. *The Origins of the French Revolution*. New York and London: Oxford University Press, 1981.

DD/AN   Durant, Will and Ariel. *The Age of Napoleon*. New York: Simon and Schuster, 1975.

DD/RR   Durant, Will and Ariel. *Rousseau and Revolution*. New York: Simon and Schuster, 1967.

Lefebvre, Georges. *The Coming of the French Revolution*. Trans. R. R. Palmer. Princeton: Princeton University Press, 1947.

SS   Schama, Simon. *Citizens: A Chronicle of the French Revolution*. New York: Vintage Books, 1990.

Soboul, Albert. *The French Revolution*. Trans. Alan Forrest and Colin Jones. New York: New Left Books, 1974.

4 _____

Thomas Carlyle's
The French Revolution

Whenever any reference (however slight) is made here to the condition of the French people before or during the Revolution, it is truly made, on the faith of trustworthy witnesses. It has been one of my hopes to add something to the popular and picturesque means of understanding that terrible time, though no one can hope to add anything to the philosophy of Mr CARLYLE's wonderful book.

Charles Dickens, preface to *A Tale of Two Cities*

INTRODUCTION

Thomas Carlyle (1795–1881) was in many important ways his times' most outstanding intellectual figure. A Scotsman of modest background, Carlyle through his brilliance of thought and literary perseverance over a long lifetime became a towering figure in the field today called Political Philosophy. Charles Dickens revered him and was greatly influenced by him, as were many others.

Carlyle's first great popular success was *The French Revolution*, published in 1837. Thoroughly researched and written with rare intensity and compelling vividness of imagination, it is extraordinary in its blend of historical fact and philosophical perspective. Reading it, we feel we are actually present, observing the events he describes. (Dickens, in the preface quoted above, does not mention that he owed much of the factual basis and even plot elements of his novel to it; see Chapter 5, "Dickens and Carlyle: Common Threads.")

The book is, in fact, a prose poem: indeed, Carlyle postulated that a "right *History* (that impossible thing I mean by History) of the French Revolution were the grand Poem of our Time." Fred Kaplan says, "his fascination with both personal and public images of fire, electricity, and revolution were beginning to draw together, beaming intensely, like a torchlight, on the French Revolution, revealing it as the key event of modern times" (FK 98). "He wanted to write impressionistic and apocalyptic history, to create a 'flame-picture.' "He wanted to write a masterpiece, an achievement that would be a work of art rather than a work of expository logic or historical fact" (FK 216).

After a shattering interruption when the first third of the book was destroyed and had to be rewritten, Carlyle finished on January 12, 1837. He thought it "a wild savage Book, itself a kind of French Revolution" that "has come out of my own soul; born in blackness, whirl-wind and sorrow." He was not sanguine about its success, but it was the phenomenon of its day.

The book is not an easy read for us today: one cannot browse in it very readily. It is written in the old "classical" style, full of apostrophe and declamation, but it amply repays a reader willing to concentrate intensely over a stretch of time to visualize and absorb the scenes Carlyle describes.

FACT AND PERSPECTIVE IN CARLYLE'S
THE FRENCH REVOLUTION

Below is a selection of passages from *The French Revolution*, abridged and somewhat simplified: some, long historical extracts; others, short vignettes. References are to Part (upper-case Roman), Book (lower-case Roman) and Chapter (Arabic) in *The French Revolution*. We have not tried to eliminate the Victorian flavor of the book, except for some old-fashioned turns of phrase. See the Glossary for any terms that puzzle you.

Dickens describes aspects of the September Massacres in his chapter "The Grindstone." Other connections with *A Tale of Two Cities* run through this material and will become apparent with a little study. See Topics for Written and Oral Discussion at the end of this chapter, and Chapter 5.

Space prevents our including the fall of Robespierre, which ended the Terror. Go and read it in Carlyle: no more exciting, suspenseful, higher-stakes historical story has ever been told, or told better.

FROM THOMAS CARLYLE, *THE FRENCH REVOLUTION*
London: James Fraser, 1837

The American Revolution

Alas, much more lies sick than poor Louis XV: not the French King only, but the French Kingship; this too, after long rough tear and wear, is breaking down. The world is all so changed; so much that seemed vigorous has sunk decrepit, so much that was not is beginning to be!— Borne over the Atlantic, to the closing ear of Louis, what sounds are these; muffled ominous, new in our centuries? Boston Harbor is black with unexpected Tea: behold a Pennsylvanian Congress gather; and ere long, on Bunker Hill, DEMOCRACY announcing, in rifle-volleys death-winged, under her Star-Banner, to the tune of Yankee-doodle-doo, that she is born, and, whirlwind-like, will envelop the whole world! (I i 2).

Observe, however, beyond the Atlantic, has not the new day verily dawned! Democracy, as we said, is born; storm-girt, is struggling for life and victory. A sympathetic France rejoices over the Rights of Man; in all saloons, it is said, What a spectacle! Now too behold our Deane, our

Franklin, American Plenipotentiaries, here in person soliciting: the sons of the Saxon Puritans, with their Old-Saxon temper, Old-Hebrew culture, sleek Silas, sleek Benjamin, here on such errand, among the light children of Heathenism, Monarchy, Sentimentalism, and the Scarlet-woman. A spectacle indeed; over which saloons may cackle joyous.

Squadrons cross the ocean: Gateses, Lees, rough Yankee Generals, "with woollen night-caps under their hats," present arms to the far-glancing Chivalry of France; and new-born Democracy sees, not without amazement, "Despotism tempered by Epigrams" fight at her side. So, however it is. King's forces and heroic volunteers; Rochambeaus, Bouil-lés, Lameths, Lafayettes, have drawn their swords in this sacred quarrel of mankind (I ii 5).

Poverty and Hunger in France

With the working people it is not so well. Unlucky! For there are from twenty to twenty-five millions of them. Whom, however, we lump to-gether into a kind of dim compendious unity, monstrous but dim, far off, as the *canaille* [rabble]; or, more humanely, as "the masses." Masses indeed; and yet, singular to say, if, with an effort of imagination, you follow them, over Broad France, into their clay hovels, into their garrets and hutches, the masses consist all of units. Every unit of whom has his own heart and sorrows; stands covered there with his own skin, and if you prick him he will bleed. What a thought: that every unit of these masses is a miraculous Man, struggling, with vision or with blindness, for his infinite Kingdom (this life which he has got, once only, in the middle of Eternities); with a spark of the Divinity, what you call an immortal soul, in him!

Dreary, languid do these struggle in their obscure remoteness; their hearth cheerless, their diet thin. For them, in this world, rises no era of Hope; hardly now in the other—if it be not hope in the gloomy rest of Death, for their faith too is failing. Untaught, uncomforted, unfed! A dumb generation; their voice only an inarticulate cry; spokesman, in the King's Council, in the world's forum, they have none that finds credence. At rare intervals they will fling down their hoes and hammers; and, to the astonishment of thinking mankind, flock hither and thither, danger-ous, aimless; get the length even of Versailles.

And so, on the second day of May 1775, these waste multitudes do here, at Versailles Château, in wide-spread wretchedness, in sallow faces, squalor, winged raggedness, present their Petition of Grievances. The Château gates have to be shut; but the King will appear on the bal-cony, and speak to them. They have seen the King's face; their Petition of Grievances has been, if not read, looked at. For answer, two of them are hanged, on a "new gallows forty feet high"; and the rest driven back to their dens—for a time (I ii 2).

—*on word of national elections*: How the whole People shakes itself, as if it had one life; and, in thousand-voiced rumor, announces that it is awake, suddenly out of long death-sleep, and will thenceforth sleep no more! The long looked-for has come at last; wondrous news, of Victory, Deliverance, Enfranchisement, sounds magical through every heart. To the proud strong man it has come; whose strong hands shall no more be manacled; to whom boundless unconquered continents lie disclosed.

The weary day-drudge has heard of it; the beggar with his crust moistened in tears. What! To us also has hope reached; down even to us? Hunger and hardship are not to be eternal? The bread we extorted from the rugged earth, and, with the toil of our sinews, reaped and ground, and kneaded into loaves, was not wholly for another, then; but we also shall eat of it, and be filled? Glorious news but all too unlikely! (I iv 2).

Starvation has been known among the French Commonalty, known and familiar. Did not we see them, in the year 1775, presenting, in sallow faces, in wretchedness and raggedness, their Petition of Grievances; and, for answer, getting a brand-new Gallows forty feet high? Hunger and Darkness through long years!

Or has the Reader forgotten that "flood of savages," which descended from the mountains? Lank-haired haggard faces; shapes raw-boned, in high sabots, in woollen tunics, with leather girdles studded with copper nails! They rocked from foot to foot, and beat time with their elbows too, as the quarrel and battle went on; shouting fiercely; the lank faces distorted into similitude of a cruel laugh. For they were darkened and hardened: long had they been the prey of excise-men and tax-men, of "clerks with the cold spurt of their pen."

The harvest is reaped and garnered; yet still we have no bread. Urged by despair and by hope, what can Drudgery do, but rise, as predicted, and produce the General Overturn?

Fancy, then, some Five full-grown Millions of such gaunt figures, with their haggard faces; starting v⁻ to ask, as in forest-roarings, their washed Upper-Classes, after long unreviewed centuries, virtually this question: How have ye treated us; how have ye taught us, fed us and led us, while we toiled for you? The answer can be read in flames, over the nightly summer-sky. *This* is the feeding and leading we have had of you: EMPTINESS,—of pocket, of stomach, of head and of heart. Behold there is *nothing in us*; nothing but what nature gives her wild children of the desert: Ferocity and Appetite; Strength grounded on Hunger. Did ye mark among your Rights of Man, that man was not to die of starvation, while there was bread reaped by him? It is among the Mights of Man (I vi 3).

The Fall of the Bastille

The twelfth of July morning is Sunday: the streets are well placarded with an enormous-sized *De par le Roi* [king's proclamation], "inviting peaceable citizens to remain within doors," to feel no alarm, to gather in no crowd. Why so? what means this clatter of military; dragoons, hussars, rattling in from all points of the compass?

Have the destroyers descended on us, then? Alarm, of the vague unknown, is in every heart. Hark! a human voice reporting articulately: *Necker, People's Minister, Saviour of France, is dismissed.* Impossible; incredible! Treasonous of the public peace! Such a voice ought to be choked in the waterworks;—had not the news-bringer quickly fled. Nevertheless, friends, make of it what you will, the news is true. Necker is gone. Necker hies northward incessantly, in obedient secrecy, since yesternight. We have a new Ministry, including Foulon who said the people might eat grass!

But see Camille Desmoulins rushing out, sybilline in face; his hair streaming, in each hand a pistol! Friends! shall we die like hunted hares? Like sheep hounded into their pinfold; bleating for mercy, where is no mercy, but only a whetted knife? The hour is come; the supreme hour of Frenchman and Man; when Oppressors are to try conclusions with the Oppressed; and the word is, swift Death, or Deliverance forever. To Arms! Let universal Paris, universal France, as with the throat of the whirlwind, sound only: To arms!—"To arms!" yell responsive the innumerable voices; like one great voice, as of a Demon yelling from the air: for all faces wax fire-eyed, all hearts burn up into madness.

France, so long shaken and wind-parched, is probably at the right inflammable point. The wax-bust of Necker, the Wax-bust of D'Orléans, helpers of France; these, covered with crape, as in funeral procession, or after the manner of suppliants appealing to Heaven, to Earth, and Tartarus itself, a mixed multitude bears off.

In this manner march they, a mixed, continually increasing multitude; armed with axes, staves and miscellanea; grim through the streets. Be all Theatres shut; let all dancing, on planked floor, or on the natural greensward, cease! Instead of a Christian Sabbath, it shall be a Sorcerer's Sabbath; and Paris, gone rabid, dance,—with Fiend for piper!

What a Paris, when the darkness fell! A European metropolitan City hurled suddenly forth from its old combinations and arrangements; to crash tumultuously together, seeking new. Use and wont will now no longer direct any man; each man, with what of originality he has, must begin thinking; or following those that think. Seven hundred thousand individuals, on the sudden, find all their old paths, old ways of acting and deciding, vanish from under their feet. And so there go they, with

The Storming of the Bastille, July 14, 1789.

clangor and terror, they know not as yet whether running, swimming or flying,—headlong into the New Era.

On Monday the huge City has awoke, not to its week-day industry: to what a different one! The working man has become a fighting man; has one want only: that of arms. The industry of all crafts has paused;— except it be the smith's, fiercely hammering pikes; and, in a faint degree, the kitchener's, cooking offhand victuals. Women too are sewing cockades;—not now of *green*, but of *red* and *blue*, our old Paris colors: these, once based on a ground of constitutional *white*, are the famed TRI-COLOR,—which "will go round the world."

All shops, unless it be the Bakers' and Vintners', are shut: Paris is in the streets;—rushing, foaming like some Venice wine-glass into which you had dropped poison. The tocsin, by order, is pealing madly in all steeples. Arms, give us arms! Also an order to all Smiths to make pikes with their whole soul.

And so it roars, and rages, and brays; drums beating, steeples pealing, criers rushing with hand-bells: "Oyez, oyez, All men to their Districts to be enrolled!" The Districts have met in gardens, open squares; are getting marshalled into volunteer troops. Deserters with their arms are continually dropping in: nay now, joy of joys, at two in the afternoon, the Gardes Françaises have come over in a body! It is a fact worth many. Three thousand six hundred of the best fighting men, with complete accoutrement; with cannoneers even, and cannon! Their officers are left standing alone; could not so much as succeed in "Spiking the guns."

Meanwhile, the faster, O ye black-aproned Smiths, smite; with strong arm and willing heart. This man and that, all stroke from head to heel, shall thunder alternating, and ply the great forge-hammer, till stithy [anvil] reel and ring again. Pikes are fabricated; fifty thousand of them, in six-and-thirty hours. Dig trenches, unpave the streets, ye others, assiduous, men and maid cram the earth in barrel-barricades, at each of them a volunteer sentry; pile the whinstones in window-sills and upper rooms. Have scalding pitch, at least boiling water ready, ye weak old women, to pour it and dash it with your old skinny arms: your shrill curses along with it will not be wanting!

Old Marquis de Launay of the bastille, has pulled up his drawbridges long since, "and retired into his interior"; with sentries walking on his battlements, under the midnight sky, aloft over the glare of illuminated Paris;—whom a National Patrol, passing that way, takes the liberty of firing at: "seven shots towards twelve at night," which do not take effect. This was the 13th day of July 1789 (I v 5).

To the living and the struggling, a new Fourteenth morning dawns. Under all roofs of this distracted City is the nodus of a drama, not untragical, crowding towards solution. The bustlings and preparings, the tremors and menaces; the tears that fell from old eyes! This day, my sons, ye shall quit you like men. By the memory of your fathers' wrongs, by the hope of your children's rights! Tyranny impends in red wrath: help for you is none, if not in your own right hands. This day ye must do or die.

Behold, about nine in the morning, our National Volunteers rolling in long wide flood to the *Hôtel des Invalides*; in search of the one thing needful. Patriotism rushes in, tumultuous, through all rooms and passages; rummaging distractedly for arms. What cellar, or what cranny can escape it? The arms are found; all safe there; lying packed in straw,— apparently with a view to being burnt! More ravenous than famishing lions over dead prey, the multitude, with clangor and vociferation, pounces on them; struggling, dashing, clutching:—to the jamming-up, to the pressure, fracture and probable extinction of the weaker Patriot. And so, with such protracted crash of deafening, most discordant Orchestra-music, the Scene is changed; and eight-and-twenty thousand sufficient firelocks are on the shoulders of as many National Guards, lifted thereby out of darkness into fiery light. And now, to the Bastille, ye intrepid Parisians! There grapeshot still threatens: thither all men's thoughts and steps are now tending.

Old De Launay, as we hinted, withdrew "into his interior" soon after midnight of Sunday. He remains there ever since, hampered as all military gentlemen now are, in the saddest conflict of uncertainties. The Hôtel-de-Ville [Paris town hall] "invites" him to admit National Soldiers, which is a soft name for surrendering. On the other hand, His Majesty's orders were precise. His garrison is but eighty-two old Invalides [soldiers], re-inforced by thirty-two young Swiss; his walls indeed are nine feet thick, he has cannon and powder; but, alas, only one day's provision of victuals. The city too is French, the poor garrison mostly French. Rigorous old De Launay, think what thou wilt do!

All morning, since nine, there has been a cry everywhere: To the Bastille! Repeated "deputations of citizens" have been here, passionate for arms; whom De Launay has got dismissed by soft speeches through port-holes. Elector Thuriot de la Rosière gains admittance; finds De Launay indisposed for surrender; nay disposed for blowing up the place rather. Thuriot mounts with him to the battlements: heaps of paving-stones, old iron and missiles lie piled; cannon all duly levelled; in every embrasure a cannon,—only drawn back a little! But outwards, behold, O Thuriot, how the multitude flows on, welling through every street: tocsin furiously pealing, all drums beating the *générale*: the Suburb Saint-Antoine rolling hitherward wholly, as one man! *"Que voulez-vous?"* said De Launay, turn-ing pale at the sight, with an air of reproach, almost of menace. "Mon-sieur," said Thuriot, rising into the moral-sublime, "what mean *you*?

Consider if I could not precipitate *both* of us from this height,"—say only a hundred feet, exclusive of the walled ditch! Whereupon De Launay fell silent.

Thuriot shows himself from some pinnacle, to comfort the multitude becoming suspicious: then descends; departs with protest; with warning addressed also to the Invalides,—on whom, however, it produces but a mixed indistinct impression. The old heads are none of the clearest; besides, it is said, De Launay has been profuse of beverages. They think, they will not fire,—if not fired on, if they can help it; but must, on the whole, be ruled considerably by circumstances.

Woe to you, De Launay, in such an hour, if you cannot, taking some one firm decision, *rule* circumstances! Soft speeches will not serve; hard grapeshot is questionable; but hovering between the two is *un*questionable. Ever wilder swells the tide of men; their infinite hum waxing ever louder, into imprecations, perhaps into crackle of stray musketry,—which latter, on the walls nine feet thick, cannot do execution. The Outer Drawbridge has been lowered for Thuriot; new *deputation of citizens* (it is the third, and noisiest of all) penetrates that way into the Outer Court; soft speeches producing no clearance of these, De Launay gives fire; pulls up his Drawbridge. A slight sputter;—which has *kindled* the too combustible chaos; made it a roaring fire-chaos! Bursts forth Insurrection, at sight of its own blood (for there were deaths by that sputter of fire), into endless rolling explosion of musketry, distraction, execration;—and overhead, from the Fortress, let one great gun, with its grapeshot, go booming, to show what we *could do*. The Bastille is besieged!

On then, all Frenchmen, that have hearts in your bodies! Roar with all your throats, of cartilage and metal, ye Sons of Liberty; stir spasmodically whatsoever of utmost faculty is in you, soul, body, or spirit; for it is the hour! Smite, thou Louis Tournay, cartwright and old-soldier, smite at that Outer Drawbridge chain, though the fiery hail whistles round thee! Never did your axe strike such a stroke. Down with it, man; down with it to Orcus: let the whole accursed Edifice sink thither, and Tyranny be swallowed up forever! Mounted, some say, on the roof of the guard-room, some "on bayonets stuck into joints of the wall," Tournay smites: the chain yields, breaks; the huge Drawbridge slams down, thundering. Glorious; and yet, alas, it is still but the outworks. The Eight grim Towers, with their Invalide musketry, their paving-stones and cannon-mouths, still soar aloft intact;—Ditch yawning impassable, stone-faced; the inner Drawbridge with its *back* towards us: the Bastille is still to take!

To describe this Siege of the Bastille (thought to be one of the most important in History) perhaps transcends the talent of mortals. Could one but, after infinite reading, get to understand so much as the plan of the building! But there is open Esplanade, at the end of the Rue

Saint-Antoine; there are such Forecourts, arched Gateway (where Louis Tournay now fights); then new drawbridges, dormant-bridges, rampant-bastions, and in the grim Eight Towers: a labyrinthic Mass, high-frowning there, of all ages from twenty years to four hundred and twenty;—beleaguered, in this its last hour, by mere Chaos come again! Ordnance of all calibres; throats of all capacities; men of all plans, every man his own engineer: seldom since the war of Pygmies and Cranes was there seen so anomalous a thing. The roar of the multitude grows deep. Paris wholly has got to the acme of its frenzy; whirled, all ways, by panic madness. At every street-barricade, there whirls simmering a minor whirlpool,—strengthening the barricade, since God knows what is coming; and all minor whirlpools play distractedly into that grand Fire-Maelstrom which is lashing round the Bastille.

And so it lashes and it roars. Cholat the wine-merchant has become an impromptu cannoneer. See Georget, of the Marine Service, ply the King of Siam's cannon. Singular: Georget lay, last night, taking his ease at his inn; the King of Siam's cannon also lay, knowing nothing of *him*, for a hundred years. Yet now, at the right instant, they have got together, and discourse eloquent music. Gardes Françaises also will be here, with real artillery: were not the walls so thick!—Upwards from the Esplanade, horizontally from all neighboring roofs and windows, flashes one irregular deluge of musketry, without effect. The Invalides lie flat, firing comparatively at their ease from behind stone; hardly through portholes show the tip of a nose. We fall, shot; and make no impression.

Let conflagration rage; of whatsoever is combustible! Guard-rooms are burnt, Invalides mess-rooms. A distracted wigmaker with two fiery torches is for igniting the powder-magazine of the Arsenal;—had not a woman run screaming; had not a Patriot instantly struck the wind out of him (butt of musket on pit of stomach), overturned barrels, and stayed the devouring element. Straw is burnt; three cartloads of it, hauled thither, go up in white smoke: almost to the choking of Patriotism itself. Smoke as of Tophet; confusion as of Babel; noise as of the Crack of Doom!

Blood flows; the aliment of new madness. The wounded are carried into houses; the dying leave their last mandate not to yield till the accursed Stronghold fall. And yet, alas, how fall? The walls are so thick! Deputations, three in number, arrive from the Hôtel-de-Ville. These wave their Town-flag in the arched Gateway; and stand, rolling their drum; but to no purpose. In such Crack of Doom, De Launay cannot hear them, dare not believe them: they return, with justified rage, the whew of lead still singing in their ears. What to do? The Firemen are here, squirting with their fire-pumps on the Invalides cannon, to wet the touchholes; they unfortunately cannot squirt so high; but produce only clouds of spray. Individuals of classical knowledge propose *catapults*. Every man his own engineer! And still the fire-deluge abates not: even women are firing. Gardes Françaises have come: real cannon, real cannoneers.

How the great Bastille Clock ticks (inaudible) in its Inner Court there, at its ease, hour after hour; as if nothing special, for it or the world, were passing! It tolled One when the firing began; and is now pointing towards Five, and still the firing slakes not.—Far down, in their vaults, the seven Prisoners hear muffled din as of earthquakes; their Turnkeys answer vaguely.

Woe to thee, De Launay, with thy poor hundred Invalides! Hast thou considered how each man's heart is so tremulously responsive to the hearts of all men; hast thou noted how omnipotent is the very sound of many men? How their shriek of indignation palsies the strong soul; their howl of contumely withers with unfelt pangs? Gluck confessed that the ground-tone of the noblest passage, in one of his noblest Operas, was the voice of the Populace he had heard at Vienna, crying to their Kaiser: Bread! Bread! Great is the combined voice of men; the utterance of their *instincts*, which are truer than their *thoughts*: it is the greatest a man encounters, among the sounds and shadows which make up this World of Time. He who can resist that, has his footing somewhere *beyond* Time. De Launay could not.

For four hours now has the World-Bedlam roared: call it the World-Chimæra, blowing fire! The poor Invalides have sunk under their battlements, or rise only with reversed muskets: they have made a white flag of napkins. The very Swiss at the Portcullis look weary of firing; disheartened in the fire-deluge: a porthole at the drawbridge is opened, as by one that would speak. On this plank, swinging over the abyss of that stone Ditch; plank resting on parapet, balanced by weight of Patriots,— Maillard hovers perilous: such a Dove towards such an Ark! Deftly thou shifty Usher: one man already fell; and lies smashed, far down there, against the masonry! Usher Maillard falls not; deftly, unerring he walks, with outspread palm. The Swiss holds a paper through his porthole; the shifty Usher snatches it, and returns. Terms of surrender: Pardon, immunity to all! Are they accepted?—"*Foi d'officer*, On the word of an officer," answers half-pay Hulin,—or half-pay Elie, for men do not agree on it,—"they are!" Sinks the drawbridge,—rushes-in the living deluge: the Bastille is fallen! *Victoire! La Bastille est prise!* (I v 6).

—*after-comment*: In Court, all is mystery, not without whispering of terror; though ye dream of lemonade and epaulettes, ye foolish women! His Majesty, kept in happy ignorance, perhaps dreams of double-barrels and the Woods of Meudon. Late at night, the Duke de Liancourt, having official right of entrance, gains access to the Royal Apartments, unfolds, with earnest clearness, the Job's-news. "*Mais*," said poor Louis, "*c'est une révolte,* Why, that is a revolt!"—"Sire," answered Liancourt, "it is not a revolt,—it is a revolution" (I v 7).

So many highest superlatives achieved by man are followed by new higher; and dwindle into comparatives and positives! The Siege of the Bastille, weighed with which, in the Historical balance, most other sieges, including that of Troy Town, are gossamer, cost, as we find in killed and mortally wounded, on the part of the Besiegers, some eighty-three persons: on the part of the Besieged, after all that straw-burning, fire-pumping, and deluge of musketry, One poor solitary Invalide, shot stone dead on the battlements! The Bastille Fortress, like the City of Jericho, was overturned by miraculous *sound* (I v 9).

Power of Woman

Sullen is the male heart, repressed by Patrollotism [Lafayette's patrols to prevent "effervescence"]; vehement is the female, irrepressible. Men know not what the pantry is, when it grows empty; only house-mothers know. O women, wives of men that will only calculate and not act! Patrollitism is strong; but Death, by starvation and military onfall, is stronger. Patrollotism represses male Patriotism; but female Patriotism? Will Guards named National thrust their bayonets into the bosoms of women? Such thought, or rather such dim unshaped raw material of a thought, ferments universally under the female nightcap; and, by earliest daybreak, on slight hint, will explode (I vii 3).

In squalid garret, on Monday morning Maternity awakes, to hear children weeping for bread. Maternity must forth to the streets, to the herb-markets and Bakers'-queues; meets there with hunger-stricken Maternity, sympathetic, exasperative. O we unhappy women! But, instead of Bakers'-queues, why not to Aristocrats' palaces, the root of the matter? *Allons!* Let us assemble (I vii 4).

One thing we will specify: the aspect under which the Patriotism of the softer sex presents itself in 1793. There are Female Patriots, whom the Girondins call Megæras, and count to the extent of eight thousand; with serpent-hair, all out of curl; who have changed the distaff for the dagger. They are of "the Society called Brotherly," *Fraternelle,* say *Sisterly,* which meets under the roof of the Jacobins. "Two thousand daggers," or *so,* have been ordered,—doubtless for them (III iii 8).

The September Massacres

This month of September 1792, which has become one of the memorable months of History, presents itself under two most diverse aspects; all of black on the one side, all of bright on the other. Whatsoever is cruel in the panic frenzy of Twenty-five million men, whatsoever is great in the

The departure of the Volunteers, July 1792 (painting by Edouard Detaille in the *Musée de l'Armée*).

simultaneous death-defiance of Twenty-five million men, stand here in abrupt contrast, near by one another. As indeed is usual when a man, how much more when a Nation of men, is hurled suddenly beyond the limits. For Nature, as green as she looks, rests everywhere on dread foundations, were we farther down; and Pan, to whose music the Nymphs dance, has a cry in him that can drive all men distracted.

Very frightful it is when a Nation, rending asunder its Constitutions and Regulations which were grown dead cerements [shrouds] for it, becomes *trans*cendental; and must now seek its wild way through the New, Chaotic,—where Force is not yet distinguished into Bidden and Forbidden, but Crime and Virtue welter unseparated! Sansculottism reigning in all its grandeur and in all its hideousness: the Gospel (God's-message) of Man's Rights, Man's *mights* or strengths, and still louder for the time, the fearfulest Devil's-Message of Man's weaknesses and sins;—and all on such a scale, and under such aspect: cloudy "death-birth of a world": huge smoke-cloud, streaked with rays as of heaven on one side; girt on the other as with hell-fire! History tells us many things: but for the last thousand years and more, what thing has she told us of a sort like this?

It is unfortunate, though very natural, that the history of this Period has so generally been written in hysterics. Exaggeration abounds, execration, wailing; and, on the whole, darkness. One finds it difficult to imagine that the Sun shone in this September month, as he does in others. Nevertheless it is an indisputable fact that the Sun did shine.

He had been a wise Frenchman, who, looking close at hand on this waste aspect of France all stirring and whirling, in ways new, untried, had been able to discern where the cardinal movement lay; which tendency it was that had the rule and primary direction of it then! But at forty-four years' distance, it is different. To all men now, two cardinal movements or grand tendencies, in the September whirl, have become discernible enough: that stormful effluence towards the Frontiers; and that frantic crowding towards Town-houses and Council-halls in the interior. Wild France dashes, in desperate death-defiance, towards the Frontiers, to defend itself from foreign Despots; and crowds towards Townhalls and Election Committee-rooms, to defend itself from domestic Aristocrats.

Two great movements: a rushing against domestic Traitors, a rushing against foreign Despots. Mad movements both, restrainable by no known rule; strongest passions of human nature driving them on: love, hatred, vengeful sorrow, braggart Nationality also vengeful,—and pale Panic over all! Twelve hundred slain Patriots, do they not, from their dark catacombs there, in Death's dumb-show plead (O ye Legislators) for vengeance? Such was the destructive rage of these Aristocrats on the ever-memorable Tenth of August. Nay, apart from vengeance, are there not still in this

Paris (in round numbers) "Thirty-thousand Aristocrats," of the most ma-
lignant humor; driven now to their last trump-card? Be patient, ye Patriots: our new High Court sits; each Section has sent Four Jurymen; and
Danton, extinguishing improper judges, improper practices wheresover
found: with such a Minister of Justice, shall not Justice be done?—Let it
be swift, then, answers universal Patriotism; swift and sure!—(III i 1).

Danton had come over, last night, and demanded a Decree to *search*
for arms, since they were not yielded voluntarily. Let "Domiciliary visits,"
with rigor of authority, be made to this end. To search for arms; for
horses,—Aristocratism rolls in its carriage, while Patriotism cannot trail
its cannon. To search generally for munitions of war, "in the houses of
persons suspect,"—and even, if it seem proper, to seize and imprison
the suspect persons themselves! In the Prisons their Plots will be harmless; in the Prisons they will be as hostages for us, and not without use.
This Decree the energetic Minister of Justice demanded last night, and
got; and this same night it is to be executed. Two-thousand stand of arms,
as they count, are foraged in this way; and some four-hundred head of
new Prisoners; and, on the whole, such a terror and damp is struck
through the Aristocrat heart, as all but Patriotism, and even Patriotism
were it out of this agony, might pity. Yes, Messieurs! if Brunswick blast
Paris to ashes, he probably will blast the Prisons of Paris too: pale Terror,
if we have got it, we will also give it, and the depth of horrors that lie in
it; the same leaky bottom, in these wild waters, bears us all.

One can judge what stir there was now among the "thirty-thousand
Royalists": how the Plotters, or the accused of a Plotting, shrank each
closer into his lurking-place. From five in the afternoon, a great city is
struck suddenly silent; except for the beating of drums, for the tramp of
marching feet; and ever and anon the dread thunder of the knocker at
some door, a Tricolor Commissioner with his blue Guards (*black-
guards!*) arriving. All Streets are vacant, beset by Guards at each end: all
Citizens are ordered to be within doors. On the River float sentinel
barges, lest we escape by water: the Barriers hermetically closed. Frightful! The Sun shines; serenely westering, in smokeless mackerel-sky; Paris
is as if sleeping, as if dead:—Paris is holding its breath, to see what stroke
will fall on it; all logic reduced to this one primitive thesis, An eye for an
eye, a tooth for a tooth!

Of "thirty-thousand" naturally great multitudes were left unmolested:
but, as we said, some four-hundred, designated as "persons suspect,"
were seized; and an unspeakable terror fell on all. Woe to him who is
guilty of plotting, who, guilty or not guilty, has an enemy in his Section
to call him guilty! Poor old M. de Cazotte is seized; his young loved
Daughter with him, refusing to quit him. Poor old M. de Sombreuil is
seized; a man seen askance by Patriotism ever since the Bastille days;

whom also a fond Daughter will not quit. With young tears hardly suppressed, and old wavering weakness rousing itself once more,—O my brothers, O my sisters!

The famed and named go; the nameless, if they have an accuser. What with the arrestments on this night of the twenty-ninth, what with those that have gone on more or less, day and night, ever since the Tenth, one may fancy what the Prisons now were. Crowding and confusion; jostle, hurry, vehemence and terror! (III i 2).

And terror is on these streets of Paris; terror and rage, tears and frenzy: tocsin pealing through the air; fierce desperation rushing to battle; mothers, with streaming eyes and wild hearts, sending forth their sons to die. "Carriage-horses are seized by the bridle," that they may draw cannon; "the traces cut, the carriages left standing." In such murky bewilderment of Frenzy, are not Murder and all Furies near at hand? On slight hint—who knows on how slight?—may not Murder come; and, with *her* snaky-sparkling head, illuminate this murk!

How it was and went, what part might be premeditated, what was improvised and accidental, man will never know, till the great Day of Judgment make it known. In this Paris there are as wicked men, say a hundred or more, as exist in all the Earth: to be hired, and set on; to set on, of their own accord, unhired.—And yet we will remark that premeditation itself is not performance, is not surety of performance; that it is perhaps, at most, surety of *letting* whosoever wills perform. From the purpose of crime to the act of crime there is an abyss; wonderful to think of. The finger lies on the pistol; but the man is not yet a murderer: may his whole nature staggering at such consummation, is there not a confused pause rather,—one last instant of possibility for him? Not yet a murderer; it is at the mercy of light trifles whether the most fixed idea may not yet become unfixed. One slight switch of a muscle, the death-flash bursts; and he is it, and will for Eternity be it; his horizon girdled now not with golden hope, but with red flames of remorse; voices from the depths of Nature sounding, Woe, woe on him!

Of such stuff are we all made; on such powder-mines of bottomless guilt and criminality,—"if God restrained not," as is well said,—does the purest of us walk. There are depths in man that go the length of lowest Hell, as there are heights that reach highest Heaven;—for are not both Heaven and Hell made out of him, made by him, everlasting Miracle and Mystery as he is?—But looking on the tent-buildings and frantic enrolments; on this murky-simmering Paris, with its crammed Prisons (supposed about to burst), with its tocsin, its mothers' tears, and soldiers' farewell shoutings,—the pious soul might have prayed, that day, that God's grace would restrain, and greatly restrain; lest on slight hest or hint, Madness, Horror and Murder rose, and this Sabbathday of September became a Day black in the Annals of men.

The tocsin is pealing its loudest, the clocks inaudibly striking *Three*, when along the streets fare some thirty Priests, in six carriages, from their preliminary House of Detention towards the Prison of the Abbaye. Carriages enough stand deserted on the streets; these six move on,—through angry multitudes, cursing as they move. Accursed! Aristocrat hypocrites, this is the pass ye have brought us to! Frantic Patriots mount even on the carriage-steps; the very Guards hardly refraining. Pull up your carriage-blinds?—No! answers Patriotism, clapping its horny paw on the carriage-blind, and crushing it down again. Patience in oppression has limits: we are close on the Abbaye, it has lasted long: a Priest, of quicker temper than others, smites the horny paw with his cane; nay, finding solacement in it, smites the unkempt head, sharply and again more sharply, twice over,—seen clearly of us and of the world. It is the last that we see clearly. Alas, next moment the carriages are locked and blocked in endless raging tumults; in yells deaf to the cry for mercy, which answer the cry for mercy with sabre-thrusts through the heart. The thirty Priests are torn out, are massacred about the Prison-Gate, one after one—and Murder's snaky-sparkling head *has* risen in the murk!—

From Sunday after noon (exclusive of intervals and pauses not final) till Thursday evening, there follow consecutively a Hundred Hours. Which hundred hours are to be reckoned with the hours of the Bartholomew Butchery, of the Armagnac Massacres, Sicilian Vespers, or whatsoever is savagest in the annals of this world. Horrible the hour when man's soul, in its paroxysm, spurns asunder the barriers and rules; and shows what dens and depths are in it! For Night and Orcus, as we say, as was long prophesied, have burst forth, here in this Paris, from their subterranean imprisonment: hideous, dim-confused; which it is painful to look on; and yet which cannot, and indeed which should not, be forgotten.

In this Abbaye Prison, the sudden massacre of the Priests being once over, a strange Court of Justice, or call it Court of Revenge and Wild-Justice, swiftly fashions itself. At *La Force*, at the *Châtelet*, the *Conciergerie*, the like Court forms itself; the thing that one man does, other men can do. There are Seven Prisons in Paris, full of Aristocrats with conspiracies; and there are seventy times seven hundred Patriot hearts in a state of frenzy. Scoundrel hearts also there are; as perfect, say, as the Earth holds,—if such are needed. To whom, in this mood, law is as no-law; and killing, by what name soever called, is but work to be done.

So sit these sudden Courts of Wild-Justice, with the Prison-Registers before them; unwonted wild tumult howling all round; the Prisoners in dread expectancy within. Swift: a name is called; bolts jingle, a Prisoner is there. A few questions are put; swiftly this sudden Jury decides: Royalist Plotter or not? Clearly not: in that case, let the Prisoner be enlarged with *Vive la Nation*. Probably yea; then still, Let the Prisoner be enlarged, but without *Vive la Nation*; or else it may run, Let the Prisoner be conducted to La Force. Volunteer bailiffs seize the doomed man; he is at the outer-gate; "enlarged," or "conducted," not into La Force, but into a howling sea; forth, under an arch of wild sabres, axes and pikes, hewn asunder. And another sinks, and another; and there forms itself a piled heap of corpses, and the gutters begin to run red.

Fancy the yells of these men, their faces of sweat and blood; the crueler shrieks of these women and a fellow-mortal hurled naked into it all! Man after man is cut down; the sabres need sharpening, the killers refresh themselves from wine-jugs. Onward and onward goes the butchery; the loud yells wearying down into bass growls. A sombre-faced shifting multitude looks on; in dull approval, or dull disapproval; in dull recognition that it is Necessity. The brave are not spared, nor the beautiful, nor the weak. The circuit of the Temple is guarded by a long stretched tricolor riband; terror enters, and the clangor of infinite tumult; hitherto not regicide, though that too may come.

But of thrillings of affection, fragments of wild virtues turning up in this shaking asunder of man's existence: of these too there is a proportion. Note old M. de Sombreuil, who had a Daughter:—My Father is not an Aristocrat: O good gentlemen, I will swear it, and testify it, and in all ways prove it; we are not; we hate Aristocrats! "Wilt thou drink Aristocrats' blood?" The man lifts blood (if universal Rumor can be credited); the poor maiden does drink. "This Sombreuil is innocent, then!" Yes, indeed,—and note, most of all, how the bloody pikes, at this news, do rattle to the ground; and the tiger-yells become bursts of jubilee over a brother saved; the old man and his daughter are clasped to bloody bosoms, with hot tears; and borne home in triumph of *Vive la Nation*, the killers refusing even money! Does it seem strange, this temper of theirs? It seems very certain, and very significant (III i 4).

"O everlasting infamy," one exclaims, "that Paris stood looking on in stupor for four days, and did not interfere!" Very desirable indeed that Paris had interfered; yet not unnatural that it stood even so, looking on in stupor. Paris is in death-panic, the enemy and gibbets at its door: whosoever in Paris has the heart to front death, finds it more pressing to do it fighting the Prussians, than fighting the killers of Aristocrats. Indignant abhorrence may be here; gloomy sanction, premeditation or not, may be there; dull disapproval, dull approval, and acquiescence in Necessity and Destiny, is the general temper. The Sons of Darkness, "two-hundred or so," risen from their lurking-places, have scope to do their work. Urged on by fever-frenzy of Patriotism, and the madness of Terror;

—urged on by lucre, and the gold louis of wages? Nay, not lucre; for the gold watches, rings, money of the Massacred, are punctually brought to the Townhall, by Killers who higgle afterwards for their twenty shillings of wages.

But the temper, as we say, is dull acquiescence. Not till the Patriotic or Frenetic part of the work is finished for want of material; and Sons of Darkness, bent clearly on lucre alone, begin wrenching watches and purses, brooches, "to equip volunteers," in daylight, on the streets,— does the temper grow vehement; does the Constable raise his truncheon, and striking heartily (like a cattle-driver in earnest) beat the "course of things" back into its old regulated drove-roads.

This is the September Massacre, otherwise called "Severe Justice of the People." These are the Septemberers (*Septembriseurs*); a name of some note and lucency,—but lucency of the Nether-fire sort; very different from that of our Bastille Heroes, who shone, disputable by no Friend of Free- dom, as in Heavenly light-radiance: to such a stage of the business have we advanced since then! The numbers massacred are in the Historical *fantasy* "between two and three thousand"; or indeed they are "upwards of six thousand"; nay finally they are "twelve thousand" and odd hun- dreds,—not more than that. In Arithmetical ciphers, and Lists drawn up by an accurate advocate, the number, including two-hundred and two priests, three "persons unknown," and "one thief," is a Thousand and Eighty-nine,—not less than that (III i 6).

—*after-comment*: That a shriek of inarticulate horror rose over this thing, not only from French Aristocrats and Moderates, but from all Eu- rope, and has prolonged itself to the present day, was most natural and right. The thing lay done, irrevocable; a thing to be counted beside some other things, which lie very black in our Earth's Annals, yet which will not erase therefrom. For man, as was remarked, stands in the intersection of primeval Light with the everlasting Dark!—Thus have there been very miserable things done. Sicilian Vespers, and "eight thousand slaughtered in two hours," [history now says two thousand] are a known thing. Kings themselves, not in desperation, but only in difficulty, have sat hatching, for year and day, their Bartholomew Business; and then, at the right moment, also on an Autumn Sunday; this very Bell was set a-pealing— with effect.

Nay the same black boulder-stones of these Paris Prisons have seen Prison-massacres before now; Burgundies massacring Armagnacs, whom they had suddenly imprisoned, till, as now, there were piled heaps of carcasses, and the streets ran red;—the mayor speaking the austere lan- guage of the law, and answered by the Killers, "Sir, God's malison on your 'justice,' your 'pity,' your 'right reason.' Cursed be of God whoso shall have pity on these false traitorous Armagnacs; dogs they are; they have destroyed us, wasted this realm of France, and sold it to the English." And so they slay, and fling aside the slain, to the extent of "fifteen hundred and eighteen, among whom are found four Bishops and two Presidents of Parlement."

For though it is not Satan's world this that we live in, Satan always has his place in it (underground properly); and from time to time bursts up. Well may mankind shriek, inarticulately anathematizing as they can. Shriek ye; acted have they (III i 6).

The Guillotine

For, lo, the great *Guillotine*, wondrous to behold, now stands there; the Doctor's *Idea* has become Oak and Iron; the huge cyclopean axe "falls in its grooves like the ram of the Pile-engine," swiftly snuffing-out the light of men! (III i 1).

Terror of the Guillotine was never terrible till now. Systole, diastole, swift and ever swifter goes the Axe of Samson. Indictments cease by degrees to have so much as plausibility: Fouquier chooses from the Twelve Houses of Arrest what he calls Batches, "*Fournées*," a score or more at a time. Swift and ever swifter goes Samson; up, finally, to threescore and more at a Batch. It is the highday of Death: none but the Dead return not (III vi 3). [See Chapter 10 for more on the guillotine and Samson.]

The Revolutionary Tribunal

Very notable also is the *Tribunal Extraordinaire*: for do not we all hate Traitors, O ye people of Paris? Five Judges; a standing Jury, which is named from Paris and the Neighborhood, that there be not delay in naming it: they are subject to no Appeal; to hardly any Law-forms, but must "get themselves convinced" in all readiest ways; and for security are bound "to vote audibly"; audibly, in the hearing of a Paris Public. This is the *Tribunal Extraordinaire*; which, in few months, getting into most lively action, shall be entitled *Tribunal Révolutionaire*; as indeed it from the very first has entitled itself; with a Judge-President, a Fouquier-Tinville for Attorney-General, and a Jury of such as Citizen Leroi, who has surnamed himself *Dix-Août*, "Leroi *August-Tenth*," it will become the wonder of the world. Herein has Sansculottism fashioned for itself a Sword of Sharpness: a weapon magical; tempered in the Stygian hell-waters; to the edge of it all armor, and defence of strength or of cunning shall be soft; it shall mow down Lives and Brazen-gates; and the waving of it shed terror through the souls of men (III iii 5). [See Chapter 7 for the words of Jourgniac, an eyewitness.]

The Terror

They [the Committee of Public Safety] ride this Whirlwind; they, raised by force of circumstances, insensibly, very strangely, thither to that dread height;—and guide it, and seem to guide it. Stranger set of Cloud-Compellers the Earth never saw. A Robespierre, a Billaud, a Collot, Couthon, Saint-Just: these are your Cloud-Compellers. Small intellectual talent is necessary: indeed where among them, except in the head of Carnot, busied organizing victory, would you find any? The talent is one of instinct rather. It is that of divining aright what this great dumb Whirlwind wishes and wills; that of willing, with more frenzy than any one, what all the world wills. To stand at no obstacles; to heed no considerations, human or divine; to know well that, of divine or human, there is one thing needful, Triumph of the Republic, Destruction of the Enemies of the Republic! With this one spiritual endowment, and so few others, it is strange to see how a dumb inarticulately storming Whirlwind of things puts, as it were, its reins into your hand, and invites and compels you to be leader of it (III v 5).

Nor with heroic daring against the Foreign foe, can black vengeance against the Domestic be wanting. Deputy Merlin of Douai, named subsequently Merlin *Suspect*, comes in August 1793 with his world-famous *Law of the Suspect*; ordering all Sections, by their Committees, instantly to arrest all Persons Suspect; and explaining: "Are suspect," says he, "all who by their actions, by their connections, speakings, writings have"—in short become Suspect. Municipal Placards and Proclamations will bring it about that you may almost recognize a Suspect on the streets, and clutch him there,—off to Committee and Prison. Watch well your words, watch well your looks: if Suspect of nothing else, you may grow, as came to be a saying, "Suspect of being Suspect!" For are we not in a state of Revolution?

No frightfuler Law ever ruled in a Nation of men. All Prisons and Houses of Arrest in French land are getting crowded to the ridge-tile: Forty-four thousand Committees, like as many companies of reapers or gleaners, gleaning France, are gathering their harvest, and storing it in these Houses. And we are to have an ambulant "Revolutionary Army": six-thousand strong, under right captains, this shall perambulate the country at large, and strike-in wherever it finds such harvest-work slack. Let Aristocrats, Federalists, Monsieurs vanish, and all men tremble: "the Soil of Liberty shall be purged,"—with a vengeance!

Daily the great Guillotine has its due. Like a black Spectre, daily at eventide, glides the Death-tumbril through the variegated throng of things. The variegated street shudders at it, for the moment; next moment forgets it: The Aristocrats! They were guilty against the Republic; their death, were it only that their goods are confiscated, will be useful to the Republic; *Vive la République!* (III iv 6).

We are now, therefore, got to that black precipitous Abyss; whither all things have long been tending; where, having now arrived on the giddy verge, they hurl down, in confused ruin; headlong, pellmell, down, down;—till Sansculottism have consummated itself; and in this wondrous French Revolution, as in a Doomsday, a World have been rapidly, if not born again, yet destroyed and engulfed. Terror has long been terrible: but to the actors themselves it has now become manifest that their appointed course is one of Terror; and they say, Be it so. *"Que la Terreur soit à l'ordre du jour."* "Let Terror be the Order of the Day"

So many centuries had been adding together, century transmitting it with increase to century, the sum of Wickedness, of Falsehood, Oppression of man by man. Kings were sinners, and Priests were, and People. Open Scoundrels rode triumphant, bediademed, becoronetted, bemitred; or the still fataler species of Secret-Scoundrels, in their fair-sounding formulas, speciosities, respectabilities, hollow within: the race of Quacks was grown many as the sands of the sea. Till at length such a sum of Quackery had accumulated itself as, in brief, the Earth and the Heavens were weary of. Slow seemed the Day of Settlement; coming on, all imperceptible, across the bluster and fanfaronade: behold it has come, suddenly, unlooked for by any man!

The harvest of long centuries was ripening and whitening so rapidly of late; and now it is grown *white*, and is reaped rapidly, as it were, in one day. Reaped, in this Reign of Terror; and carried home, to Hades and the Pit!—Unhappy Sons of Adam: it is ever so; and never do they know it, nor will they know it. With cheerfully smoothed countenances, day after day, and generation after generation, they, calling cheerfully to one another, Well-speed-ye, are at work, *sowing the wind*. And yet, as God lives, they *shall reap the whirlwind*: no other thing, we say, is possible,—since God is a Truth, and His World is a Truth.

Now surely not realization, of Christianity or of aught earthly, do we discern in their Reign of Terror, in this French Revolution of which it is the consummating. Destruction rather we discern,—of all that was destructible. It is as if Twenty-five millions, risen at length into the Pythian mood, had stood up simultaneously to say, with a sound which goes through far lands and times, that the Untruth of an Existence had become insupportable. O ye Hypocrisies and Speciosities, Royal mantles, Cardinal plush-cloaks, ye Credos, Formulas, Respectabilities, fair-painted Sepulchres full of dead men's bones,—behold, ye appear to us to be altogether a Lie. Yet our Life is not a Lie; yet our Hunger and Misery is not a Lie! Behold we lift up, one and all, our Twenty-five million right-hands; and take the Heavens, and the Earth and also the Pit of Tophet to witness, that either ye shall be abolished, or else we shall be abolished!

No inconsiderable Oath, truly; forming the most remarkable transaction in these last thousand years. Wherefrom likewise there follow, and will follow, results. The fulfilment of this Oath; the black desperate battle of Men against their whole Condition and Environment,—a battle, alas, withal, against the Sin and Darkness that was in themselves as in others: this is the Reign of Terror. Transcendental despair was the purport of it, though not consciously so. False hopes, of Fraternity, Political Millennium, and what not, we have always seen: but the unseen heart of the whole, the transcendental despair, was not false; neither has it been of no effect. Despair, pushed far enough, completes the circle, so to speak; and becomes a kind of genuine productive hope again.

A nation of men, full of wants and void of habits! The old habits are gone to wreck because they were old: men, driven forward by Necessity and fierce Pythian Madness, have, on the spur of the instant, to devise for the want the *way* of satisfying it. The Wonted tumbles down; by imitation, by invention, the Unwonted hastily builds itself up. What the French National head has in it comes out: if not a great result, surely one of the strangest.

Neither shall the Reader fancy that it was all black, this Reign of Terror: far from it. How many hammermen and squaremen, bakers and brewers, washers and wringers, over this France, must ply their old daily work, let the Government be one of Terror or one of Joy! In this Paris there are Twenty-three Theatres nightly; some count as many as Sixty Places of Dancing. The Playwright manufactures,—pieces of a strictly Republican character. Ever fresh Novel-garbage, as of old, fodders the Circulating Libraries. Business speculation exhales from itself "sudden fortunes," like Aladdin-Palaces: really a kind of miraculous Fata-Morganas, since you *can* live in them, for a time. Terror is as a sable ground, on which the most variegated of scenes paints itself. In startling transitions, in colors all intensified, the sublime, the ludicrous, the horrible succeed one another; or rather, in crowding tumult, accompany one another (III v 1). [Ninety percent of all the executions in the Terror took place in twenty of the eighty-six departments, all of which except Paris were in the war zone; in thirty departments there were fewer than ten killings, and many sizeable towns were almost entirely spared.]

But the grand and indeed substantially primary and generic aspect of the Consummation of Terror remains still [after descriptions of numerous executions of luckless politicians and atrocities against the populations of many cities and towns across France] to be looked at; nay blinkard History has for most all but *over*looked this aspect, the soul of the whole; that which makes it terrible to the Enemies of France. Let Despotism and Cimmerian Coalitions consider. All French men and French things are in a State of Requisition; Fourteen Armies are got on foot; Patriotism, with all that it has of faculty in heart or in head, in soul or body or breeches-pocket, is rushing to the Frontiers, to prevail or die! Not swifter pulses that Guillotine, in dread systole-diastole in the Place de la Révolution, than smites the Sword of Patriotism, smiting Cimmeria back to its own borders, from the sacred soil.

In fact, the Government is what we can call Revolutionary; and some men are *"à la hauteur,"* on a level with the circumstances; and others are not *à la hauteur,*—so much the worse for them. But the Anarchy, we may say, has *organized* itself: Society is literally overset; its old forces working with mad activity, but in the inverse order; destructive and self-destructive (III v 5).

On the whole, is it not, O Reader, one of the strangest Flame-Pictures that ever painted itself; flaming off there, on its ground of Guillotine-black? And the nightly Theatres are Twenty-three; and the *Salons de danse* are Sixty; full of mere *Egalité, Fraternité* and *Carmagnole.* And the Houses of Arrest are Twelve, for Paris alone; crowded and even crammed. And at all turns, you need your "certificate of Civism"; be it for going out, or for coming in; nay without it you cannot, for money, get your daily ounces of bread. For we still live, waited on by these two, Scarcity and Confusion. The faces of men are darkened with suspicion; with suspecting, or being suspect. The streets lie unswept; the ways unmended. Law has shut her Books; speaks little, save impromptu. Crimes go unpunished; not crimes against the Revolution.

How silent now sits Royalism; sits all Aristocratism; Respectability that kept its Gig! The honor now, and the safety, is to Poverty, not to Wealth. Aristocratism crouches low, in what shelter is still left; submitting to all requisitions, vexations; too happy to escape with life. Ghastly châteaus stare on you by the wayside; disroofed, diswindowed.

And daily, we say, like a black Spectre, silently through that Life-tumult, passes the Revolution Cart; writing on the walls its MENE, MENE, *Thou are weighed, and found wanting!* A Spectre with which one has grown familiar. Men have adjusted themselves: complaint issues not from that Death-tumbril. Weak women and *ci-devants*, their plumage and finery all tarnished, sit there; with a silent gaze, as if looking into the Infinite Black. The once light lip wears a curl of irony, uttering no word; and the Tumbril fares along. They may be guilty before Heaven, or not; they are guilty, we suppose, before the Revolution. Then, does not the Republic "coin money" of them, with its great axe? Red Nightcaps [worn by many in the mob] howl dire approval: the rest of Paris looks on; if with a sigh, that is much: Fellow-creatures whom sighing cannot help; whom black Necessity and the prosecutor have clutched.

Two other things, we will mention: The Blond Perukes; the Tannery at Meudon. Great talk is of these *Perruques blondes*: O Reader, they are made from the Heads of Guillotined women! The locks of a Duchess, in this way, may come to cover the scalp of a Cordwainer; her blonde German Frankism his black Gaelic poll, if it be bald. Or they may be worn affectionately, as relics; rendering one suspect? Citizens use them, not without mockery; of a rather cannibal sort.

Still deeper into one's heart goes that Tannery at Meudon; not mentioned among the other miracles of tanning! "At Meudon," says a witness with considerable calmness, "there was a Tannery of Human Skins; such of the Guillotined as seemed worth flaying: of which perfectly good wash-leather was made"; for breeches, and other uses. The skin of the men, he remarks, was superior in toughness and quality to chamois; that of the women was good for almost nothing, being so soft in texture!— History looking back over Cannibalism will perhaps find no terrestrial Cannibalism of a sort, on the whole, so detestable. It is a manufactured, soft-feeling, quietly elegant sort; a sort *perfide!* Alas, then, is man's civilization only a wrappage, through which the savage nature of him can still burst, infernal as ever? Nature still makes him; and has an Infernal in her as well as a Celestial (III v 7).

The Prisons

In these Twelve Houses of Arrest there have now accumulated twelve-thousand persons. They are Ci-devants, Royalists; in far greater part, they are Republicans, of various Girondin, Fayettish, Un-Jacobin color. Perhaps no human Habitation or Prison ever equalled in squalor, in noisome horror, these Twelve Houses of Arrest.

Very singular how a kind of order rises up in all conditions of human existence; there are formed modes of existing together, habitudes, observances, nay gracefulness, joys!

One citizen will explain fully how our lean dinner was consumed not without politeness and *place-aux-dames*: how Seigneur and Shoeblack, Duchess and Doll-Tearsheet, flung pell-mell into a heap, ranked themselves according to method: at what hour "the Citoyennes took to their needlework"; and we, yielding the chairs, endeavored to talk gallantly standing, or even to sing and harp more or less. Jealousies, enmities, are not wanting; nor flirtations, of an effective character.

Alas, by degrees, even needlework must cease: Plot in the Prison rises, by Preternatural Suspicion. Rigor grows, stiffens into horrid tyranny; Plot in the Prison getting ever rifer. This Plot in the Prison is now the stereotype formula of prosecutor Fouquier-Tinville: against whomsoever he knows no crime, this is a ready-made crime. His Judgment-bar has become unspeakable; a recognized mockery; known only as the wicket one passes through, towards Death. His Indictments are drawn out in blank; you insert the Names after. Nightly come his Tumbrils to the Luxembourg, with the fatal Roll-call; list of the condemned of to-morrow. Men rush towards the Grate; listen, if their name be in it? One deep-drawn breath, when the name is not in; we live still one day! And yet some score or scores of names were in. Quick these, they clasp their loved ones to their heart, one last time; with brief adieu, wet-eyed or dry-eyed, they mount, and are away. This night to the Conciergerie; through the Palais misnamed *of Justice*, to the Guillotine to-morrow.

And still the Prisons fill, and the Guillotine goes faster. On all high roads march Prisoners, wending towards Paris. Not *Ci-devants* now; they, the noisy of them, are mown down; it is Republicans now. Chained they march; in exasperated moments singing their *Marseillaise*. They are way-worn, weary of heart; can only shout: *Live the Republic*; we, as under horrid enchantment, dying in this way for it!

How long, O Lord! Not forever, no. All Anarchy, all Evil, Injustice, is, by the nature of it, *dragon's-teeth*; suicidal, and cannot endure (III v 6).

TOPICS FOR WRITTEN AND ORAL DISCUSSION

1. Was France's aid to the Americans a serious mistake in terms of her interests? Was it a fatal one? From your knowledge of the American Revolution, how would things have worked out for the colonies if France had not come in?

2. Two "disturbers of the peace," were hanged at Versailles when they protested that they were hungry and desperate. Why were extreme measures taken? What does it suggest about the state of mind in the palace?

3. Comment on the phrase "the Mights of Man" in Carlyle's discussion of the state of things when people grow food for others but starve themselves. What is the difference between a "Might" in this sense and a "Right"? Is there now a Right to be fed, at least at subsistence level? Should there be?

4. One of the brilliant aspects of the Carlyle book is the way he evokes the dizzying feeling of a world made new, where old habits, connections, ways of governance are suddenly out the window. Have we seen anything like that in the twentieth century? What happened?

5. According to some historians, that slight "sputter of fire" ordered by the Bastille's governor killed forty people to whom the governor had given safe-conduct. Why do you think Carlyle soft-pedals this? Does Dickens refer to it?

6. Study Dickens's description of the siege of the Bastille. How does his narrative technique differ from Carlyle's? Do you prefer one or the other?

7. "Cholat the wine-merchant has become an impromptu cannoneer." What character in *A Tale of Two Cities* does this individual remind you of? What, if any, elements in the Carlyle description of the Bastille's fall did Dickens use?

8. There were only seven prisoners in the Bastille. Why all the fuss?

9. What conversation in *A Tale of Two Cities* does "Power of Woman" remind you of?

10. Carlyle laments the way emigrant nobility behaved. Is he realistic? What was the terrible thing these emigrants did to France and those they left behind?

11. Carlyle paints a picture of France ringed by enemies and fearing enemies within. Is it convincing? Does it make you feel any differently about the Terror from the way Dickens would have you feel?

12. Comment on the two forces Carlyle sees at work in France in the fall

of 1792. He seems to find one producing admirable results, the other despicable. Did they need each other?

13. "The sabres need sharpening." Dickens had other sources for his novel, though we have little information about them. But it seems possible that this little phrase inspired a complete picture in his mind. What do you think of the device he uses in his chapter "The Grindstone" to convey the horror of the September Massacres, covered so extensively in the Carlyle book?

14. What does Carlyle mean about the importance of instinct, as opposed to intellect, in the Revolution? Do you see echoes of this idea in *A Tale of Two Cities*?

15. Carlyle seems to think the Terror has a good side. What does he mean? Do you think Dickens shares this view? Is it within the scope of his novel?

16. How do the horrors of the French Revolution compare with more recent horrors in quantity and quality? What do you think Carlyle would have made of the twentieth century?

SUGGESTED READINGS AND WORKS CITED

Carlyle, Thomas. *The French Revolution*. London: James Fraser, 1837.
FK   Kaplan, Fred. *Thomas Carlyle: A Biography*. Berkeley: University of California Press, 1993.

5

Dickens and Carlyle: Common Threads

INTRODUCTION

Charles Dickens's preface to *A Tale of Two Cities* deferentially acknowledges the "philosophy" of Thomas Carlyle's *The French Revolution* (see introductory quotation for Chapter 4), but it does not hint at any debt to the book for material in his novel. Dickens was not a humble man and in some ways far from a mature one. But in this case he may have thought the debt too obvious to need mentioning.

    A Tale of Two Cities was not his first historical novel. Nearly two decades earlier he had written *Barnaby Rudge: A Tale of the Riots of 'Eighty*, about the Gordon Riots in London in 1780. (This novel is discussed and extensively quoted in Chapter 6.) He had done a great deal of homework for that book, and it is obvious that he did a great deal for his second effort in the genre. We know, for instance, that he appealed to Carlyle early on to suggest source materials he might consult. Dickens was (in his biographer Edgar Johnson's words) "grateful but staggered when Carlyle sardonically chose two cartloads of books at the London Library and had them all sent to him. The more of them that Dickens waded through, however, the more he felt with amazed admiration that

Carlyle had torn out the vitals of them all and fused them into his fulginous masterpiece'' (EJ 947–48).

This chapter provides an opportunity to examine the way Dickens created his book. Given all the material he had at hand, what choices did he make? What facts did he suppress? What emphases did he alter? What new elements did he introduce? Were it possible to do so in a readable way in a book of this size, it would have been preferable to set up Dickens and Carlyle side by side; but as it is not, open the novel at the places indicated and study it as you read this chapter.

DICKENS'S INSPIRATIONS
AND CONNECTIONS

Dickens blended a great deal of detailed historical fact with his story. Indeed, some historical figures and localities described by Carlyle appear in *A Tale of Two Cities*, sometimes in modified form. Some minor factual elements that might have inspired Dickens are King Louis XVI's hobby of lockmaking (III i 7), echoed in Doctor Manette's shoemaking; Philippe Egalité's emigrant son's career, under an assumed name, as a teacher of mathematics (III v 2), reminding us of Charles Darnay's career in England as a tutor and translator; and the gallows forty feet high erected for Gaspard, seemingly directly inspired by Carlyle's early story of a forty-foot gallows erected to hang troublemakers at Versailles. Here are some more important connections, presented in somewhat abridged and simplified passages from Carlyle's work.

FROM THOMAS CARLYLE, *THE FRENCH REVOLUTION*
London: James Fraser, 1837

Foulon (compare *A Tale of Two Cities* ii 22)

Already old Foulon, with an eye to be war-minister himself, is making underground movements. This is that same Foulon named *âme damnée* [damned soul] *du Parlement*; a man grown gray in treachery, in griping, projecting, intriguing and iniquity: who once when it was objected, to some finance-scheme of his, "What will the people do?"—made answer, in the fire of discussion, "The people may eat grass": hasty words, which fly abroad irrevocable,—and will send back tidings! (I iii 9).

As for old Foulon, one learns that he is dead; at least "a sumptuous funeral" is going on; the undertakers honoring him, if no other will. Intendant Berthier, his son-in-law, is still living; lurking . . . now fled no man knows whither (I v 8).

We are but at the 22nd of the month, hardly above a week since the Bastille fell, when it suddenly appears that old Foulon is alive; nay, that he is here, in early morning, in the streets of Paris: the extortioner, the plotter, who would make the people eat grass, and was a liar from the beginning!—It is even so. The deceptive "sumptuous funeral" (of some domestic that died); the hiding-place at Vitry towards Fontainebleau, have not availed that wretched old man. Some living domestic or dependent, for none loves Foulon, has betrayed him to the Village. Merciless boors of Vitry unearth him; pounce on him, like hell-hounds: Westward, old Infamy; to Paris, to be judged at the Hôtel-de-Ville! His old head, which seventy-four years have bleached, is bare; they have tied an emblematic bundle of grass on his back; a garland of nettles and thistles is round his neck: in this manner; led with ropes; goaded on with curses and menaces, must he, with his old limbs, sprawl forward; the pitiablest, most unpitied of all old men.

Sooty Saint-Antoine, and every street, musters its crowds as he passes; —the Hall of the Hôtel-de-Ville, the Place de Grève itself, will scarcely hold his escort and him. Foulon must not only be judged righteously, but judged there where he stands, without any delay. Appoint seven judges, ye Municipals, or seventy-and-seven; name them yourselves, or we will name them: but judge him! Electoral rhetoric, eloquence of Mayor Bailly, is wasted, for hours, explaining the beauty of the Law's delay. Delay, and still delay! Behold, O Mayor of the People, the morning has worn itself into noon: and he is still unjudged!—Lafayette, pressingly sent for, arrives; gives voice: This Foulon, a known man, is guilty almost beyond doubt; but may he not have accomplices? Ought not the truth to be cunningly pumped out of him,—in the Abbaye Prison? It is a new light! Sansculottism claps hands;—at which handclapping, Foulon (in his faintness, as his Destiny would have it) also claps.

"See! they understand one another!" cries dark Sansculottism, blazing into fury of suspicion.—"Friends," said a person in good clothes, stepping forward, "what is the use of judging this man? Has he not been judged these thirty years?" With wild yells, Sansculottism clutches him, in its hundred hands: he is whirled across the Place de Grève, to the "*Lanterne*," Lamp-iron which there is at the corner of the *Rue de la Vannerie*; pleading bitterly for life,—to the deaf winds. Only with the third rope—for two ropes broke, and the quavering voice still pleaded— can he be so much as got hanged! His Body is dragged through the streets; his Head goes aloft on a pike, the mouth filled with grass: amid sounds as of Tophet, from a grass-eating people (I v 9).

Foulon's son-in-law (compare *A Tale of Two Cities* ii 22)

Word comes that Berthier has also been arrested; that he is on his way thither from Compiègne. Berthier, Intendant (say *Tax-levier*) of Paris; sycophant and tyrant; forestaller of Corn; contriver of Camps against the people;—accused of many things: is he not Foulon's son-in-law; and, in that one point, guilty of all? In these hours, too, when Sansculottism has its blood up! The shuddering Municipals send one of their number to escort him, with mounted National Guards.

At the fall of day, the wretched Berthier, still wearing a face of courage, arrives at the Barrier; in an open carriage; with the Municipal beside him; five hundred horsemen with drawn sabres; unarmed footmen enough: not without noise! Placards go brandished round him; bearing legibly his indictment, as Sansculottism with unlegal brevity, "in huge letters," draws it up. Paris is come forth to meet him: with hand-clappings, with windows flung up; with dances, triumph-songs, as of the Furies. Lastly, the Head of Foulon; this also meets him on a pike. Well might his "look become glazed," and sense fail him, at such sight!—Nevertheless, be the man's conscience what it may, his nerves are of iron. At the Hôtel-de-Ville he will answer nothing. He says he obeyed superior orders; they have his papers; they may judge and determine: as for himself, not having closed an eye these two nights, he demands, before all things, to have sleep. Leaden sleep, thou miserable Berthier! Guards ride with him, in motion towards the Abbaye. At the very door of the Hôtel-de-Ville, they are clutched; flung asunder, as by a vortex of mad-arms; Berthier whirls towards the Lanterne. He snatches a musket; fells and strikes, defending himself like a mad lion: he is borne down, trampled, hanged, mangled: his Head too, and even his Heart, flies over the City on a pike (I v 9).

Governor of the Bastille (compare *A Tale of Two Cities* ii 21 and see discussion of Helen Maria Williams's letter in Chapters 6 and 9)

What shall De Launay do? One thing only De Launay could have done: what he said he would do. Fancy him sitting, from the first, with lighted taper, within arm's-length of the Powder-Magazine; motionless, like old Roman Senator, or Bronze Lamp-holder; coldly apprising . . . all men, by a slight motion of his eye, what his resolution was:—Harmless he sat there, while unharmed; but the King's Fortress, meanwhile, could, might, would, or should in nowise by surrendered, save to the King's Messenger: one old man's life is worthless, so it be lost with honor; but think, ye brawling *canaille*, how it will be when a whole Bastille springs skyward!—In such statuesque, taper-holding attitude, one fancies De Launay might have left all the tag-rag-and-bobtail of the world, to work their will.

And yet, withal, he could not do it. Distracted, he hovers between two; hopes in the middle of despair; surrenders not his Fortress; declares that he will blow it up, seizes torches to blow it up, and does not blow it. Unhappy old De Launay, it is the death-agony of thy Bastille and thee! Jail, Jailoring and Jailor, all three, such as they may have been, must finish (I v 6).

Let all Prisoners be marched to the Townhall, to be judged!—Alas, already one has his right hand slashed off him; his maimed body dragged to the Place de Grève and hanged there. This same right hand, it is said, turned back De Launay from the Powder-Magazine, and saved Paris.

De Launay, "discovered in gray frock with poppy-colored riband," is for killing himself with the sword of his cane. He shall to the Hôtel-de-Ville; Hulin, Maillard and others escorting him; Elie marching foremost "with the capitulation-paper on his sword's point." Through roarings and cursings; through hustlings, clutchings, and at last through strokes! Your escort is hustled aside, felled down; Hulin sinks exhausted on a heap of stones. Miserable De Launay! He shall never enter the Hôtel-de-Ville: only his "bloody hair-queue, held up in a bloody hand"; that shall enter, for a sign. The bleeding trunk lies on the steps there; the head is off through the streets; ghastly, aloft on a pike.

Rigorous De Launay has died; crying out, "O friends, kill me fast!" Merciful De Losme must die; though Gratitude embraces him, in this fearful hour, and will die for him; it avails not. One other officer is massacred; one other Invalide [soldier] is hanged on the Lamp-iron; with difficulty, with generous perseverance, the Gardes Françaises will save the rest (I v 7).

Knitting women (compare *A Tale of Two Cities* iii 15)

Anarchy, September Massacre: it is a thing that lies hideous in the general imagination; very detestable to the undecided Patriot, of Respectability: a thing to be harped on as often as need is. Harp on it, denounce it, trample it, ye Girondin Patriots:—and yet behold, the black-spot will not trample down; it will only, as we say, trample blacker and wider: fools, it is no black-spot of the surface, but a well-spring of the deep!

In the Jacobin Society, therefore, the decided Patriot complains that there are men who with their private ambitions and animosities will ruin Liberty, Equality, and Brotherhood, all three: they check the spirit of Patriotism; throw stumbling-blocks in its way; and instead of pushing on, all shoulders at the wheel, will stand idle there, spitefully clamoring what foul ruts there are, what rude jolts we give! To which the Jacobin Society answers with angry roar;—with angry shriek, for there are Citoyennes too, thick crowded in the galleries [of the hall of the Convention] here. Citoyennes who bring their seam with them, or their knitting-needles; and shriek or knit as the case needs; famed *Tricoteuses*, Patriot Knitters; *Mère Duchesse*, or like Deborah [a famous Old Testament fighter] and Mother of the Faubourgs [neighborhoods], giving the key-note. It is a changed Jacobin Society; and a still changing. Where Mother Duchess now sits, authentic Duchesses have sat. High-rouged dames went once in jewels and spangles; now, instead of jewels, you may take the knitting-needles and leave the rouge: the rouge will gradually give place to natural brown, clean washed or even unwashed (III ii 5).

Letter found in the Bastille
(compare *A Tale of Two Cities* iii 10)

Ashlar stones of the Bastille continue thundering through the dusk; its paper archives shall fly white. Old secrets come to view; and long-buried Despair finds voice. Read this portion of an old Letter: "If for my consolation Monseigneur would grant me, for the sake of God and the Most Blessed Trinity, that I could have news of my dear wife; were it only her name on a card, to show that she is alive! It were the greatest consolation I could receive; and I should forever bless the greatness of Monseigneur." Poor Prisoner, who namest thyself *Quéret-Démery*, and hast no other history,—she is *dead*, that dear wife of thine, and thou art dead! 'Tis fifty years since thy breaking heart put this question; to be heard now first, and long heard, in the hearts of men (I v 7)

Prison spy (compare *A Tale of Two Cities* iii 8)

The prosecutor has his *moutons* [sheep], detestable traitor jackals, who report and bear witness; that they themselves may be allowed to live,—for a time (III vi 5).

Remarkable sufferer by the axe (compare *A Tale of Two Cities* iii 15; and see Chapter 7)

Marie-Jeanne Philipon, the Wife of Roland. Queenly, sublime in her uncomplaining sorrow, seemed she in her Prison. She has been in Prison, liberated once, but recaptured the same hour, ever since the first of June: in agitation and uncertainty; which has gradually settled down into the last stern certainty, that of death. And now, short preparation soon done, she too shall go her last road. There went with her a certain Lamarche, "Director of Assignat-printing"; whose dejection she endeavored to cheer. Arrived at the foot of the scaffold, she asked for pen and paper, "to write the strange thoughts that were rising in her"; a remarkable request; which was refused. Looking at the Statue of Liberty which stands there, she says bitterly: "O Liberty, what things are done in thy name!" For Lamarche's sake, she will die first; show him how easy it is to die: "Contrary to the order," said Samson.—"Pshaw, you cannot refuse the last request of a Lady"; and Samson yielded.

Noble white Vision, with its high queenly face, its soft proud eyes, long black hair flowing down to the girdle; and as brave a heart as ever beat in woman's bosom! Like a white Grecian Statue, serenely complete, she shines in that black wreck of things. Biography will long remember that trait of asking for a pen "to write the strange thoughts that were rising in her." It is a little light-beam, shedding softness, and a kind of sacredness, over all that preceded (III iv 2).

Saint-Antoine (compare *A Tale of Two Cities* i 5)

Trading Speculation, Commerce of all kinds, has as far as possible come to a dead pause; and the hand of the industrious lies idle in his bosom. Frightful enough, when now the rigor of seasons has also done its part, and to scarcity of work is added scarcity of food! In the opening spring, there come . . . troops of ragged Lackalls, and fierce cries of starvation! These are the thrice-famed *Brigands*: an actual existing quotity [quantity] of persons; who, long reflected and reverberated through so many millions of heads, as in concave multiplying mirrors, become a whole Brigand World; and, like a kind of Supernatural Machinery, wondrously move the Epos of the Revolution. The Brigands are here; the Brigands are there; the Brigands are coming!

If poor famishing men shall, prior to death, gather in groups and crowds, as the poor fieldfares [thrushes] and plovers do in bitter weather, were it but that they may chirp mournfully together, and misery look in the eyes of misery; if famishing men (what famishing fieldfares cannot do) should discover, once congregated, that they need not die while food is in the land, since they are many, and with empty wallets have right hands: in all this, what need we there of Preternatural Machinery?

Be that as it may, the Brigands are clearly got to Paris, in considerable multitudes: with sallow faces, lank hair (the true enthusiast complexion), with sooty rags; and also with large clubs, which they smite angrily against the pavement! These mingle in the Election tumult; would fain sign any Petition whatsoever, could they but write. Their enthusiast complexion, the smiting of their sticks bodes little good to any one; least of all to rich master-manufacturers of the Suburb Saint-Antoine, with whose workmen they consort (I iv 2).

Alas, it is no Montgolfier [hot-air balloon] rising there to-day; but Drudgery, Rascality and the Suburb that is rising!

Saint-Antoine has arisen anew, grimmer than ever;—reinforced by the unknown Tatterdemalion Figures [trouble-makers from other districts], with their enthusiast complexion and large sticks. The City, through all streets, is flowing thitherward to see: "two cartloads of paving-stones, that happened to pass that way," have been seized as a visible godsend. Another detachment of Gardes Françaises must be sent. Then still another; they hardly, with bayonets and menace of bullets, penetrate to the spot. What a sight! A street choked up, with lumber, tumult and the endless press of men. A Paper-Warehouse eviscerated by axe and fire: mad din of Revolt; musket-volleys responded to by yells, by miscellaneous missiles, by tiles raining from roof and window,—tiles, execrations and slain men!

The Gardes Françaises like it not, but have to persevere. All day it continues, slackening and rallying; the sun is sinking, and Saint-Antoine has not yielded. The City flies hither and thither.

At fall of night, as the thing will not end, Besenval takes his resolution: orders out the *Gardes Suisses* with two pieces of artillery. At sight of the lit matches, of the foreign red-coated Switzers, Saint-Antoine dissipates; hastily, in the shades of dusk (I iv 3).

—*in the Insurrection of Women*: Tumultuous; with or without drum-music: for the Faubourg Saint-Antoine also has tucked-up its gown; and with besom-staves [brooms], fire-irons, and even rusty pistols (void of ammunition), is flowing on. Sound of it flies, with a velocity of sound, to the utmost Barriers (I vii 4).

The Versailles Esplanade, over all its spacious expanse, is covered with groups of squalid dripping Women; of lankhaired male Rascality, armed with axes, rusty pikes, old muskets, iron-shod clubs (*batons ferrés*, which end in knives or swordblades, a kind of extempore billhook);—looking nothing but hungry revolt (I vii 6).

—*in the Insurrection of 1 Prairial*: Sansculottism has risen, yet again, from its death-lair; waste, wild-flowing, as the unfruitful Sea. Saint-Antoine is afoot: "Bread and the Constitution of Ninety-three," so sounds it; so stands it written with chalk on the hats of men. They have their pikes, their firelocks; Paper of Grievances; standards; printed Proclamation, drawn-up in quite official manner,—considering this, and also considering that, they, a much-enduring Sovereign People, are in Insurrection; will have Bread and the Constitution of Ninety-three. And so the Barriers are seized, and the *générale* beats, and tocsins discourse discord. Black deluges overflow the Tuileries; spite of sentries, the Sanctuary itself is invaded: enter, to our Order of the Day, a torrent of dishevelled women, wailing, "Bread! Bread!" President may well cover himself; and have his own tocsin rung in "the Pavilion of Unity"; the ship of the State again labors and leaks; overwashed, near to swamping, with unfruitful brine.

The oak doors have become as oak tambourines, sounding under the axe of Saint-Antoine; plaster-work crackles, wood-work booms and jingles; door starts up;—bursts-in Saint-Antoine with frenzy and vociferation, with Rag-standards, printed Proclamation, drum-music: astonishment to eye and ear. Gendarmes, loyal Sectioners charge through the other door; they are re-charged; musketry exploding; Saint-Antoine cannot be expelled. We have no Bread, no Constitution! They wrench poor Féraud; they tumble him, trample him, wrath waxing to see itself work; they drag him into the corridor, dead or near it; sever his head, and fix it on a pike (III vii 5).

Samson, the executioner (compare *A Tale of Two Cities* iii 5)

Executioner Samson shows the Head of the King: fierce shout of *Vive la République* rises, and swells; caps raised on bayonets, hats waving: students take it up, on the far Quais; fling it over Paris. D'Orléans drives off in his cabriolet: the Townhall Councillors rub their hands, saying, "It is done, It is done." There is dipping of handkerchiefs, of pike-points in the blood. Headman Samson, though he afterwards denied it, sells locks of the hair: fractions of the puce coat are long after worn in rings.—And so, in some half-hour it is done; and the multitude has all departed. Pastry-cooks, coffee-sellers, milkmen sing out their trivial quotidian [everyday] cries: the world wags on, as if this were a common day. In the coffeehouses that evening Patriot shook hands with Patriot in a more cordial manner than usual. Not till some days after did public men see what a grave thing it was (III ii 8). [See also Chapter 10.]

A self-sacrificing father (compare *A Tale of Two Cities* iii 15)

The notable person is Lieutenant-General Loiserolles, a nobleman by birth and by nature; laying down his life here for his son. In the Prison of Saint-Lazare, the night before last, hurrying to the Grate to hear the Death-list read, he caught the name of his son. The son was asleep at the moment. "I am Loiserolles," cried the old man: an error in the Christian name is little; small objection was made (III vi 7).

Wife of a prisoner (compare *A Tale of Two Cities* iii 5)

Camille [Desmoulin]'s young beautiful Wife, who had made him rich not in money alone, hovers round the Luxembourg, like a disembodied spirit, day and night (III vi 2).

TOPICS FOR WRITTEN AND ORAL DISCUSSION

1. Dickens omits the story of the prison governor being seated, poised to blow up the Bastille (and quite a bit of Paris, and a lot of people), and then refraining from doing so. Why do you think he made this judgment in writing his account of the siege?

2. Neither Dickens nor Carlyle tells us (Carlyle hints at it) that De Launay had earlier fired on a flag of truce and then had his soldiers gun down forty people to whom he had promised safe-conduct. Carlyle softens, almost obscures these facts. Why do you think he does so? And Dickens neglects or overlooks them. What is the impact, in fictional terms, of this important suppression on Dickens's version of the death of the prison governor? If his story had included these details, would that have affected your reaction to the picture of Madame Defarge? Of the Mob? Of the Terror that came later?

3. Dickens describes the deaths of Foulon and his son-in-law rather differently from the way Carlyle does. What might be the reasons for his expanding some elements and abridging others? When a writer of fiction takes a historical event for his subject, is it legitimate for him to make such changes in emphasis? In these particular examples, does Dickens fictionalize or merely expand on (or omit) material already present in the record? How successfully does he use this material? Does he misrepresent any of the facts as Carlyle relates them? Does he tell the story of Berthier's death clearly, or do you find it confusing?

4. In the novel, Madame Defarge and the Vengeance are depicted knitting while watching the guillotine's grisly operations. Carlyle has no such scene, but he does show the passionate revolutionary women knitting as they watch the proceedings of the Convention. Why do you think Dickens moved them out of doors? Do you think this choice enhances the story? How? In historical terms, is what he does fair to the women?

5. Discuss Carlyle's depiction of the residents of the Paris quarter Saint-Antoine, which he describes as originally an upscale manufacturing district, essentially middle-class. Compare it with Dickens's version. Do you think Dickens was fictionalizing? Did he just borrow a name? When Carlyle uses it, is he always talking about the residents of that particular part of Paris? If not, what literary device is he using? Did Dickens use it in this instance?

6. Samson, the only executioner Carlyle mentions by name (his actual name was Charles-Henri Sanson), is given considerable space in *The French Revolution* but gets a different treatment in the Dickens ver-

sion (*TTC* iii 5). Comment on these differences. What is the ironic coincidence in this name?

7. Many think the most remarkable passage in *A Tale of Two Cities* is Sidney Carton's soliloquy at the end of the book. Dickens seems to have been inspired to write it by the story Carlyle tells about Madame Roland's request for the chance to write down her thoughts just prior to her execution. Discuss the interaction of fact and fiction here. What does Dickens's use of this ingredient tell you about his fictional method? Are there other elements in the depiction of Madame Roland which remind you of story details in the novel? Do you think Dickens would have thought of writing the soliloquy if the lady had not made her request?

8. Do you see in these extracts from *The French Revolution* other connections with fictional elements in *A Tale of Two Cities*?

SUGGESTED READINGS AND WORKS CITED

Carlyle, Thomas. *The French Revolution*. London: James Fraser, 1837.
EJ Johnson, Edgar. *Charles Dickens: His Tragedy and Triumph*. 2 vols. New York: Simon and Schuster, 1952.

6

The Mob in Two Cities
and the Terror

> Rumour is a pipe
> Blown by surmises, jealousies, conjectures,
> And of so easy and so plain a stop
> That the blunt monster with uncounted heads,
> The still-discordant wavering multitude,
> Can play upon it.
>> Shakespeare, *Henry IV, Part II; Induction*

INTRODUCTION: THE TWO CITIES

During most of the eighteenth and nineteenth centuries, Paris and London were probably the two most populous cities in the world (Tokyo, known as Edo, may have competed). The cities had much in common: leadership was held predominantly by the old aristocracy (though not in the enclave of the City of London); merchant classes were growing in importance; and the spreading central districts were increasingly overcrowded by wage earners, craftsmen, petty tradesmen, and the poor. Each city had its underclass, as cities have always had.

London had the larger population, the larger port, the more affluent commercial class. Its suburbs were more developed, its wage earners more independent and class-conscious. It was largely self-governing. The City of London (known today as The City, the central financial district) was overseen by its own corps of merchants, shopkeepers, and craftsmen. They had political authority there, and they guarded it jealously.

In the seventeenth century, England had had a Civil War; had dethroned and executed a king; had even had an eleven-year period of no king at all. Its hostility to Roman Catholicism, combined with the arrogance and stupidity of a restored monarch, had led in 1688 to another, this time nearly bloodless, upheaval. Later, it imported Protestant royalty from Hanover. The Georges chose able native ministers, and the government rode the tide of accelerating economic change in relative stability. Most important, it fought and defeated France and took exclusive control of substantially all the New World.

During most of the eighteenth century London was more turbulent, more militant, more politically conscious than Paris. The climax came with the "anti-Popery" riots of 1780. Much of the agitation grew out of resentment at the influx of cheap Irish labor which competed for available jobs, but the trigger was a Parliamentary proposal to ease restrictions on Catholics.

Though the greatest city of France, Paris was not the seat of government. That was at Versailles, where Louis XIV had built his great palace. After centuries of pulling and hauling between the monarch who wanted to centralize power, and the aristocracy and rising merchant class who resisted, France was fractured along scores of faultlines, with districts for this, jurisdictions for that, taxing entities (largely private concessions) of all sorts, bureaucracies petty and grand. The Seven Years' War (1756–63) had exposed it as a pitiful, helpless giant in some things, though not in all.

As Simon Schama shows in his story of the French Revolution, *Citizens*, French political and commercial consciousness was rising rapidly during the eighteenth century. Possibly, but for the tremendous financial drain of the Seven Years' War and the injury to its pride, France might have stumbled along and, with luck and the English example, adapted her government to new conditions. But that pride seduced it into a try for vengeance in a venture it could not afford.

Charmed by Benjamin Franklin, hooked by dreams of punishing England for past humiliation, French society supported Lafayette and other Frenchmen who wanted to help the colonials throw off their London masters. The people too were enthusiastic. French treasure poured out, and Admiral De Grasse's arrival off Yorktown helped Washington inflict the *coup de grâce*. But France had spent too much for its revenge: its debts mandated new taxation, and no one wanted to pay.

THE MOB IN LONDON: THE GORDON RIOTS OF 1780

Charles Dickens, eighteen years before publication of *A Tale of Two Cities*, told of an English uprising in 1780, less deadly and much briefer than the convulsion in France which began nine years later. *Barnaby Rudge*, today probably read less than any other of his novels, has been highly influential in its description of the behavior and "madness" of crowds. Dickens's picture of how a mob forms and conducts itself is nowhere surpassed in detail and drama. Having written it once, he did not need to write it again, but we can suppose that the scenes he depicted in the London of 1780 were not very different from the ones in the back of his mind as he wrote about the Paris of 1789 and after.

In the eight days of the Gordon Riots (a dim-witted peer, Lord George Gordon, was their figurehead), forty thousand zealots, opportunists, and riffraff injured few (though several hundred of their own died when the militia at last fired on them), but they inflicted great destruction on property and the public order. The mob's siege of Newgate Prison found a more famous echo in Paris nine years later, and the rough treatment members of Parliament received had its parallel in recurring intimidations of the Assembly by Paris *sansculottes*.

Shakespeare's "blunt monster with uncounted heads" was the same "still-discordant wavering multitude" in London nearly two centuries after he flourished. (Numbers at the end of passages refer to chapter numbers in *Barnaby Rudge*. Side captions in italics are the editor's.) The selections have been abridged.

FROM CHARLES DICKENS, *BARNABY RUDGE*
London: Chapman and Hall, 1841

Rumour. When the air was filled with whispers of a confederacy among the Popish powers to degrade and enslave England, establish an inquisition in London, and turn the pens of Smithfield market into stakes and cauldrons; when terrors and alarms which no man understood were perpetually broached, and bygone bugbears [superstitions] which had lain

quietly in their graves for centuries, were raised again to haunt the ignorant and credulous; when secret invitations to join the Great Protestant
Association in defence of religion, life, and liberty, were dropped in the
public ways, thrust under the house-doors, tossed in at windows, and
pressed into the hands of those who trod the streets by night, urging all
men to join together blindfold in resistance of they knew not what, they
knew not why;—the mania spread, and the body, still increasing every
day, grew forty thousand strong (*BR* 37).

On to Parliament. The mob had been divided from its first assemblage
into four divisions. It was not without its method for, in a very short
space of time after being put in motion, the crowd had resolved itself
into three great parties, and were prepared to cross the river by different
bridges, and make for the House of Commons in separate detachments.

At the head of that division which had Westminster Bridge for its approach to the scene of action, Lord George Gordon took his post. The
conduct of a second party, whose route lay by Blackfriars, was entrusted
to a committee of management, including perhaps a dozen men: while
the third was to go by London Bridge, and through the main streets, in
order that their numbers and their serious intentions might be the better
known and appreciated by the citizens. That which went through the city
greatly exceeded the others in number, and was of such prodigious extent that when the rear began to move, the front was nearly four miles
in advance, notwithstanding that the men marched three abreast and
followed very close upon each other (*BR* 49).

It was between two and three o'clock in the afternoon when the three
great parties met at Westminster, and, uniting into one huge mass, raised
a tremendous shout. This was not only done in token of their presence,
but as a signal to those on whom the task devolved, that it was time to
take possession of the lobbies of both Houses, and of the various avenues
of approach, and of the gallery stairs. Their followers pressing on behind,
they were borne as on a great wave to the very doors of the gallery,
whence it was impossible to retreat, even if they had been so inclined,
by reason of the throng which choked up the passages.

Through this vast throng, sprinkled doubtless here and there with honest zealots, but composed for the most part of the very scum and refuse
of London, whose growth was fostered by bad criminal laws, bad prison
regulations, and the worst conceivable police, such of the members of
both Houses of Parliament as had not taken the precaution to be already
at their posts, were compelled to fight and force their way. Their carriages
were stopped and broken; the wheels wrenched off; the glasses shivered
to atoms; the panels beaten in; drivers, footmen, and masters, pulled
from their seats and rolled in the mud.

Lords, commoners, and reverend bishops, with little distinction of person or party, were kicked and pinched and hustled; passed from hand to hand through various stages of ill-usage; and sent to their fellow-senators at last with their clothes hanging in ribands about them, their bagwigs torn off, themselves speechless and breathless, and their persons covered with the powder which had been cuffed and beaten out of their hair. The noise and uproar were on the increase every moment. The air was filled with execrations, hoots, and howlings. The mob raged and roared, like a mad monster as it was, unceasingly, and each new outrage served to swell its fury.

Thus the members were not only attacked in their passage through the streets, but were set upon within the very walls of Parliament; while the tumult, both within and without, was so great, that those who attempted to speak could scarcely hear their own voices: far less, consult upon the course it would be wise to take in such extremity, or animate each other to dignified and firm resistance. So sure as any member, just arrived, with dress disordered and dishevelled hair, came struggling through the crowd in the lobby, it yelled and screamed in triumph; and when the door of the House, partially and cautiously opened by those within for his admission, gave them a momentary glimpse of the interior, they grew more wild and savage, like beasts at the sight of prey, and made a rush against the portal which strained its locks and bolts in their staples, and shook the very beams (*BR* 49).

The First Night. [The streets] were filled with people, for the rumour of that day's proceedings had made a great noise. Those persons who did not care to leave home, were at their doors or windows, and one topic of discourse prevailed on every side. Some reported that the riots were effectually put down; others that they had broken out again: some said that Lord George Gordon had been sent under a strong guard to the Tower; others that an attempt had been made upon the King's life, that the soldiers had been again called out, and that the noise of musketry in a distant part of the town had been plainly heard within an hour. As it grew darker, these stories became more direful and mysterious; and as much consternation engendered, as if the city were invaded by a foreign army (*BR* 50).

[The crowd] had torches among them, and the chief faces were distinctly visible. That they had been engaged in the destruction of some building was sufficiently apparent, and that it was a Catholic place of worship was evident from the spoils they bore as trophies. Covered with soot, and dirt, and dust, and lime; their garments torn to rags; their hair hanging wildly about them; their hands and faces jagged and bleeding with the wounds of rusty nails, the dense throng came fighting on: some singing; some shouting in triumph; some quarrelling among themselves; some menacing the spectators; some with great wooden fragments, on which they spent their rage as if they had been alive, rending them limb from limb, and hurling the scattered morsels high into the air; some in a drunken state, unconscious of the hurts they had received from falling bricks, and stones, and beams; one borne upon a shutter, in the very midst, covered with a dingy cloth, a senseless, ghastly heap.

Thus—a vision of coarse faces, with here and there a blot of flaring, smoky light; a dream of demon heads and savage eyes, and sticks and iron bars uplifted in the air, and whirled about; a bewildering horror, in which so much was seen, and yet so little, which seemed so long, and yet so short, in which there were so many phantoms, not to be forgotten all through life, and yet so many things that could not be observed in one distracting glimpse—it flitted onward, and was gone (*BR* 50).

The Mob in Suspension. The people who were boisterous at Westminster upon the Friday morning, and were eagerly bent upon the work of devastation in Duke Street and Warwick Street at night, were, in the mass, the same. Allowing for the chance accession of which any crowd is morally sure in a town where there must always be a large number of idle and profligate persons, one and the same mob was at both places. Yet they spread themselves in various directions when they dispersed in the afternoon, made no appointment for re-assembling, had no definite purpose or design, and indeed, for anything they knew, were scattered beyond the hope of future union.

The experience of one evening had taught the reckless leaders of disturbance, that they had but to show themselves in the streets, to be immediately surrounded by materials which they could only have kept together when their aid was not required, at great risk, expense, and trouble. Once possessed of this secret, they were as confident as if twenty thousand men, devoted to their will, had been encamped about them, and assumed a confidence which could not have been surpassed, though that had really been the case (*BR* 52).

Looting Freely. Without the slightest preparation, saving that they carried clubs and wore the blue cockade, [the leaders] sallied out into the streets; and paraded [the crowd] at random. Their numbers rapidly increasing, they soon divided into parties; and scoured the town in various directions. The largest body took its way towards Moorfields, where there was a rich chapel, and in which neighbourhood several Catholic families were known to reside.

Beginning with the private houses so occupied, they broke open the doors and windows; and while they destroyed the furniture and left but the bare walls, made a sharp search for tools and engines of destruction, such as hammers, pokers, axes, saws, and such like instruments. Many of the rioters made belts of cord, of handkerchiefs, or any material they found at hand, and wore these weapons as openly as pioneers upon a field-day. This Sunday evening's recreation they pursued like workmen who had a certain task to do and did it.

They marched to the rendezvous, made great fires in the fields, and reserving the most valuable of their spoils, burnt the rest. They danced and howled, and roared about these fires till they were tired, and were never for an instant checked (*BR* 52).

No Turning Back. The leaders of the riot, rendered still more daring by the success of last night, kept steadily together, and only thought of implicating the mass of their followers so deeply that no hope of pardon or reward might tempt them to betray their more notorious confederates into the hands of justice.

Indeed, the sense of having gone too far to be forgiven, held the timid together no less than the bold. Many who would readily have pointed out the foremost rioters and given evidence against them, felt that escape by that means was hopeless, when their every act had been observed by scores of people who had taken no part in the disturbances, and whom the government would, no doubt, prefer to any King's evidence that might be offered (*BR* 53).

The Mob as a Force of Nature. From the moment of their first outbreak at Westminster, every symptom of order or preconcerted arrangement among them vanished. When they divided into parties and ran to different quarters of the town, it was on the spontaneous suggestion of the moment. Each party swelled as it went along, like rivers as they roll towards the sea; new leaders sprang up as they were wanted, disappeared when the necessity was over, and reappeared at the next crisis.

Each tumult took shape and form from the circumstances of the moment; sober workmen, going home from their day's labour, were seen to cast down their baskets of tools and become rioters in an instant; mere boys on errands did the like. In a word, a moral plague ran through the city. The noise, and hurry, and excitement, had for hundreds and hundreds an attraction they had no firmness to resist. The contagion spread like a dread fever: an infectious madness, as yet not near its height, seized on new victims every hour, and society began to tremble at their ravings (*BR* 53).

Madness at a House-burning. If Bedlam gates had been flung open wide, there would not have issued forth such maniacs as the frenzy of that night had made. There were men there, who danced and trampled on the beds of flowers as though they trod down human enemies, and wrenched them from the stalks, like savages who twisted human necks. There were men who cast their lighted torches in the air, and suffered them to fall upon their heads and faces, blistering the skin with deep unseemly burns.

There were men who rushed up to the fire, and paddled in it with their hands as if in water; and others who were restrained by force from plunging in, to gratify their deadly longing. On the skull of one drunken lad—not twenty, by his looks—who lay upon the ground with a bottle to his mouth, the lead from the roof came streaming down in a shower of liquid fire, white hot; melting his head like wax.

When the scattered parties were collected, men—living yet, but singed as with hot irons—were plucked out of the cellars, and carried off upon the shoulders of others, who strove to wake them as they went along, with ribald jokes, and left them, dead, in the passages of hospitals. But of all the howling throng not one learnt mercy from, nor sickened at, these sights; nor was the fierce, besotted, senseless rage of one man glutted (*BR* 55).

The Mob Ascendant. The regulars and militia, in obedience to the orders which were sent to every barrack and station within twenty-four hours' journey, began to pour in by all the roads. But the disturbance had attained to such a formidable height, and the rioters had grown, with impunity, to be so audacious, that the sight of their great force, continually augmented by new arrivals, instead of operating as a check, stimulated them to outrages of greater hardihood than any they had yet committed; and helped to kindle a flame in London, the like of which had never been beheld.

Large bodies of the soldiery were despatched to the Mansion House to await [the Mayor's] orders: but as he could, by no threats or persuasions, be induced to give any, and as the men remained in the open street, fruitlessly for any good purpose, and thrivingly for a very bad one; these laudable attempts did harm rather than good. For the crowd, becoming speedily acquainted with the Lord Mayor's temper, did not fail to take advantage of it by boasting that even the civil authorities were opposed to the Papists, and could not find in their hearts to molest those who were guilty of no other offence.

These vaunts they took care to make within the hearing of the soldiers; and they, being naturally loth to quarrel with the people, received their advances kindly enough: answering, when they were asked if they desired to fire upon their countrymen, "No, they would be damned if they did;" and showing much honest simplicity and good nature. Rumours of their disaffection, and of their leaning towards the popular cause, spread from mouth to mouth with astonishing rapidity; and whenever they were drawn up idly in the streets or squares, there was sure to be a crowd about them, cheering and shaking hands, and treating them with great confidence and affection.

The [rioters] assembled in the streets, traversed them at their will and pleasure, and publicly concerted their plans. Business was quite suspended; the greater part of the shops were closed. *The crowd was the law, and never was the law held in greater dread, or more implicitly obeyed* (emphasis added) (*BR* 63).

Invasion and Fire at Newgate. And now the strokes began to fall like hail upon the gate, and on the strong building; for those who could not reach the door, spent their fierce rage on anything—even on the great blocks of stone, which shivered their weapons into fragments, and made their hands and arms to tingle as if the walls were active in their stout resistance, and dealt them back their blows.

The clash of iron ringing upon iron, mingled with the deafening tumult and sounded high above it, as the great sledge-hammers rattled on the mailed and plated door: the sparks flew off in showers; men worked in gangs, and at short intervals relieved each other, that all their strength might be devoted to the work; but there stood the portal still, as grim and dark and strong as ever, and, saving for the dints upon its battered surface, quite unchanged.

While some brought all their energies to bear upon the toilsome task; and some, rearing ladders against the prison, tried to clamber to the summit of the walls they were too short to scale; and some again engaged a body of police a hundred strong, and beat them back and trod them under foot by force of numbers; others besieged the house on which the jailer had appeared, and driving in the door, brought out his furniture, and piled it up against the prison-gate, to make a bonfire which should burn it down.

As soon as this device was understood, all those who had laboured hitherto, cast down their tools and helped to swell the heap; which reached halfway across the street, and was so high, that those who threw more fuel on the top, got up by ladders. When all the keeper's goods were flung upon this costly pile, to the last fragment, they smeared it with the pitch, and tar, and rosin they had brought, and sprinkled it with turpentine. To all the woodwork round the prison-doors they did the like, leaving not a joist or beam untouched. This infernal christening performed, they fired the pile with lighted matches and with blazing tow, and then stood by, awaiting the result.

They never slackened in their zeal, or kept aloof, but pressed upon the flames so hard, that those in front had much ado to save themselves from being thrust in; if one man swooned or dropped, a dozen struggled for his place, and that although they knew the pain, and thirst, and pressure to be unendurable. Those who fell down in fainting-fits, and were not crushed or burnt, were carried to an inn-yard close at hand, and dashed with water from a pump; of which buckets full were passed from man to man among the crowd; but such was the strong desire of all to drink, and such the fighting to be first, that for the most part, the whole contents were spilled upon the ground, without the lips of one man being moistened.

Meanwhile, and in the midst of all the roar and outcry, those who were nearest to the pile, heaped up again the burning fragments that came toppling down, and raked the fire about the door, which although a sheet of flame, was still a door fast locked and barred, and kept them out. Great pieces of blazing wood were passed, besides, above the people's heads to such as stood about the ladders, and some of these, climbing up to the topmost stave, and holding on with one hand by the prison wall, exerted all their skill and force to cast these fire-brands on the roof, or down into the yards within.

In many instances their efforts were successful; which occasioned a new and appalling addition to the horrors of the scene: for the prisoners within, seeing from between their bars that the fire caught in many places and thrived fiercely, and being all locked up in strong cells for the night, began to know that they were in danger of being burnt alive. This terrible fear, spreading from cell to cell and from yard to yard, vented itself in such dismal cries and wailings, and in such dreadful shrieks for help, that the whole jail resounded with the noise; which was loudly heard even above the shouting of the mob and roaring of the flames, and was so full of agony and despair, that it made the boldest tremble.

The women who were looking on, shrieked loudly, beat their hands together, stopped their ears; and many fainted; the men who were not near the walls and active in the siege, rather than do nothing, tore up the pavement of the street, and did so with a haste and fury they could not have surpassed if that had been the jail, and they were near their object. Not one living creature in the throng was for an instant still. The whole great mass were mad.

A shout! Another! Another yet, though few knew why, or what it meant. But those around the gate had seen it slowly yield, and drop from its topmost hinge. It hung on that side by but one, but was upright still, because of the bar, and its having sunk, of its own weight, into the heap of ashes at its foot. There was now a gap at the top of the doorway, through which could be descried a gloomy passage, cavernous and dark. Pile up the fire!

It burnt fiercely. The door was red-hot, and the gap wider. They vainly tried to shield their faces with their hands, and standing as if in readiness for a spring, watched the place. Dark figures, some crawling on their hands and knees, some carried in the arms of others, were seen to pass along the roof. It was plain the jail could hold out no longer. The keeper, and his officers, and their wives and children, were escaping. Pile up the fire!

The door sank down again: it settled deeper in the cinders—tottered—yielded—was down! (*BR* 64).

The Crisis. At last, at seven o'clock in the evening, the Privy Council issued a solemn proclamation that it was now necessary to employ the military. There was then delivered out to every soldier on duty, thirty-six rounds of powder and ball; the drums beat; and the whole force was under arms at sunset. The streets were comparatively clear, and were guarded at all the great corners and chief avenues by the troops: while parties of the officers rode up and down in all directions, ordering chance stragglers home.

It being now quite dark, those in command awaited the result in some anxiety: and not without a hope that such vigilant demonstrations might of themselves dishearten the populace, and prevent any new outrages. But in this reckoning they were cruelly mistaken, for in half an hour, or less, as though the setting in of night had been their preconcerted signal, the rioters rose like a great sea; and that in so many places at once, and with such inconceivable fury, that those who had the direction of the troops knew not, at first, where to turn or what to do.

One after another, new fires blazed up in every quarter of the town, as though it were the intention of the insurgents to wrap the city in a circle of flames, which, contracting by degrees, would burn the whole to ashes; the crowd swarmed and roared in every street; and none but rioters and soldiers being out of doors, it seemed to the latter as if all London were arrayed against them, and they stood alone against the town.

In two hours, six-and-thirty fires were raging. In almost every street, there was a battle; and in every quarter the muskets of the troops were heard above the shouts and tumult of the mob. The firing began in the Poultry, where nearly a score of people were killed on the first discharge. Their bodies having been hastily carried into St Mildred's Church by the soldiers, the latter fired again, and following fast upon the crowd, charged them at the point of the bayonet.

The streets were now a dreadful spectacle. The shouts of the rabble, the shrieks of women, the cries of the wounded, and the constant firing, formed a deafening and an awful accompaniment to the sights which every corner presented. Wherever the road was obstructed by chains, there the fighting and the loss of life was greatest; but there was hot work and bloodshed in almost every leading thoroughfare. (*BR* 67).

Depth of Horror. The reflections in every quarter of the sky, of deep, red, soaring flames, as though the last day had come and the whole universe was burning; the dust, and smoke, and drift of fiery particles, scorching and kindling all it fell upon; the hot unwholesome vapour, the blight on everything; the stars, and moon, and very sky, obliterated;—

made up such a sum of dreariness and ruin, that it seemed as if the face of Heaven were blotted out, and night, in its rest and quiet, and softened light, never could look upon the earth again.

But there was a worse spectacle than this. The gutters of the street, and every crack and fissure in the stones, ran with scorching spirit, which being dammed up by busy hands, overflowed the road and pavement, and formed a great pool, into which the people dropped down dead by dozens. They lay in heaps all round this fearful pond, husbands and wives, fathers and sons, mothers and daughters, women with children in their arms and babies at their breasts, and drank until they died. While some stooped with their lips to the brink and never raised their heads again, others sprang up from their fiery draught, and danced, half in a mad triumph, and half in the agony of suffocation, until they fell, and steeped their corpses in the liquor that had killed them.

Nor was even this the worst or most appalling kind of death. From the burning cellars, where they drank out of hats, pails, buckets, tubs, and shoes, some men were drawn, alive, but all alight from head to foot; who, in their unendurable anguish and suffering, making for anything that had the look of water, rolled, hissing, in this hideous lake, and splashed up liquid fire which lapped in all it met with as it ran along the surface, and neither spared the living nor the dead. On this last night of the great riots, the wretched victims of a senseless outcry, became themselves the dust and ashes of the flames they had kindled, and strewed the public streets of London (*BR* 68).

THE MOB IN PARIS

After 1780, political ferment and popular enthusiasms rose in France, as they subsided in England. The growth of a mercantile class brought with it increasing impatience with anachronistic governmental structures, the feudal attitudes of much of the aristocracy, and the fumbling cross-purposes at the center in Versailles. This impatience was not limited to the affluent middle class—the *bourgeoisie*—it was shared by the little people: the local shopkeepers, the wine-merchants and their clerks, the small employers and their wage-earners.

The great hailstorm of July 13, 1788 had devastated the truck farms around Paris which had fed the city over the years. Government confusion had hampered corrective measures. The creaking taxation system entailed customs barriers at the entrances to Paris which inhibited delivery of such food as could be gathered. At last, on July 12, 1789, the populace, hungry and furious, stormed the warehouse at the St. Lazare monastery in Paris. Police records show that this was done by local people: small tradesmen, craftsmen, and workers living near the borderline between the faubourgs (districts) of St. Denis and St. Lazare, to the north of the center of Paris.

The attack came in two stages: in the first the crowd broke in and seized stored grain and flour, which it carried to the Corn Market; it destroyed the registers; and it liberated prisoners. (Religious houses in Paris often functioned in part as holding pens for petty criminals and other offenders; later, no longer "religious," they held prisoners of the Terror.) This first phase appears to have been thoughtfully planned and was carried out by armed citizens supported by soldiers of the *Gardes Françaises* and directed by *bourgeois* leaders. But then the hotheads gained ascendancy. They ransacked rooms, destroyed furniture, and pillaged wine, food, and altar furniture, making off with any object which took their fancy.

Among the twenty-three men and women against whom arrest warrants were later issued, there were quarrymen, housewives, a groom, laborers, a carter, a water-carrier, a ribbon-weaver, a button-maker, a mason, a joiner, a journeyman shoemaker, and a wheel-wright; also a master shoemaker and his wife, a market-woman, a shopkeeper and the wife of a cork-seller. They all lived locally. No one went to jail. Looting and lawlessness had happily tasted blood.

A day later, it was the turn of the *"Vainqueurs de la Bastille,"* the nearly one thousand victorious citizens who shouted down the walls and took the prison. The first official list of *vainqueurs* was published by the Assembly on June 17, 1790. It contained the names of 871 assailants, sixteen widows, and eleven children. A second official summary has 954 names, alphabetized. The records of the Parisian National Guard contain a list of 662 individuals issued muskets, bayonets, swords, bandoliers, and other weapons in 1790 by order of the Assembly in recognition of their historic exploit.

This last list included occupation details. There were manufacturers and merchants, a brewer, thirty-five tradesmen (some probably wealthy), and others described as *bourgeois*. There were three naval officers, sixty-three soldiers, and fourteen cavalrymen of the

National Guard. The rest were small tradesmen and artisans, shop-keepers and small businessmen—nearly all self-employed. The French, inspired by a worthy deed, memorialized it thoroughly.

The bourgeois participants included:

11 wine-merchants	21 storekeepers of various kinds
2 innkeepers	3 café proprietors
9 hatters	3 manufacturers
4 businessmen	1 brewer

The "little people" who took the Bastille were:

49 joiners	48 cabinet-makers
41 locksmiths	28 shoemakers
20 sculptors and modelers	11 metal-chasers
10 turners	17 porters
12 stonemasons	21 gauze-workers
9 gardeners	10 hairdressers and wigmakers
7 potters	9 monumental masons
9 nailsmiths	9 dealers in fancy ware
8 printers	7 braziers
7 tailors	9 founders
5 jewelers	5 goldsmiths
5 stove-makers	3 upholsterers
4 stone-cutters	3 ribbon-weavers
3 carpenters	5 shipyard workers
8 river workers, bargemen	2 laborers
4 hatter's workmen	6 coachmen and carters
2 navvies (unskilled laborers)	2 clerks
2 cooks	1 brewer's boy
1 ex-postman	1 silk worker
1 shop assistant	1 laundress
1 glassworker	

Plus tinsmiths, blacksmiths, watchmakers, dyers, wheelwrights, sawyers, saddlers, bakers, butchers, pastrycooks, and others.

We are told that about 400 of the *vainqueurs* on the 1790 list had come originally from the provinces, but they and most of the rest had become settled inhabitants of the Faubourg St. Antoine. Of the civilians on that list, 425 had St. Antoine addresses, mostly in the streets immediately adjoining the Bastille. Of these, 102 were wage earners. Few lived more than a mile and a half from the Bastille.

The 1790 list, of course, did not include the over one hundred dead, but other reports indicate that several were wage earners. One was a journeyman shoemaker, another a street lamplighter (with heavy shoes attached with string; a shirt of rough cloth), another a journeyman edged-tool maker. Over thirty left their families in a state of great financial distress, suggesting that they had been unemployed. Substantial monetary contributions were made for the relief of the Faubourg St. Antoine after an appeal by public officials soon after the Bastille fell.

So the historical evidence shows that the taking of the Bastille was largely achieved by the inhabitants of the Faubourg St. Antoine, with some aid from adjacent districts. Four-fifths of the victors lived within half a mile of the prison. About two-thirds of the civilians were independent craftsmen, small masters and their apprentices. Wage earners were only about one-fourth of the total: the faubourg was essentially an area of small workshops and cafés, not of factories with large workforces.

The mob which marched on Versailles on October 5, 1789 and brought the royal family back to Paris suffered few casualties and arrests, so records do not tell us anything exact about them, though we know that women took the lead (believing the police would be restrained in dealing with them) and the men came behind.

The assault of August 10, 1792, on the Tuileries, when the king's Swiss guard was massacred and the monarchy effectively ended, has been documented from hospital and army records. The invaders included merchants and workers all across the spectrum of Paris life, but they came from elsewhere as well, particularly Marseilles. Five hundred men had marched to Paris singing a song Rouget de Lisle had written at Strasbourg for the French Army of the Rhine. It became their song, known forever as the *Marseillaise*. When the Assembly did not promptly act against the King, the people took matters into their own hands. Because the achievement of the Tuileries invaders, however bloody, was held to be honorable, many of their names and histories are in the Paris files.

THE BASTILLE AND ITS FALL DESCRIBED

A year after the fall of the Bastille, an Englishwoman, Helen Maria Williams (1762–1827), visited Paris and wrote home a series of letters describing what she had seen and learned. These letters were collected and printed in London in 1792. They are valuable to us, not only for their contemporaneity but because they exemplify an English point of view and an English sensibility, before the Revolution's excesses dramatically changed public opinion across the Channel.

It is striking that Carlyle nowhere mentions the Williams letters: it seems impossible that he should not have known of them, but perhaps he thought them too unreliable to be recognized.

Williams's description of a visit to the Bastille has the interest of being one of the last contemporaneous depictions of the prison before its demolishment. Some of her statements may not have turned out to be historically accurate, but she seems honestly to have believed what she was reporting, and that belief, widely shared in England then and later, has its own great importance for our purposes. For extensive quotes on the *lettre de cachet*, see Chapter 9.

FROM HELEN MARIA WILLIAMS, *LETTERS ON THE FRENCH REVOLUTION, WRITTEN IN FRANCE, IN THE SUMMER OF 1790, TO A FRIEND IN ENGLAND*
London: G. G. and J. Robinson, 1792

Letter IV

Before I suffered my friends at Paris to conduct me through the usual routine of convents, churches, and palaces, I requested to visit the Bastille; feeling a much stronger desire to contemplate the ruins of that building than the most perfect edifices of Paris. When we got into the carriage, our French servant called to the coachman, with an air of triumph, "A la Bastille—mais nous n'y resterons pas."[1] We drove under that porch which so many wretches have entered never to repass, and alighting from the carriage descended with difficulty into the dungeons, which were too low to admit of our standing upright, and so dark that we were obliged at noon-day to visit them with the light of a candle. We saw the hooks of those chains by which the prisoners were fastened round the neck, to the walls of their cells; many of which being below the level of the water, are in a constant state of humidity; and a noxious vapour issued from them, which more than once extinguished the candle, and was so insufferable that it required a strong spirit of curiosity to tempt one to enter. Good God!—and to these regions of horror were human creatures dragged at the caprice of despotic power.

There appears to be a greater number of these dungeons than one could have imagined the hard heart of tyranny itself would contrive; for, since the destruction of the building, many subterraneous cells have been discovered underneath a piece of ground which was inclosed within the walls of the Bastille, but which seemed a bank of solid earth before the horrid secrets of this prison-house were disclosed. Some skeletons were found in these recesses, with irons still fastened on their decaying bones.

After having visited the Bastille, we may indeed be surprized, that a nation so enlightened as the French, submitted so long to the oppressions of their government; but we must cease to wonder that their indignant spirits at length shook off the galling yoke.

Those who have contemplated the dungeons of the Bastille, without rejoicing in the French revolution, may, for aught I know, be very respectable persons, and very agreeable companions in the hours of prosperity; but, if my heart were sinking with anguish, I should not fly to those persons for consolation. [Laurence] Sterne says, that a man is incapable of loving one woman as he ought, who has not a sort of an affection for the whole sex; and as little should I look for particular sympathy from those who have no feelings of general philanthropy. If the splendour of a despotic throne can only shine like the radiance of lightning, while all around is involved in gloom and horror, in the name of heaven let its baleful lustre be extinguished for ever. May no such strong contrast of light and shade again exist in the political system of France!

The Bastille, which Henry the Fourth and his veteran troops assailed in vain, the citizens of Paris had the glory of taking in a few hours. The avarice of Mons. de Launay had tempted him to guard this fortress with only half the complement of men ordered by government; and a letter which he received the morning of the 14th of July, commanding him to sustain the siege till evening, when succour would arrive, joined to his own treachery towards the assailants, cost him his life.

The courage of the besiegers was inflamed by the horrors of famine, there being at this time only twenty-four hours provision of bread in Paris. For some days the people had assembled in crouds [*sic*] round the shops of the bakers, who were obliged to have a guard of soldiers to protect them from the famished multitude; while the women, rendered furious by want, cried, in the resolute tone of despair, "Il nous faut du pain pour nos enfans [*sic*]."[2] Such was the scarcity of bread, that a French gentleman told me, that, the day preceding the taking of the Bastille, he was invited to dine with a Negotiant, and, when he went, was informed that a servant had been out five hours in search of bread, and had at last been able to purchase only one loaf.

It was at this crisis, it was to save themselves the shocking spectacle of their wives and infants perishing before their eyes, that the citizens of Paris flew to arms, and, impelled by such causes, fought with the daring intrepidity of men who had all that renders life of any value at stake, and who determined to die or conquer. The women too, far from indulging the fears incident to our feeble sex, in defiance of the cannon of the Bastille, ventured to bring victuals to their sons and husbands; and, with a spirit worthy of Roman matrons, encouraged them to go on. Women mounted guard in the streets, and, when any person passed, called out, "Qui va la?" [Who goes there?]

A gentleman, who had the command of fifty men in this enterprize, told me, that one of his soldiers being killed by a cannon-ball, the people, with great marks of indignation, removed the corpse, and then, snatching up the dead man's hat, begged money of the bystanders for his interment, in a manner characteristic enough of that gaiety, which never forsakes the French, even on such occasions as would make any other people on earth serious. "Madame, pour ce pauvre diable qui s'est fait tué pour la Nation!—Mons. pour ce pauvre chien qui s'est fait tué pour la nation!" This mode of supplication, though not very pathetic, obtained the end desired; no person being sufficiently obdurate to resist the powerful plea, "qu'il s'est fait tué pour la Nation."[3]

When the Bastille was taken, and the old man, of whom you have no doubt heard, and who had been confined in a dungeon thirty-five years, was brought into day-light, which had not for so long a space of time visited his eyes, he staggered, shook his white beard, and cried faintly, "Messieurs, vous m'avez rendu un grand service, rendez m'en un autre, tuez moi! je ne fais pas où aller"—"Allons, allons," the croud answered with one voice, "la Nation te nourrira."[4]

As the heroes of the Bastille passed along the streets after its surrender, the citizens stood at the doors of their houses loaded with wine, brandy, and other refreshments, which they offered to these deliverers of their country. But they refused to taste any strong liquors, considering the great work they had undertaken as not yet accomplished, and being determined to watch the whole night, in case of any surprize.

I have heard several persons mention a young man, of a little insignificant figure, who, the day before the Bastille was taken, got up on a chair in the Palais Royal, and harangued the multitude, conjuring them to make a struggle for their liberty, and asserting, that now the moment was arrived. They listened to his eloquence with the most eager attention; and, when he had instructed as many as could hear him at one time, he requested them to depart, and repeated his harangue to a new set of auditors.[5]

Among the dungeons of the Bastille are placed, upon a heap of stones, the figures of the two men who contrived the plan of this fortress, where they were afterwards confined for life. These men are represented chained to the wall, and are beheld without any emotion of sympathy.

The person employed to remove the ruins of the Bastille, has framed of the stones eighty-three complete models of this building, which, with a true patriotic spirit, he has presented to the eighty-three departments of the kingdom, by way of hint to his countrymen to take care of their liberties in the future.

Letter X published in the same volume is the source of the following two extracts, the first giving some inaccurate, though not perfectly fanciful, background leading up to the Bastille assault, the second a reflection on the subsequent street lynchings at "la Lanterne." In the latter, Miss Williams's words present as apt an example of "prophetic irony," to coin a phrase, as one is ever likely to come by.

Letter X

A few days before the taking of the Bastille, a croud of the Parisians assembled at the Hopital [*sic*] des Invalides, and demanded arms of the old soldiers; who answered, that they were the friends of their fellow citizens, but durst not deliver up their arms without the appearance of a contest; and therefore desired that the people would assemble before the gates in greater numbers the next day, when, after firing a little powder upon them, they would throw down their arms. The people accordingly returned the following day; and the invalids, after a faint shew of resistance, threw down their arms, which the citizens took up, embraced the old men, and then departed.[6]

• • •

As we came out of La Maison de Ville, we were shewn, immediately opposite, the far-famed lanterne, at which, for want of a gallows, the first victims of popular fury were sacrificed. I own that the sight of La Lanterne chilled the blood within my veins. At that moment, for the first time, I lamented the revolution; and, forgetting the imprudence, or the guilt, of those unfortunate men, could only reflect with horror on the dreadful expiation they had made. I painted in my imagination the agonies of their families and friends, nor could I for a considerable time chase these gloomy images from my thoughts.

It is for ever to be regretted, that so dark a shade of ferocious revenge was thrown across the glories of the revolution. But, alas! where do the records of history point out a revolution unstained by some actions of barbarity? When do the passions of human nature rise to that pitch which produces great events, without wandering into some irregularities? *If the French revolution should cost no further bloodshed, it must be allowed, notwithstanding a few shocking instances of public vengeance, that the liberty of twenty-four millions of people will have been purchased at a far cheaper rate than could ever have been expected from the former experience of the world* (emphasis added).

NOTES

1. The servant's joke, "But we are not going to remain there" sounds a touch nervous, and perhaps appropriately so.

2. "We must have bread for our children." This quotation is obviously more generic than specifically accurate. From what we know and can infer, the women were considerably more graphic and importunate; but this doubtless was the burden of their complaints.

3. The humor of which Helen Maria Williams speaks is a little hard to discern in "Madam, for this poor devil, who died for the Nation! Sir, for this unfortunate dog who died for the Nation!" Perhaps, to an English-woman, calling a dead man a poor devil or a poor dog has to reflect lighthearted courage in the presence of death; otherwise it is in poor taste.

4. This apocryphal tale of the old prisoner who pled for death because he had now nowhere to go for shelter (and the grandiose reply, "The nation will provide for you") is a fine example of the pitfalls always await-ing historians. This was the kind of story which arose spontaneously among the people, in the rumormongering (better, myth making) which accompanies great and dramatic events.

5. The individual described must be Camille Desmoulins (1760–94), whose oratory did indeed inflame those who subsequently assaulted the Bastille. Like so many other revolutionary heroes, he died on the guil-lotine, being too much a moderate for Robespierre.

6. Christopher Hibbert states the facts now accepted by historians: the day before the assault, the Governor of the Invalides "had referred an earlier request for arms from a deligation of Electors to the Swiss General Baron de Besenval . . . who had told him he must do nothing without authority from Versailles and had taken the precaution of ordering the pensioners on duty at the Invalides to render the muskets useless by

unscrewing the hammers. The pensioners, unwilling to help their masters, set about this task with such extreme laboriousness that in six hours they had unscrewed scarcely more than twenty hammers of the 32,000 muskets awaiting their attention."

THE TERROR IN FRANCE

When troubles had once begun in the cities, those who followed carried the revolutionary spirit further and further, and determined to outdo the report of all who had preceded them by the ingenuity of the enterprises and the atrocity of their revenges. The meaning of words had no longer the same relation to things, but was changed by them as they thought proper. Reckless daring was held to be loyal courage; prudent delay was the excuse of a coward; moderation was the disguise of unmanly weakness; to know everything was to do nothing. Frantic energy was the true quality of a man. A conspirator who wanted to be safe was a recreant in disguise. The lover of violence was always trusted, and his opponent suspected. He who succeeded in a plot was deemed knowing, but a still greater master in craft was he who detected one. On the other hand, he who plotted from the first to have nothing to do with plots was a breaker up of parties and a poltroon who was afraid of the enemy. In a word, he who could outstrip another in a bad action was applauded, and so was he who encouraged to evil one who had no idea of it. . . . The tie of party was stronger than the tie of blood, because a partisan was more ready to dare without asking why.

Thucydides (in about 400 B.C.E.)

There is no new thing under the sun.

Ecclesiastes 1:9

By Terror we mean a condition of human mob psychology so steeped in fear that it must lash out, feeling that killing those who seem to represent or personify what is feared is the only way to ensure safety and survival. The result is indiscriminate butchery, totally animalistic behavior—sometimes mob-inflicted but, appallingly enough, often fomented by government and sometimes indeed actually a reflection of deliberate policy set by those who rule.

"The Terror was a recurrent mood as well as a specific time." So begins the Durants' description of the great Terror in Paris, which is usually held to have begun with the passage of the Law of Suspects in September 17, 1793, and which ended with the deaths of Robespierre and his cohorts. This is the Terror which pervades Book The Third of *A Tale of Two Cities* and the Carlyle extracts in this book in Chapters 4 and 7. We will pass over it in this chapter, in part because its perpetrators were not the "mob" but the government, and in no way anonymous.

There had been earlier Terror: the massacre of September 1792, when Marat's Oversight Committee called for the slaughter Dickens describes in Book ii, Chapter 2, "The Grindstone" and which Carlyle depicts over several chapters. Twelve to fourteen hundred prisoners died, of whom thirty-seven were women. Of the rest, fewer than four hundred were priests, nobles, or political prisoners: most were ordinary criminals and vagrants.

We know some things about how the massacres were engendered. Some in government thought the prisoners were secretly allied with the Duke of Brunswick, several hundred miles away but just now victorious at Verdun (September 2, 1792). Rumor spread that they were only waiting for the volunteers to leave for the front: they would then break out and annihilate the aged, the women, and the children left behind. But the hysteria was not a sudden eruption. Already on August 11, the day after the Tuileries investiture, the police were alerting the National Guard that a plot was afoot to invade the prisons, remove the prisoners, and inflict "prompt justice" on them. On receiving news of Verdun's fall, the general assembly of one Paris district circulated a resolution to all: "There is no other way to avoid the danger and to augment the zeal of the citizenry to volunteer for the front but to inflict prompt justice on all malefactors and conspirators detained in the prisons" (SL).

That afternoon, prisoners being brought under escort to the Abbaye prison were torn from the soldiers by a furious, terrified crowd and slaughtered in the street. The massacre spread first to Carmes, then to the Conciergerie, the Châtelet, and the Hôtel du Force. It continued for days. Executions occurred at the monastery of Saint-Firmin and at the Bernardine monastery, where common criminals were waiting to be transported to the galleys. The slaughter continued at Bicêtre, a prison hospital for the poor, vagrants, and lunatics. It spread to the Salpêtrière, where female prisoners, thieves, and prostitutes were held. Out of a total of 2,800 prisoners in nine localities, nearly half died. The rest of those processed by the hastily organized courts of justice, some 1,500 or so, kept their lives.

While the killings were going on, ministers Danton and Roland turned their backs, and a circular sent to the outlying parts of the country by the Paris Commune applauded them as acts of necessary justice and an example to be followed. But once the crisis was past, and particularly after the astounding news arrived that the invaders had been thrown back at Valmy, no one wanted to claim credit for what had gone on. Indeed, there were charges and countercharges between the Montagnards and the Girondins: who started the massacre? who failed to stop it? Even after Robespierre fell two years later recriminations continued.

In fact, it was very difficult to pinpoint responsibility anywhere. Exhaustive studies have been done, and all that can be said, based upon proceedings brought four years later against thirty-nine individuals (nearly all of the cases were dismissed for lack of evidence), was that the two hundred or so murderers probably included some criminals, but were mostly shop assistants, artisans, guardsmen, and police. The tale was told that many of them, back at work afterwards, apparently thought they had done the state good service by eliminating a threat to its rear at a time of peril at the front. They showed off swords and axes, stained with blood, to their friends and customers. Later, when *septembriseur* became a term of contempt, they claimed they had dipped their weapons in the buckets of the real perpetrators in order to impress their girlfriends.

Revenge can also engender Terror, as a reaction from the previous fear. After Robespierre fell, known and suspected Jacobins were hunted down relentlessly. A "White Terror" (white was the royal, or conservative, color) raged in May–June 1795. In Lyons, ninety-seven were massacred in prison; at Aix-en-Provence thirty died butchered, and others were slaughtered in Arles, Avignon, and Marseilles. At Tarascon, two hundred masked men seized the prison, bound the prisoners, and threw them into the Rhône. When workers at Toulon rose against these new atrocities, they were wiped out. The Terror had not ended; it had changed hands.

A second "White Terror" after Napoléon's fall in 1815 killed many in Avignon, Marseilles, Nîmes, Montpellier, and Toulouse, some in scenes of bloody carnage and cruelty worthy of the "Red Terror" of 1793–94. While some of the killings were in retribution for the earlier Terror, those who cried *Vive l'Empereur!* but had no blood on their consciences were dealt with as mercilessly, for politics had changed.

Terror is not obsolete. The horrors of "ethnic cleansing" in Turkey early in this century, when Armenians may have been exterminated under government policy (this is denied or called "unproved" by some), found their echoes in Yugoslavia after the death of Tito. Millions were massacred in the partition of India, and recently we have been edified by the likes of Pol Pot in Cambodia, ghastliness in Rwanda-Burundi, and the devastations in Bosnia and other areas of the former country of Yugoslavia. Topping them all, in an unprecedented conflagration of scapegoating, hatred, and fear, was Hitler's Holocaust.

ROBESPIERRE, DEAN OF TERRORISTS

Charles Dickens's contemporary, Anthony Trollope, in a writing life about as long as that of Dickens, wrote forty-seven novels (Dickens wrote fourteen and a half). In his third book, *La Vendée*, Trollope tried his hand at historical romance. As a subject, he chose the most serious revolt against the French Revolution, that in the western province of the *Vendée*. It is a failure as a novel— stilted and overdramatic—but it contains an astute portrait of the Terrorist of Terrorists, Maximilien Robespierre. The passage below presents an authoritative, balanced view and typifies intelligent English opinion (Trollope was more enlightened than most of his countrymen). Reading them carefully, we learn much about revolution when it becomes radical: when blood and death come to seem moral imperatives.

FROM ANTHONY TROLLOPE, *LA VENDÉE*
London: Henry Colburn, 1850

. . . : in the Convention and in the Committee, Robespierre was omnipotent; but he also had his master, and he knew it. He knew that he could only act, command, and be obeyed, in union with, and dependence on, the will of the populace of Paris; and the higher he rose in that path of life which he marked out for himself with so much precision, and followed with so much constancy, the more bitterly his spirit chafed at the dependence. He knew it was of no avail to complain of the people to the people, and he seldom ventured to risk his position by opposing the wishes of the fearful masters whom he served, but at length he was driven to do so, and at length he fell.

Half a century has passed since Robespierre died, and history has become peculiarly conversant with his name. Is there any one whose character suffers under a more wide-spread infamy? The abomination of whose deeds has become more notorious? The tale of whose death has been oftener told; whose end, horrid, fearful, agonized, as was that of this man, has met with less sympathy? For fifty years the world has talked of, condemned, and executed Robespierre. Men and women, who have barely heard the names of Pitt and Fox, who know not whether Metternich is a man or a river, or one of the United States, speak of Robespierre as of a thing accursed. They know, at any rate, what *he* was—the demon of the revolution; the source of the fountain of blood with which Paris was deluged; the murderer of the thousands whose bodies choked the course of the Loire and the Rhone. Who knows not enough of Robespierre to condemn him? Who abstains from adding another malediction to those which already load the name of the King of the Reign of Terror!

I am not the bold man who will dare to face the opinion of the world, and attempt to prove that Robespierre has become infamous through prejudice. He must be held responsible for the effects of the words which he spoke, and the things which he did, as other men are. He made himself a scourge and a pestilence to his country; therefore, beyond all other men, he has become odious, and therefore, historian after historian, as they mention his name, hardly dare, in the service of truth, to say one word to lessen his infamy.

Yet Robespierre began his public life with aspirations of humanity, which never deserted him; and resolutions as to conduct, to which he adhered with a constancy never surpassed. What shall we say are the qualifications for a great and good man?—Honesty. In spite of his infamy, Robespierre's honesty has become proverbial. Moral conduct—the life he led even during the zenith of his power, and at a time when licentiousness was general, and morality ridiculous, was characterized by the simplicity of the early Quakers. Industry—without payment from the State, beyond that which he received as a member of the Convention, and which was hardly sufficient for the wants of his simple existence, he worked nearly night and day in the service of the State. Constancy of purpose—from the commencement of his career, in opposition at first to ridicule and obscurity, then to public opinion, and lastly to the combined efforts of the greatest of his countrymen, he pursued only one idea; convinced of its truth, sure of its progress, and longing for its success. Temperance in power—though in reality governing all France, Robespierre assumed to himself none of the attributes or privileges of political power. He took to himself no high place, no public situation of profit or grandeur. He was neither haughty in his language, nor imperious in his demeanour. Love of country—who ever showed a more devoted love? For his country he laboured, and suffered a life which surely in itself could have had nothing attractive; the hope of the future felicity of France alone fed his energies, and sustained his courage.

Courage—those who have carefully studied his private life, and have learnt what he endured, and dared to do in overcoming the enemies of his system, can hardly doubt his courage. Calumny or error has thrown an unmerited disgrace over his last wretched days. He has been supposed to have wounded himself in an impotent attempt to put an end to his life. It has been ascertained that such was not the fact, the pistol by which he was wounded having been fired by one of the soldiers by whom he was arrested. He is stated also to have wanted that firmness in death which so many of his victims displayed. They triumphed even in their death. Louis [XVI] and Vergniaud, Marie Antoinette, and Madame Roland, felt that they were stepping from life into glory, and their step was light and elastic. Robespierre was sinking from existence into infamy. During those fearful hours, in which nothing in life was left him but to suffer, how wretched must have been the reminiscences of his career! He, who had so constantly pursued one idea, must then have felt that that idea had been an error; that he had all in all been wrong; that he had waded through the blood of his countrymen to reach a goal, which, bright and luminous as it had appeared, he now found to be an *ignis fatuus*. Nothing was then left to him. His life had been a failure, and for the future he had no hope. His body was wounded and in tortures; his spirit was dismayed by the insults of those around him, and his soul had owned no haven to which death would give it an escape. Could his eye have been lit with animation as he ascended the scaffold? Could his foot have then stepped with confidence? Could he have gloried in his death? Poor mutilated worm, agonised in body and in soul. Can it be ascribed to want of courage in him, that his last moments were passed in silent agony and despair?

Honesty, moral conduct, industry, constancy of purpose, temperance in power, courage, and love of country: these virtues all belonged to Robespierre; history confesses it, and to what favoured hero does history assign a fairer catalogue? Whose name does a brighter galaxy adorn? With such qualities, such attributes, why was he not the Washington of France? Why, instead of the Messiah of freedom, which he believed himself to be, has his name become a bye-word, a reproach, and an enormity? Because he wanted faith! He believed in nothing but himself, and the reasoning faculty with which he felt himself to be endowed. He thought himself perfect in his own human nature, and wishing to make others perfect as he was, he fell into the lowest abyss of crime and misery in which a poor human creature ever wallowed. He seems almost to have been sent into the world to prove the inefficacy of human reason to effect human happiness. He was gifted with a power over common temptation, which belongs to but few. His blood was cool and temperate, and yet his heart was open to all the softer emotions. He had no appetite for luxury; no desire for pomp; no craving for wealth. Among thousands who were revelling in sensuality, he kept himself pure and immaculate. If any could have said, I will be virtuous; I, of myself, unaided, trusting to my own power, guarding myself by the light of my own reason; I will walk uprightly through the world, and will shed light from my path upon my brethren, he might have said so. He attempted it, and history shows us the result. He attempted, unassisted, to be perfect among men, and his memory is regarded as that of a loathsome plague, defiling even the unclean age in which he lived (V 23).

Robespierre, sketched by Jacques-Louis David. An inscription notes his green eyes and pale skin.

TOPICS FOR WRITTEN AND ORAL DISCUSSION

1. Shakespeare's view that the mob is led by rumor and, by implication, acts on irrational impulse, may find support in the factual situation in the moments of greatest crowd violence in France. What do you think? How do you think it applied in England? What did Dickens think?

2. The parallels and differences between the mob actions in *Barnaby Rudge* and those of *A Tale of Two Cities* could be grist for many essays. For example, there is the frenzy of the English not to waste spilled whiskey. What does that remind you of? For extra credit, do some work with *Barnaby Rudge* (especially the chapters cited in the above extracts) for more insight into the ways the novels parallel each other (e.g., Newgate Prison and the Bastille).

3. The timidity of the authorities in London had its match at Versailles and in Paris. Does Dickens make this connection? From your knowledge of the French Revolution developed by your reading in this and other books, discuss other similarities and differences.

4. Do you have an impression of the cultural and socio-economic background of the mob figures in *A Tale of Two Cities*? From the foregoing chapter, do you think Dickens "stacked the deck" in the way he depicted them?

5. It seems evident that the fall of the Bastille became a seminal myth for the French. Is it based on fact? Were the *vainqueurs* heroes or accidents? Were women involved in the siege? If not, where does Dickens get the idea of Madame Defarge as a leader and an executioner? Is this legitimate "novelist's license"?

6. Helen Maria Williams gives no active role to women in the storming of the Bastille. Was she right? If not, why does she speak as she does?

7. Discuss the last paragraph of the Williams extract in light of what happened later. There is an irony here. Can you explain it? Do you think the subsequent events of the Revolution teach any lesson about the human costs of progress? Can you think of a place in the world today where that lesson might profitably be remembered? What is appeasement?

8. Can you find any elements in Helen Maria Williams's letters that are also to be found in *A Tale of Two Cities*?

9. Having read Trollope's characterization of Robespierre, do you have sympathy for him? If not, why not?

SUGGESTED READINGS AND WORKS CITED

BR   Dickens, Charles. *Barnaby Rudge: A Tale of the Riots of 'Eighty.* London: Chapman and Hall, 1841.

DD/RR   Durant, Will and Ariel. *Rousseau and Revolution.* New York: Simon and Schuster, 1967.

Hibbert, Christopher. *The Days of the French Revolution.* New York: William Morrow, 1980.

SL   Loomis, Stanley. *Paris in the Terror: June 1793–July 1794.* Philadelphia: Lippincott, 1964.

Peltier, Jean-Gabriel. *Dernier Tableau de Paris, ou Récit Historique de la Révolution du 10 Août.* London: by the author, 1792–93.

Rudé, George. *The Crowd in the French Revolution.* London and New York: Oxford University Press, 1967.

———. *Paris and London in the Eighteenth Century: Studies in Popular Protest.* London: Collins, 1970.

Soboul, Albert. *The Parisian Sans-Culottes and the French Revolution, 1793–4.* Translated by Gwynne Lewis. Oxford: Clarendon Press, 1964.

Trollope, Anthony. *La Vendée.* London: Henry Colburn, 1850.

7

Voices from the Prisons of Paris in the Terror

INTRODUCTION: THE STATE OF THINGS

During the Terror of 1793–94, there were about forty prisons in Paris, many of them set up on short notice to deal with the tremendous influx of those arrested under the Law of Suspect (September 17, 1793). Private houses were commandeered in some cases. Barracks, monasteries, nunneries, and asylums for the insane were also used.

Nearly seven thousand people were incarcerated during this period. Apart from a small minority of prisoners suspected or convicted of conventional crimes, the inmates fell into three categories:

—those who had appeared before the Revolutionary Tribunal and been condemned, either to the *gêne* (a long prison term) or to the *fers* (transportation overseas for a term at hard labor: the destination was usually French Guiana);

—those who were waiting to be heard by the Tribunal: records indicate that these waits ranged from forty-eight hours to six months; and

—"suspects" not formally "arrested" but simply haled into prison under the Law of Suspect: this group constituted the bulk of all prisoners during the period and included emi-

grants who had voluntarily returned, relying on judicial ac-
quittals or other clearances obtained *before* the adoption of
the Law of Suspect.

Formal charges, which applied to the first two categories, usually
cited offenses such as hoarding (of commodities or precious met-
als); financial subversion of the Revolution (as by distributing
counterfeit money or exporting wealth in the form of gold or silver
bars, or jewels); or such things as "federalism"—espousing the
view that the provinces should have qualified autonomy in the
management of their affairs; "treason," which might mean anything; "corruption"—another catchall, though often enough there
might have been bribery or attempts at bribery with the goal of
concealing suspect transactions or exporting valuables or loved
ones; undeclared correspondence with persons living abroad; and
statements, publicly made or reported by spies or enemies, critical
of the Revolution or its representatives.

The Law of Suspect made it easy to identify enemies of the Revolution: they were anyone who by their behavior, their associations, or their words appeared to be "advocates of tyranny or
federalism and enemies of liberty." Emigration was, without more,
a declaration of guilt, and there was a great deal of forgery of
documents intended to prove continuous residence in France by
people who had, either earlier or when frightened by the events
of September 1792, thought it expedient to get out of the country
for a while. Often, they returned in order to forestall confiscation
and sale of their landed property, and the forgeries (necessarily
entailing corruption of officialdom) were generally known of even
if difficult to prove in particular cases. The Law of Suspect vaulted
over mundane requirements of proof, and the law of II Prairial
Year II (June 10, 1794) simplified the prosecutor's job immensely
by abolishing defendants' rights to *make* any defense.

Even though returned and believing themselves safe, former emigrants continued to send assets abroad or get them out of the
government's way by transferring them to friends or other individuals, perhaps of lowly estate, who presumably ran no risk: devoted
family retainers, for example, who would become record owners
and would (presumably) give the property back if and when the
political climate made it safe to do so. Sympathetic stockbrokers
(often dealing with foreign banks) and notaries would assist in
these efforts, and the difficulty required to pursue and uncover

these transactions was doubtless part of the reason why impatient and frustrated patriots finally adopted blunt instruments like the Law of Suspect to stop the financial hemorrhaging of the republic in its time of perceived great danger.

There was much counterfeiting of the currency: the assignats (issued by the revolutionary government and backed by state lands, notably those seized from the Church). England and Germany in particular were sources of floods of this paper, which often passed through Switzerland and was distributed in the frontier departments of the new government. The effect was highly destructive to an already weak currency and was doubtless a greater threat to the survival of revolutionary France than a whole host of coalition powers wringing their hands at the border.

We can then picture a little the state of mind of those unfortunate detainees: many of them living in constant fear of denunciation by a former friend or a servant (perhaps by confession under duress), or of the discovery of a damning document like a letter from overseas or a false residence certificate. The presence in the house of a forged assignat, perhaps innocently taken by a servant in the market, might instantly transform a "suspect" into an immediate candidate for the tumbril. The agony of the suspense must have been terrific.

LETTERS NEVER DELIVERED

It would be useful, fascinating, and doubtless heartrending (if it were possible) to present to American students of *A Tale of Two Cities* some authentic, translated extracts of the diaries of executed victims of the Terror. Unfortunately, as far as can be determined, no extended diaries (other than those of Madame Roland, discussed below) survived, or at least none is accessible to us, though there are some fragments which give a picture of conditions in the prisons. A great many letters are extant, however: confiscated by prison administrators and turned over to the prosecutor, they were buried in his files. Those who waited at home waited with no word.

FROM OLIVIER BLANC, *LAST LETTERS: PRISONS AND PRISONERS OF THE FRENCH REVOLUTION, 1793–1794*
Alan Sheridan, trans.
London: Andre Deutsch, 1987

As to prison life and atmosphere, we have an anonymous account from a surprisingly lighthearted inmate of the Luxembourg, the most "upscale" of the prisons:

> It is a rather entertaining sight to see arriving in some wretched carriage two marquises, a duchess, a marchioness, a count, an abbé and two countesses who have a headache on getting in and faint on getting out. Not long ago I saw the wife of Philippe, who was recently guillotined, arrive; her room is next to that of Basire and Chabot, who are still in solitary confinement, and are filled with gloom whenever they hear the shrill voice of a pedlar crying, "Old Duchesne's [*Père Duchesne* was a Revolutionary tabloid of the day] great anger against the monk Chabot."
>
> In the same corridor are M. de la Borde de Méréville, M. le Président Nicolair and Mélin, a former civil servant in the Ministry of War under Ségur. In the other corridor, on the left, are M. de la Ferté, M. le Duc de Lévi, M. le Marquis de Fleury, M. le Comte de Mirepoix; every morning, on rising, they get out their telescopes and are delighted to see that their houses are still standing in the Rue de l'Université. At the end of the corridor, in the library, is a bunch of generals who recount their victories to one another.

In a room on the left, living in conjugal peace, are M. le Maréchal and Mme la Maréchale de Mouchy, who declare that the revolutionary committee have no sense locking up people of their quality, who have handed over their horses to the army and given five hundred *livres* for the widows of the section.

The marshal wears a square-cut brown coat, a knee-length jacket, has white hair and always looks like a protestant minister. His wife has adopted the pleasant costume of a female *sans-culotte*, while keeping the shape of the *caraco* of '77, with its two furbelows behind. It is quite common to encounter the aforementioned *maréchale* wearing a bum-freezer [a bustle?], a candle in her left hand, a cane in her right, climbing the stairs with the haste of a shepherdess from Suresnes climbing the Mont Valérien.

The prisoners are ten or twelve to a room; each of them makes whatever arrangements he can, like Robinson Crusoe when he had given up hope of ever seeing a ship enter the bay; everybody has his own trestle bed and little mattress. Some cook and hang the leg of lamb at the window to make it more tender, others have recourse to the perpetual soup pot of the traitor Coste. The rich look after the poor, with good grace and without prompting. Everybody fraternizes.

Another paints a different social picture:

The nobility usually kept themselves to themselves, having very little to do with the citizens of the sections of Paris. The Rues de l'Université, de Grenoble, Saint-Dominique, which were heavily represented in the Luxembourg, kept up the strictest etiquette; people called one another Monsieur le Prince, Monsieur le Duc, Monsieur le Comte, Monsieur le Marquis, etc.; they held their salons with the utmost gravity and contended for precedence and visits.

One of the less-favored prisons was the Carmes, a former Carmelite convent which was converted in December 1793 to house a great many "suspects." Conditions were not wonderful:

Here the corridors are not lit; one does not always have the pleasure of seeing the garden; for a long time now I have been able to catch no more than a glimpse of the women through their windows— there are some twenty of them and they eat in the refectory after the men. The corridors are varnished; though spacious enough, they are airless and infected by the noxious fumes from the latrines. The windows are blocked up to three-quarters of their height, so that the light enters only from the top and, over the little opening there is, there are thick bars. One senses at once that this is a proper prison in all its horror. The inmates do not take care of their persons as at the Bourbe. They are not properly dressed: they are mostly without ties, wear nightshirts and dirty pantaloons, their legs bare, a handkerchief around their heads, their hair uncombed, their beards unshaven.

The women, our sad companions in misfortune, are a sorry sight. They wear a short dress or a *pierrot*, sometimes of one colour, sometimes of another. However, we are fairly well fed; at the only refectory meal, we have as much bread as we like and a half-bottle of wine each. But our keeper is harsh and unpleasant.

Life in its homely concerns and details did go on, and French appreciation of the pleasures of the table comes through the horror:

> To Citizenness Boilleau, Rue Révolutionnaire
> former Saint-Louis, at Paris, this 4 Floréal
>
> My dear friend,
>
> I beg you to do your utmost to bring a well-seasoned lettuce salad or rather the materials for making one, we have bowls; but try to make sure that it is fresh and in good condition. If you have no money, try to get hold of some for this advance. As I am writing to you by the small post, I don't want to send it to you, but I shall get it to you later. Don't forget the oil and vinegar. If you cannot get money to do this, take the trouble to come and see me and I shall give you what you need to buy what is necessary. We have salt, but bring a little pepper. Try to do this for us today, if at all possible, I shall be very obliged to you, and bring as much oil as you can. I shall be very obliged to you and embrace you with all my heart.
>
> Your husband Boilleau

And from a desperately anxious wife at home:

> I am sending you a pigeon, some red currants, apricots and a bottle of wine. I'm not sending you any linen because you did not ask for it. I embrace you with all my heart. I wish I didn't have to say so, but I kiss you in good earnest. I don't know when I will have that pleasure, I'm waiting for you with such impatience.
>
> I am your friend and wife, Fournier.

The most troubling things are the farewells, confiscated and unseen by those at home desperate for some word who never ever (for their presence late in the late twentieth century in the prosecutor's files makes that clear enough) had the comfort of these last loving words:

> My dear Anne-Lise, human nature is nothing, man appears for an instant and his soul must fly off to the bosom of his creator. Mine

will prepare your place there. Live for our dear children, I go to join my ancestors and yours.

Géant

Respect the laws, as you have always seen me do. Good behavior always comes more easily to a woman than to a man. Home life, which has always suited you most, is more fitting than ever. I do now commend our children to the best of mothers and to the most loving of wives.

Poutet

Farewell, for ever. I am overcome with regret at leaving you, but I shall bear my fate steadfastly to the end. Embrace my children for me and remember their father. Love his memory, but do not be unreasonably affected by his death.

Courtonnel

Be consoled, my very good lady and dear friend. Be consoled, I beg you I have a calm and steadfastness of soul that are a great help to me at this moment. My greatest pain is that which is being caused you. So I would beg you with all my heart to be consoled; look after yourself well, you owe it to them, you owe it to their upbringing. Share farewells with good, dear Adelaide. I might have been taken from you by some disease or accident.

Farewell, I embrace you all from the bottom of my heart. I thought that I would have more time to write to you.

Farewell once more, your friend.

L. A. Beaulieu

Farewell, I have always loved you with all my heart.

There were several who wrote at length, and we must let one of these stand for all. Louis-Henri-Marthe, Marquis de Gouy d'Arsy (1753–94), an army brigadier, was suspected of "calculated inactivity" in missions entrusted to him and accused of supporting of Lafayette. He was arrested, then released; but he was taken again under the Law of Suspect and imprisoned March 31, 1794. His final letter (he drafted it several times) to his wife is given in full as Blanc has it. (He translates "mon amie" as "my friend," but the meaning here is "my dear one.")

So what remains for me to do. . . . Ah! My friend, the most painful of acts. . . . It remains to me to leave you! Here I admit, to the shame of human weakness, but to the glory of my heart, that all my physical strength deserts me. My moral faculties are destroyed, tears flood my face; and because I feel so much, it seems to me that I have ceased to be, before suffering death. This state of nothingness and pain is horrible; the yearnings I feel are frightful. . . . To leave my family, to be separated for ever from my dear companion, to be far away from my dear children, to abandon all that in the flower of my age, without accident, without glory, without disease, to be in full possession of my faculties to appreciate what I am losing, all my affections to know what I am leaving, all my senses to struggle against the mortal stroke that is to separate me from the living, all that, my dear, is more than I can bear and is killing me in advance; so conjugal love, which has brought me so much delight, now causes all my pain! Thus fatherhood, which has brought me so many sweet moments, now gives me so many regrets! And one cannot leave it! And yet, in a few moments, I shall be in another world!

Ah! My God, where shall I find the strength to undertake such a journey. Without friends, with no one to console me, isolated from all that I love, I feel around me nothing but prisons, judges and executioners! But my conscience sustains me, my innocence consoles me, pity comforts me and God calls me: it is in his paternal bosom that I shall throw myself.

Do not pity me, my friend, in a few hours I shall be happier than you; your ills alone torment me, they will be excessive, I see from here your pain, I sense your tears flowing. . . .

Ah! How sweet it would be to wipe them away, to embrace you again, to hold my children in my arms once more. . . . But no . . .

Farewell, all my beloved children! Farewell, my dear Baptiste, my beloved; I die your friend, your husband, your lover; I excuse my judges, I forgive my executioners, I wish every happiness to our country: I shall not cease to say so, for your consolation, for your happiness and that of our children.

Farewell! Farewell! You who were everything for me in this world, and whom I shall never forget in the next, farewell, for a time; that hope sweetens this cruel moment for me. . . . Farewell, dearest half of myself; we must make an end; farewell! I tear myself from your arms, I throw myself into God's bosom; come and join me there one day, with all our children. The others await me, farewell! Receive my last kiss, it is loving, pure, it is the price of the great courage of which you have given me such honourable proof, so worthy of the esteem of my loved ones!

My body perishes, my soul flies up, my heart will not leave you. . . .

I enclose a few letters; those from my children, for example, from my mother, my sister, which I managed to hide from the searches of the investigators sent into the prison by our tyrants, our executioners. . . . Plus my hair, which I cut off myself; I didn't want it to reach you sullied by the hands of Robespierre's executioner. Farewell again, a hundred kisses for each of our children! A hundred kisses for my father and mother! A thousand for you, my friend! To my eldest son I send the key to my little case; I have wrapped it in paper, which contains a few important words for him and his brothers; you will give to all the others some other object that belonged to me and which may prove to them that I love them all equally. Let them copy out this letter and you, my dear, keep the original, for it concerns you. Can I write anything without your beloved name finding itself naturally on the paper! It is in my heart, on my lips and everywhere. Farewell, yet again: how heartrending that word would be were I not sure that you would do everything in your power to join me one day: our little ones await us; already, I hear them calling me; the others will join us later; take care to bring them up well. Ah! My friend! My beloved friend! How I owe you everything that I have demanded of you in the name of the bitter sacrifice of all my joys, all the happiness and all the compensation that perhaps I was worthy of tasting after so many ills!

What a sin it is to murder a citizen thus! But . . . what am I saying? I promised to endure my sacrifice without complaint and I am already forgetting my oath.

Ah, my God! Forgive mankind, surrounded by weakness and woe. And you, my dear wife, be comforted; I summon up all my courage to offer you the homage of all that remains of my virtue: farewell, receive my last kiss. . . . My body perishes, my soul flies up, my heart does not leave you. . . . It could never leave you. . . . O my country! . . . My country! May you soon be delivered at last from the bloody executioners who wish to dishonour you before all nations!

Gouy d'Arsy

THE LUCKIER ONES

Documents in the nature of diaries did survive, created by prisoners at risk in September 1792, who were able to take them from prison (or write them afterwards) when, as over half did, they escaped execution. None of these diaries has apparently been translated except by Carlyle himself for a chapter in his great work. Note that these are not from the Terror of 1793–94.

There follows a chapter from *The French Revolution*, based on the recollections of three prisoners tormented but spared by fate. They are soldier-journalist François Jourgniac de Saint-Méard (1745–1827), attorney Pierre-Anne-Louis Maton de la Varenne (1760–1813), and the Abbé Roch Ambroise Cucurron Sicard (1742–1822).

FROM THOMAS CARLYLE, *THE FRENCH REVOLUTION*
London: James Fraser, 1837

A Trilogy

As all Delineation, in these ages, were it never so Epic, "speaking itself and not singing itself," must either found on Belief and provable Fact, or have no foundation at all,—the Reader will perhaps prefer to take a glance with the very eyes of eye-witnesses; and see, in that way, for himself, how it was. Brave Jourgniac, innocent Abbé Sicard, judicious Advocate Maton, these, greatly compressing themselves, shall speak, each an instant. Jourgniac's *Agony of Thirty-eight Hours* went through "above a hundred editions," though intrinsically a poor work. Some portion of it may here go through above the hundred-and-first, for want of a better.

> "*Towards seven o'clock* [Sunday night at the Abbaye; for Jourgniac goes by dates]: "We saw two men enter, their hands bloody and armed with sabres; a turnkey, with a torch, lighted them; he pointed to the bed of the unfortunate Swiss, Reding. Reding spoke with a dying voice. One of them paused; but the other cried, *Allons donc*; lifted the unfortunate man; carried him out on his back to the street. He was massacred there.
>
> We all looked at one another in silence, we clasped each other's hands. Motionless, with fixed eyes, we gazed on the pavement of

our prison; on which lay the moonlight, chequered with the triple stanchions of our windows.

Three in the morning: They were breaking-in one of the prison-doors. We at first thought they were coming to kill us in our room; but heard, by voices on the staircase, that it was a room where some Prisoners had barricaded themselves. They were all butchered there, as we shortly gathered.

Ten o'clock: The Abbé L'Enfant and the Abbé de Chapt-Rastignac appeared in the pulpit of the Chapel, which was our prison; they had entered by a door from the stairs. They said to us that our end was at hand; that we must compose ourselves, and receive their last blessing. An electric movement, not to be defined, threw us all on our knees, and we received it. These two white-haired old men, blessing us from their place above; death hovering over our heads, on all hands environing us; the moment is never to be forgotten. Half an hour after, they were both massacred, and we heard their cries.

—Thus Jourgniac in his *Agony* in the Abbaye: how it ended with Jourgniac, we shall see anon.

But now let the good Maton speak, what he, over in La Force, in the same hours, is suffering and witnessing. This *Résurrection* by him is greatly the best, the least theatrical of these Pamphlets; and stands testing by documents [the editor has been unable to locate a copy]:

Towards seven o'clock [on Sunday night], prisoners were called frequently, and they did not reappear. Each of us reasoned, in his own way, on this singularity: but our ideas became calm, as we persuaded ourselves that the Memorial I had drawn up for the National Assembly was producing effect.

At one in the morning, the grate which led to our quarter opened anew. Four men in uniform, each with a drawn sabre and blazing torch, came up to our corridor, preceded by a turnkey; and entered an apartment close to ours, to investigate a box there, which we heard them break up. This done, they stepped into the gallery, and questioned the man Cuissa, to know where Lamotte was. Lamotte [a figure in an earlier scandal involving the queen], they said, had some months ago, under pretext of a treasure he knew of, swindled a sum of three-hundred livres from one of them, inviting him to dinner for that purpose. The wretched Cuissa, now in their hands, who indeed lost his life this night, answered trembling, That he remembered the fact well, but could not tell what was become of Lamotte. Determined to find Lamotte and confront him with Cuissa, they rummaged, along with this latter, through various other apartments; but without effect, for we heard them say: 'Come, search among the corpses, then; for, *nom de Dieu!* we must find where he is.'

"At this same time, I heard Louis Bardy, the Abbé Bardy's name called: he was brought out; and directly massacred, as I learnt. He had been accused, along with his concubine, five or six years before, of having murdered and cut in pieces his own Brother, Auditor of the *Chambre des Comptes* of Montpelier; but had by his subtlety, his dexterity, nay his eloquence, outwitted the judges, and escaped.

"One may fancy what terror these words, 'Come search among the corpses, then,' had thrown me into. I saw nothing for it now but resigning myself to die. I wrote my last-will; concluding it by a petition and adjuration, that the paper should be sent to its address. Scarcely had I quitted the pen, when there came two other men in uniform; one of them, whose arm and sleeve up to the very shoulder, as well as his sabre, were covered with blood, said he was as weary as a hodman that had been beating plaster.

"Baudin de la Chanaye was called; sixty years of virtues could not save him. They said, *A l'Abbaye*; he passed the fatal outer-gate; gave a cry of terror, at sight of the heaped corpses; covered his eyes with his hands, and died of innumerable wounds. At every new opening of the grate, I thought I should hear my own name called, and see Rossignol enter.

"I flung off my nightgown and cap; I put on a coarse unwashed shirt, a worn frock without waistcoat, an old round hat; these things I had sent for, some days ago, in the fear of what might happen.

"The rooms of this corridor had been all emptied but ours. We were four together; whom they seemed to have forgotten: we addressed our prayers in common to the Eternal to be delivered from this peril.

"Baptiste the turnkey came up by himself, to see us. I took him by the hands; I conjured him to save us; promised him a hundred louis, if he would conduct me home. A noise coming from the grates made him hastily withdraw.

"It was the noise of some dozen or fifteen men, armed to the teeth; as we, lying flat to escape being seen, could see from our windows. 'Upstairs!' said they: 'Let not one remain.' I took out my penknife; I considered where I should strike myself,—but reflected 'that the blade was too short,' and also 'on religion.'

"Finally, however, between seven and eight o'clock in the morning, enter the men with bludgeons and sabres!—To one of whom Gérard my companion whispered, earnestly, apart. During their colloquy I searched everywhere for shoes, that I might lay off the Ad-

vocate pumps (*pantoufles de Palais*) I had on, but could find
none.—Constant, called le Sauvage, Gérard, and a third whose
name escapes me, they let clear off: as for me, four sabres were
crossed over my breast, and they led me down. I was brought to
their bar; to the Personage with the scarf, who sat as judge there.
He was a lame man, of tall lank stature. He recognized me on the
streets and spoke to me, seven months after. I have been assured
that he was son of a retired attorney, and named Chepy. Crossing
the Court called *Des Nourrices*, I saw Manuel haranguing in tricolor
scarf." The trial, as we see, ends in acquittal and *resurrection*.

Poor Sicard, from the *violon* [locked cell] of the Abbaye, shall say but a
few words; true-looking, though tremulous. Towards three in the morning, the killers bethink them of this little *violon*; and knock from the
court. "I tapped gently, trembling lest the murderers might hear, on the
opposite door, where the Section Committee was sitting: they answered
gruffly, that they had no key. There were three of us in this *violon*; my
companions thought they perceived a kind of loft overhead. But it was
very high; only one of us could reach it by mounting on the shoulders
of both the others. One of them said to me, that my life was usefuller
than theirs: I resisted, they insisted: no denial! I fling myself on the neck
of these two deliverers; never was scene more touching. I mount on the
shoulders of the first, then on those of the second, finally on the loft;
and address to my two comrades the expression of a soul overwhelmed
with natural emotions."

The two generous companions, we rejoice to find, did not perish. But
it is time that Jourgniac de Saint-Méard should speak his last words, and
end this singular trilogy. The night had become day; and the day has
again become night. Jourgniac, worn down with uttermost agitation, was
fallen asleep, and had a cheering dream: he has also contrived to make
acquaintance with one of the volunteer bailiffs, and spoken in native
Provençal with him. On Tuesday, about one in the morning, his *Agony*
is reaching its crisis.

"By the glare of two torches, I now descried the terrible tribunal,
where lay my life or my death. The President, in gray coat, with a
sabre at his side, stood leaning with his hands against a table, on
which were papers, an inkstand, tobacco-pipes and bottles. Some
ten persons were around, seated or standing; two of whom had
jackets and aprons: others were sleeping stretched on benches. Two
men, in bloody shirts, guarded the door of the place; an old turnkey
had his hand on the lock. In front of the President three men held
a Prisoner, who might be about sixty" (seventy: he was old Marshall
Maillé, of the Tuileries and August Tenth). "They stationed me in a

corner; my guards crossed their sabres on my breast. I looked on all sides for my Provençal: two National Guards, one of them drunk, presented some appeal from the Section of Croix Rouge in favor of the Prisoner; the Man in Gray answered: 'They are useless, these appeals for traitors.' Then the Prisoner exclaimed: 'It is frightful; your judgment is a murder.' The President answered: 'My hands are washed of it; take M. Maillé away.' They drove him into the street; where, through the opening of the door, I saw him massacred.

"The President sat down to write; registering, I suppose, the name of this one whom they had finished; then I heard him say: Another, *un autre!!*"

"Behold me then haled before this swift and bloody judgment-bar, where the best protection was to have no protection, and all resources of ingenuity became null if they were not founded on truth. Two of my guards held me each by a hand, the third by the collar of my coat. 'Your name, your profession?' said the President. 'The smallest lie ruins you,' added one of the Judges.—'My name is Jourgniac Saint-Méard; I have served, as an officer, twenty years; and I appear at your tribunal with the assurance of an innocent man, who therefore will not lie.'—'We shall see that,' said the President: 'Do you know why you are arrested?'—'Yes, Monsieur le Président; I am accused of editing the Journal *De la Cour et de la Ville*. But I hope to prove the falsity.' "—But no; Jourgniac's proof of the falsity, and defence generally, though of excellent result as a defence, is not interesting to read. It is longwinded; there is a loose theatricality in the reporting of it, which does not amount to unveracity, yet which tends that way. We shall suppose him successful, beyond hope, in proving and disproving; and skip largely,—to the catastrophe, almost at two steps.

" 'But after all,' said one of the Judges, 'there is no smoke without kindling; tell us why they accuse you of that.—'I was about to do so' "—Jourgniac does so; with more and more success.

" 'Nay,' continued I, 'they accuse me even of recruiting for the Emigrants!' At these words there arose a general murmur. 'O Messieurs, Messieurs,' I exclaimed, raising my voice, 'it is my turn to speak; I beg M. le Président to have the kindness to maintain it for me; I never needed it more.'—'True enough, true enough,' said almost all the Judges with a laugh: 'Silence!'

"While they were examining the testimonials I had produced, a new Prisoner was brought in. . . . 'It was one Priest more,' they said, 'whom they had ferreted out of the Chapelle.' After very few questions: '*A la Force!*' He flung his breviary on the table; was hurled forth, and massacred. I reappeared before the tribunal.

" 'You tell us always,' cried one of the Judges, with a tone of impatience, 'that you are not this, that you are not that; what are you, then?'—'I was an open Royalist.'—There rose a general murmur; which was miraculously appeased by another of the men, who had seemed to take an interest in me: 'We are not here to judge opinions,' said he, 'but to judge the results of them.' Could Rousseau and Voltaire both in one, pleading for me, have said better?— 'Yes, Messieurs,' cried I, 'always till the Tenth of August I was an open Royalist. Ever since the Tenth of August that cause has been finished. I am a Frenchman, true to my country. I was always a man of honor.'

" 'My soldiers never distrusted me. Nay, two days before that business of Nanci, when their suspicion of their officers was at its height, they chose me for commander, to lead them to Lunéville, to get back the prisoners of the Regiment Mestre-de-Camp, and seize General Malseigne.' " Which fact there is, most luckily, an individual present who by a certain token can confirm.

"The President, this cross-questioning being over, took off his hat and said; 'I see nothing to suspect in this man: I am for granting him his liberty. Is that your vote?' To which all the Judges answered: 'Oui, Oui; it is just!'

"And there arose vivats within doors and without; escort of three, amid shoutings and embracings: thus Jourgniac escaped from jury-trial and the jaws of death. Maton and Sicard did, either by trial and no bill found, lank President Chepy finding 'absolutely nothing'; or else by evasion, and new favor of Maton the brave watchmaker [who had rescued Sicard from the mob], likewise escape; and were embraced and wept over; weeping in return, as they well might.

" 'Thus they three, in wondrous trilogy, or triple soliloquy: uttering simultaneously, through the dread night-watches, their Night-thoughts,—grown audible to us! They Three are become audible: but the other 'Thousand and Eighty-nine, of whom Two-hundred and two were Priests,' who also had Night-thoughts, remain inaudible; choked forever in black Death. Heard only of President Chepy and the Man in Gray!—' " (III i 5).

To complete the picture in a lighter vein, we call on the notes of a warder, Louis Larivière, recounting a rare escape from one of the prisons, the infamous Conciergerie. The prosecutor Fouquier-Tinville, who habitually stalked the halls of the prison in the evenings, caught sight of a gaoler moving silently along the wall.

"Where are you going?" he called.

"I've just come off work, and I'm going to have a little rest."

"Do you know me?"

"Who does not know our Tribunal's eminent prosecutor?"

"Do you know where I live?"

"Yes, I've seen you come out of the house, and once I was sent to take a note to your address."

"Then you will go to my house and tell my wife not to expect me for supper. I have work to do here and will be home late."

"But," (timidly) "they might not let me out at this time."

Fouquier escorted him to the first gate: "Let him through—he's on court business."

The order was passed on, and the keepers, though they did not recognize the man, thought he must be new and did not stop him. It did not occur to them to question the orders of the grand prosecutor.

Late that night, Fouquier-Tinville came home to find a worried wife. She had not eaten and had tried to keep supper warm while waiting for him. The messenger had never turned up.

Next morning, a furious Fouquier went to the Conciergerie, where he got some bad news: a girl accused of consorting with the émigrés had disappeared, just before she was due in court.

"We've looked for her everywhere," said the keeper.

"Well!" Fouquier growled, "find that traitor of a warder while you're at it."

The unfaithful messenger was no more to be found than was the girl. Meanwhile, another guard reported that his new suit was missing.

After a thorough investigation, the conclusion seemed inescapable: a prisoner had escaped wearing the stolen uniform.

Fouquier, who had had the gates opened to the escapee, had been his indispensable accomplice.

The warder whose uniform had been stolen was punished—on the ground that he had not notified his superiors of the theft.

Fouquier, chagrined and furious, had to seem unruffled: "After all, she was not very guilty. I would probably have acquitted her." He kept the rest to himself.

"The Revolution devours its children": The trial of Fouquier-Tinville, the revolutionary prosecutor during The Terror. He was guillotined on May 8, 1795.

TWO GREAT WOMEN OF THE REVOLUTION

MARIE GOUZE (OLYMPE DE GOUGES)

Some consider Marie Gouze, known as Olympe de Gouges (1748–93), the progenitor of modern feminism for her *Déclaration des droits de la femme* (Declaration of the Rights of Woman), a reply to the better-known Declaration of the Rights of Man. "Woman," she said, "has the right to mount the scaffold; she must also have the right to mount the tribune." Her anti-slavery play was performed at the Comédie-Française in 1789. She was an apostle of nonviolence, and her offer to be the king's official legal defender scandalized the Convention.

A Girondist, she fought for her colleagues without success. Her pamphlet *Les Trois Urnes* (The Three Ballot-boxes) suggested that the French choose their form of government by referendum: just before its publication a warrant was issued for her arrest. She was condemned to death for advocating a form of government different from the single, indivisible, centrally-governed nation-state which was the Revolutionary Republic.

Her last letter, written November 2, 1793 (she was able to have her execution postponed one day to write it), was to her son.

FROM OLIVIER BLANC, *LAST LETTERS: PRISONS AND PRISONERS OF THE FRENCH REVOLUTION, 1793–1794*
Alan Sheridan, trans.
London: Andre Deutsch, 1987

To Citizen Degouges, general officer in the army of the Rhine

I die, my dear son, a victim of my idolatry for the fatherland and for the people. Under the specious mask of republicanism, her enemies have brought me remorselessly to the scaffold.

After five months of captivity, I was transferred to a *maison de santé* [hospital] in which I was as free as I would have been at home. I could have escaped, as both my enemies and executioners know full well, but, convinced that all malevolence combining to ensnare me could not make me take a single step against the Revolution, I myself demanded to go to trial. Could I have believed that unmuzzled tigers would themselves be judges against the laws, against even that assembled public that will soon reproach them with my death?

I was presented with my indictment three days before my death; from the moment this indictment was signed the law gave me the right to see my defenders and whomsoever else I chose to assist my case. All were prevented from seeing me. I was kept as if in solitary confinement, unable to speak even to the gaoler. The law also gave me the right to choose my jurats [magistrates]; I was given the list at midnight and, the following day at 7 o'clock, I was taken to the Tribunal, weak and sick, and lacking the art of speaking to the public; like Jean-Jacques [Rousseau] and also on account of his virtues, I was all too aware of my inadequacy. I asked for the *défenseur officieux* that I had chosen. I was told that there wasn't one or that he did not wish to take on my cause; I asked for another to take his place, I was told that I had enough wit to defend myself.

Yes, no doubt I had enough to spare to defend my innocence, which was evident to the eyes of all there present. I do not deny that a *défenseur officieux* could have done much more for me in pointing out all the services and benefits that I have brought the people.

Twenty times I made my executioners pale and not knowing how to reply to each sentence that betrayed my innocence and their bad faith. They sentenced me to death, lest the people be led to consider my fate as the greatest example of iniquity the world has ever seen.

Farewell, my son, I shall be no more when you receive this letter. But leave your post, the injustice done to your mother and the crime committed against her are reason enough.

I die, my son, my dear son; I die innocent. All laws have been violated for the most virtuous woman of her century. [two illegible words] for the law, always remember the good advice that I have given you.

I leave your wife's watch as well as the receipt for her jewellery at the pawnbrokers, the jar and the keys to the trunk that I sent to Tours.

De Gouges

MARIE-JEANNE PHILIPON (MADAME ROLAND)

Marie-Jeanne Philipon, Madame Roland, born March 14, 1754 and executed November 3, 1793, was one of the transcending revolutionary figures of her time. Her *Memoirs*, written in prison, is an absorbing document which can be found in most libraries. The book will vastly repay study in its own right, particularly by those interested in feminist history. Madame Roland was an activist in politics, a committed Girondist (thus a relative moderate), and a combative, courageous, self-righteous exponent of her views. Like

De Gouges, she disdained to flee when matters got hot (as her husband did), and she marched into prison with her head high.

The first time she was arrested, on June 1, 1793, she was taken to the Abbaye prison. Her husband, Jean Marie Roland de la Platière, had resigned from the ministry of the interior four months previously, having fallen afoul of Robespierre.

FROM MARIE-JEANNE ROLAND, *MEMOIRS* (1794)
Evelyn Shuckburgh, trans. and ed.
Mount Kisco, N.Y.: Moyer Bell, 1990

The first arrest

On the throne today; tomorrow in irons.

That is the common lot of the virtuous in time of revolution. When the people first rise up against oppression, wise men who have shown them the way and helped them to recover their rights come to power. But they do not stay there long. More ambitious characters soon emerge, flatter and delude the people and turn them against their true defenders. That is what has happened here, particularly since 10 August [1792].

[Her husband has resigned.] The Convention needed a just and firm man at the Ministry of the Interior; it was the best support they had and it was inevitable that, once they lost it, they should fall into the hands of extremists. The stage was set for the emergence of the Paris Commune as a rival authority to the national House of Representatives.

I had been fast asleep for an hour when my servant came into my room to announce that the gentlemen from the section requested me to step into the salon. "I know what that means," I said. "Come along, my girl, let's not keep them waiting." I jumped out of bed and dressed. My maid came in and was surprised that I had taken the trouble to put on more than a dressing gown. "One must be decently dressed to go out in the street," I said. The poor girl stared at me and burst into tears. . . . I deliberated whether I should try to resist or not. I could, for example, appeal to the law prohibiting nocturnal arrests. If they cited the law which authorises the municipality to seize suspected persons, I could retort by questioning the legality of the municipality itself; for it had been dissolved and recreated by an arbitrary power. But . . . this arbitrary power had in a sense been sanctioned by the citizens of Paris. A "law" was now little more than a word which was being used to deprive people of their most widely recognised rights. Force was now the master.

I made up a small night case for myself. Meanwhile, fifty people, a hundred people, were pouring in and out continuously, filling the two

This portrait of Madame Roland is to be found on the cover of a candy box in the Carnavalet Museum in Paris. It was first reproduced in Ernest F. Henderson's *Symbol and Satire in the French Revolution* (New York: Knickerbocker Press, 1912).

rooms, surrounding everything and providing ample cover for any ill-intentioned person who might wish to remove something—or to plant something. The air was filled with stinking breath.

Finally, at seven o'clock in the morning I left my daughter and my people, having exhorted them to calmness and patience. . . . "Shall we close the carriage windows?" the commissioners obligingly enquired. "No thank you, gentlemen," I said. "Innocence, however sorely oppressed, will never adopt the posture of the guilty. I am not afraid of anyone's looks and ask for no protection." "You have more character than many men and you await justice calmly," they said. "Justice!" I cried.

"If justice were done, I should not be here in your power. But if this iniquitous procedure leads me to the scaffold I shall mount it calmly and firmly, as I now proceed to prison. I weep for my country; I blush for my mistake in thinking that France was ready for liberty, for happiness. But I value life; I have never feared anything but sin, I despise injustice and death." The poor commissioners understood very little of all this and probably thought it typical aristocratic talk.

In prison

It is curious to see how, every now and again, events reward a man for his labours. When Roland first came to the Ministry of the Interior he found that the state of the prisons had been horribly neglected. He looked with pity at those squalid habitations, built originally for criminals but too often occupied by innocent people, and considered that they ought to be kept salubrious and if possible comfortable even for the former. He created a special post for the surveillance of the prisons. The incumbent was expected to visit regularly, to provide the minister with an accurate list of those detained and of the orders under which they were held, to note their grievances and to transmit these promptly. He offered the modest salary of 1,000 écus, which he thought sufficient for a good man who would appreciate the value of having humanitarian duties, and he appointed Grandpré, a man of sensibility, very conscious of suffering, perfectly suited in his feelings and experience for dealing with the unfortunate. Grandpré carried out his duties to perfection.

I was given a room the same evening and got into it at ten o'clock. When I saw the four dirty walls, the pallet in the centre without curtains and the window double-barred, and became aware of the stink which anyone accustomed to a clean apartment always finds so disagreeable, I realised that this was in truth a prison and that I must not expect any comfort. On the other hand, the space was reasonably large, there was a chimneypiece, the bed cover was passable and they had given me a pillow. All things considered it was not too bad.

I got up at midday and began to consider how I should settle myself in my new quarters. There was a common little table which I covered with a white cloth and put near the window to serve as my desk. I decided to eat off the corner of the mantelpiece so as to keep my worktable clean and orderly. Two large head-combs nailed to the shelves did service as coat-hangers.

I was soon told that I had to move; there were so many new arrivals. The room I had been given could take more than one bed, so if I wanted to be alone I must go into a much smaller room. More disturbance as a result. The window of this cubby-hole looks out, I think, over the sentry who guards the front entrance of the prison. All night long I heard raucous voices shouting "Who goes there?—Kill him!—Officer!—Patrol!" The buildings were lit up and it was clear from the continuous patrols that some sort of uprising was expected or had taken place. . . . I waited impatiently for the great key to turn in the lock of my door, so that I could ask for the morning paper. It was brought to me; and there it was, the fatal news: an order of arrest had been issued against the Twenty-Two [Girondist] deputies. The paper slipped from my hands and I cried out in despair, "France is lost!"

I had received numerous visitations from functionaries with mean faces and dirty ribbons across their stomachs, some claiming to belong to the police and others to I know not what. Huge *sans-culottes* with unwashed hair and fussy little bureaucrats came to enquire whether the prisoners were satisfied with their treatment. . . . I was having dinner when someone came to announce that a group of five or six more had arrived. One man [Louvet] spoke on their behalf. I could tell before he had opened his mouth that he was an empty-headed windbag.

"Good morning, *Citoyenne*." "Good morning, Sir." "Are you satisfied with these premises? Have you any complaints regarding your treatment, or any requests to make?" "Yes. I complain of being here; I demand to be released." "Is your health affected? Are you perhaps bored?" "I am well and I am not bored. Boredom is a malady of empty souls and resourceless minds. But I know what justice is and I protest against having been arrested without charge and detained without interrogation." "Ah! But in time of revolution there is so much to do; one cannot attend to everything." "A woman to whom King Philip once made that reply answered, 'If you have no time to do me justice you have no time to be King.' I say the same to you." "Adieu, *Citoyenne*." "Goodbye, Sir." And off goes the windbag, unable to cope with the argument. These men seem to have come here just to see what I look like in my cage. It would be hard to find stupider people.

They told me that Roland, when he was at the ministry, decided that the allowance of five livres per day for the expenses of each prisoner was excessive, and reduced it to two livres. But the great rise in the price of food, trebled over the past few months, made this totally inadequate. All the nation was prepared to supply was the four walls and some straw, so that twenty sous were deducted right away to cover the keeper's room charges—that is, the bed and any furniture there might be. From the twenty sous remaining, the prisoner has to pay for light, heat if he needs it and his food. It is not enough. One is free in theory to add whatever one likes to one's expenditure.

Release and Re-arrest

[O]n 24 June, at midday, the keeper's wife came to tell me that I was wanted in her room by an administrator of the prison. I was ill and in bed, but I got up and went to her quarters. There was a man there walking up and down, and another man writing. Neither of them seemed to notice my arrival. "Is it me you asked for, gentlemen?" I said eventually. "You are *Citoyenne* Roland?" "Yes, that is my name." "Please take a seat." And the one continued to write while the other walked about. I was wondering what this comedy was in aid of when the man sitting at the table said "I have come to set you free." I do not know why, but this announcement moved me hardly at all. "I should be greatly obliged to be let out of here," I said, "but I must also be allowed to go home; there are seals on my apartment." "The administration will see to that right away," he replied. "I am writing out the order" . . . the keeper came to ask whether I was making my arrangements and I could see that he was keen to get hold of my room. It was a minute, unpleasant cubicle, with damp walls and coarse gratings and it lay alongside the butcher's yard where all the dogs of the establishment did their business. Its only advantage was that it could hold only one bed, so one could be alone.

I got out of the cab with a light step—I have never been able to come down from any vehicle without jumping—and passed through the gate like a homing pigeon, calling out gaily to the porter, "Morning, Lamarre!" I had not gone up four steps of my staircase when two men stepped out from behind me. "*Citoyenne* Roland?" "What do you want?" I asked. "We arrest you in the name of the law."

I need not describe what I felt at that moment. I made them read out the order and decided immediately what to do . . . [the local section heads were summoned and took up her cause]. . . . Jobert, another police officer as violent as Louvet but heavier and more stupid, made a pompous speech defending the administration. He admitted that my first arrest had been illegal and said that they had had to set me free in order to be able to arrest me again legally [he was executed with other members of the Paris Commune in July 1794]. . . . I withdrew from the scene and was conveyed to Sainte-Pélagie.

Under the *ancien régime* this place had been occupied by an order of nuns who were supposed to look after the victims of *lettres de cachet* and whose morals were more than suspect. It was remote and isolated, in a very undesirable quarter. Hundreds of priests had been massacred there in September. . . . They looked, but there was no single room available and I was put into one with *two* beds. But as I wanted only one and would have preferred a single room I said I would pay for only one. . . . I also bought a desk, paper and pens and settled myself in. The woman in charge came to see me to tell me the local arrangements. I learned that the State does nothing at all for the prisoners here. "How do they live then?" "There is a portion of beans and a pound and a half of bread per day, but you will not be able to eat either of them." . . . I had to have recourse to Mme Bouchaud's cooking. She had offered to feed me and I accepted. It was clean and economical compared with what I could have got from an eating house. . . . A cutlet and some spoonfuls of vegetables for dinner, some greens in the evening; no dessert, nothing for breakfast but bread and water.

I was not daunted by the new calamity that had befallen me, but I was outraged by their particular cruelty in letting me taste freedom and then binding me with new chains, their barbarous device for cloaking my detention with legality. I found myself in that state of mind in which all external sensations bite cruelly into one's being and actually endanger one's health. I could not sleep at night, I could only dream. But extreme agitation never lasts very long with me. I am hardened in self-control. Why pay my persecutors the compliment of being upset? All they had done, after all, was to add to their own crimes; they had not substantially altered the conditions which I had already learned to endure.

The building allotted to women is divided into long, very narrow corridors with cells all down one side similar to the one I have described in which I was lodged. Here, under the same roof, in the same row, separated by thin plaster boards, I live with fallen women and murderers. Next door to me is one of those creatures who seduce the young and sell the innocent. Above is a woman forger of *assignats* who tore another woman to pieces on the King's highway with a gang of her accomplices. Each cell is locked with a huge key and opened every morning by a man who leers in to see whether you are asleep or awake. The inmates crowd together for the rest of the day in the corridor, on the stairs, in the small court or in a damp, stinking hall, fit receptacle for these dregs of humanity. I stayed the whole time in my cell, but it was at such close quarters that it was impossible not to hear the conversation of these women, which was indescribable.

And that is not all. The building which houses the men has windows opposite and is very close to the women's section. Conversations take place between depraved men and women such as no decent person can imagine. There is no restraint, no fear. Gesture supplies the want of contact and these windows become theatres for the enaction of the most lewd and shameful debauchery.

I must say that my gaolers soon became more concerned about my situation than I was myself, and wanted to improve it if they could. In July it became so hot that my cell was uninhabitable. I had put paper over the grilles to try and keep out the sun but it beat so strongly on the confined walls that, although the windows were open all night, the air never cooled. The keeper's wife invited me to spend the daytime in her apartment and I accepted for the afternoons. I had the idea of installing a forte piano there, which I sometimes play.

In the midst of all these troubles it is restful to find myself in the pleasant little room where dear Mme Bouchaud has managed to isolate me from the foul atmosphere of prison life. There are, admittedly, one or two small irritations: a sentry post immediately opposite my window, against which I have to keep the curtains drawn all day (and the man sometimes creeps close enough to hear what is being said when I am not alone); the terrible barking of three large dogs in a kennel not ten paces away; and the fact that I am next door to a large room known grandly as the "council chamber," in which the police officers assemble when they come to conduct an interrogation. . . . I shall certainly not try to describe the brutish humour, the vulgarity and the indecency of these entertainments: the stupid and sarcastic repetition of the word "patriot," always in association with that of the scaffold, the bloodthirsty call for the execution of all "suspected persons," a title now applied freely to anyone who has received an education or who possesses a fortune that has not been recently stolen . . . the filthy jokes of men without morals and without shame, the mad conceit of atrocious imbeciles who live by denouncing honest men and filling the prisons with innocent people.

If I could bring myself to fork over this dunghill I would give some astonishing—and very sad—details about abuses in the prisons. I could show every menial servant and tradesman in the place compounding and abetting the crimes of the unfortunate prisoners. I could show prostitutes guilty of some awful offence released without trial in return for sleeping with the administrator on their last day; murderers rich enough to bribe the officials with their ill-gotten gains, to suppress evidence and secure immunity; professional thieves freely planning their operations, communicating with one another both inside and outside the prison and finally escaping with the connivance of the prison staff or the police officers supposed to be guarding them. Everything becomes venal and corrupt in this stinking hole, under a vicious administration whose sole passion is to keep people in, with no thought of correction.

In October, the Convention outlawed the Girondins who had fled (including Roland), charged forty-one others, and ordered the arrest of another seventy-six. When she received the news, Madame Roland decided to starve herself to death. This did not happen, and when she came at last to the guillotine, Dickens tells us she asked "to be allowed to write down the thoughts that were inspiring her." This permission was denied, but we can see something of what she had in mind in the *Memoirs* under *Final*

Thoughts, beginning, "To be or not to be: it is the question. The question will soon be answered for me."

Here are a few of her words:

—Is life a blessing which is bestowed upon us? I believe it is. But I also believe that there are conditions attached which we must observe. We are born to seek happiness and to serve the happiness of our fellow mortals. The social order merely extends the range of this objective and indeed of all our faculties; it adds nothing new.

—So long as we can see a course ahead in which we may do good and set a good example it behoves us not to abandon it. We must have the courage to persist even in misfortune.

—Two months ago I coveted the honor of going to the scaffold. It was still possible to speak and I thought that a demonstration of vigorous courage might set a useful example.

—I know that the empire of evil never lasts long. Sooner or later the wicked get their deserts. If I were unknown, tucked away in some silent corner, I might find it possible to ignore the horrors that are tearing France apart and to wait patiently for better times, keeping virtue alive in private.

—Liberty? Liberty? Liberty is for proud hearts who fear not death and are ready to die; it is not for this corrupt nation which, the moment it was rescued from debauchery and tyranny, fell into brutal licence and wallowed in blood.

—Farewell my child, my husband, my maid, my friends! Farewell glorious sun that ever filled my heart with contentment as it filled the skies with light. Farewell lone countryside, where I have sighed and dreamed, and you, rustic villagers. . . . Farewell my peaceful study, where I ever strove after truth and beauty and learned to control my senses and to despise vanity.

—Eternal Creator, Supreme Being, soul of the universe, the source of all that is great and good, I believe in thee because I cannot accept that I am simply a product of this terrible material world. I know that I am of thine essence and I return to thee!

It was reported by a contemporary that when the sentence of death (for corresponding/conspiring with insurgents in Calvados) was pronounced, she replied, "You find me worthy to share the fate of the great men whom you have assassinated. I shall do my best to mount the scaffold with the same courage as they."

TOPICS FOR WRITTEN AND ORAL DISCUSSION

1. The story of the Marquis de Gouy d'Arsy bears some resemblance to that of Darnay. His letter also strikingly has the feel of having been written by one of Darnay's background and sensibility. Do you agree?

2. The text of the "Declaration of the Rights of Woman," written by Olympe de Gouges, falls too far outside the scope of this book to be included. A project for extra credit would be to test library referral and loan systems and find a copy.

3. The life and mind of Madame Roland would be an inspiration to anyone, and probably particularly to any girl. What are the opportunities you have noticed in this book or in the novel which lend themselves especially to feminist studies?

SUGGESTED READINGS AND WORKS CITED

OB   Blanc, Olivier. *Last Letters: Prisons and Prisoners of The French Revolution, 1793–1794*. Trans. Alan Sheridan. London: Andre Deutsch, 1987.

Carlyle, Thomas. *The French Revolution*. London: James Fraser, 1837.

MR   Roland, Marie-Jeanne. *Memoirs*. 1794. Trans. and ed. Evelyn Shuckburgh. Mount Kisco, N.Y.: Moyer Bell, 1990.

Yalom, Marilyn. *Blood Sisters: The French Revolution in Women's Memory*. New York: Basic Books, 1933.

8

Revolution: When, What, and How

INTRODUCTION: FRANCE AND ENGLAND

The American and French Revolutions, in their different ways, set off a galvanic shift in the way the peoples of nations viewed their rights and their governments. The following chapter discusses Thomas Paine, one of several brilliant, influential thinkers who articulated these attitudes. Some of the others were John Locke (1632–1704), François-Marie Arouet, known as Voltaire (1694–1778), Jean-Jacques Rousseau (1712–1778) and Thomas Jefferson (1743–1826).

The American and French Revolutions so differed in their essential natures that some thought must be given here to what "revolution" means—both as a word and as a historical phenomenon. A revolution is a rapid and violent change in government, as to people and policy. A transition without violence is an evolution; a quick, violent (or illegal) change of rulers without changing policy as such is a coup d'état, or, these days, simply a coup. A rebellion or revolt is a term for open resistance to authority, which, if successful, might become a revolution.

Historians ask, "Why in France, but not in England?" By the late 1700s most English yeomen had been driven off their land and replaced by sheep, whose wool and meat made better money for the landowners. Corn Laws kept grain prices high, causing hardship. Technology and the displacement of workers to the cities combined to jump-start the Industrial Revolution, with many abuses going along. Will and Ariel Durant give the picture in *The Age of Napoleon*.

> The economic picture of Britain in 1800 showed, at the top, an aristocracy still, but decreasingly, masters of the economy through ownership of the land; cooperating with them was a Parliament overwhelmingly noble or genteel; swelling below and around them was a ruthless and enterprising bourgeoisie of merchants and manufacturers displaying their new riches and bad manners, and clamoring for more political power; below these the professions, from the most learned physician to the most courageous or virulent journalist; below them all a peasantry progressively dispossessed and dependent upon relief, and sunless miners stripping or gutting the earth, and "navvies" engaged in movable gangs to level roads and dig canals, and a labor pool of hungry, disorganized, demoralized factory workers writing their tragedy in polluted skies. (DD/AN 343)

The Factory Act of 1802 limited the employment of children to twelve hours a day but provided no funds to pay for its enforcement. In the forty years from 1782 to 1821, their condition was truly dreadful. Carlyle himself said the medieval serf had been better off.

And there was some rebellion: in 1811 bands of Luddites began destroying factory machinery, and they killed one employer who had ordered his men to fire on them. "Half of England shivered with fright, remembering the French Revolution" (DD/AN 345). But government responded with a regiment, and the Luddite leaders were deported or hanged after a mass trial in 1813.

"The basic struggle," say the Durants, "was of the capitalist to replace the aristocrat at the helm of state; in France it took a generation; in England it took centuries" (DD/AN 340). Why? No one knows for sure, but luck may have played a part (there was no disastrous weather to cause famine in London, and the Crown's ministers were resolute, not soft-headedly inconsistent like Louis XVI). There is also the question of personality: again and again we read that the French were "excitable," the English the opposite. They were habituated to defer to their "betters," their hardships were rarely so severe as to push them to desperation, and no leaders like the fiery Desmoulins sought to ignite a conflagration. (Thomas Paine was an exception, and he was chased out of the country.)

The political environment was luckily different, too. In 1688, incensed by James II's pretensions to Divine Right (his ties to Roman Catholicism may have been even more irksome), Parliament had stepped in to depose him and invite William and Mary to come and rule. This "Glorious Revolution" was neither especially glorious nor a revolution, but it did shift ultimate power from the crown to Parliament. Though in France, as its Revolution began, the electorate numbered in the millions while in England the House of Commons was chosen by fewer than 250,000, the English people could look up and see their governance coming from a group of men, chosen in a rough-and-ready fashion but not by pure accident (and to some extent representing the new middle class), rather than one individual entitled to reign by his birth. Over time, the way that group was chosen was reformed and reformed, until, near the end of the nineteenth century, the English electorate was roughly as broad as the Americans' had been for a century. This was truly evolution, not revolution, for it was gradual and (usually) nonviolent.

And it was probably critically important that, since they already had governing power through Parliament, the intellectual leadership in England felt no need to push for profound change. Their church, also, was a force for stability, not an opulent, oppressive lightning rod for unrest as in France. The dissenters—Methodists, Presbyterians, Baptists, Independents, Congregationalists, Quakers, Unitarians—could freely preach on condition that they declared themselves Christian, and their preachers were often fiery and terrifying. The downtrodden were willing to be consoled by their religion and so resisted foreign, often atheistic, revolutionary ideas.

There was also an eloquent defender of the status quo: Edmund Burke. Once a fierce defender of the Americans in Parliament, he had grown conservative with age and property, and he denounced the French Revolution and its English supporters:

Our present danger is from anarchy: a danger of being led, through an admiration of successful fraud and violence, to an imitation of the excess of an irrational, unprincipled, proscribing, confiscatory, plundering, ferocious, bloody, and tyrannical democracy. On the side of religion the danger is no longer from intolerance but from atheism—a foul, unnatural vice, a foe to all the dignity and consolation of mankind—which seems in France, for a long time, to have been embodied into a faction, accredited, and almost avowed. (DD/ AN 514)

Thomas Paine wrote his famous *The Rights of Man* in 1790 to rebut Burke's attacks on the French Revolution (see Chapter 9).

CARLYLE AND DICKENS

And what was Carlyle's attitude on revolution in general, and the risk of it in England? In his fine biography, *Thomas Carlyle* (1983), Fred Kaplan describes him as alarmed by the continuing debates over proposed reform of the franchise. "A second edition of the French Revolution is distinctly within the range of chances," he thought.

In Carlyle's opinion, the burning of hay ricks and the riots of unemployed factory workers in response to economic depression and political disenfranchisement were not the real basis of the current revolutionary threat. He was convinced that domestic tranquillity could readily be reestablished by any government that accepted its primary responsibility to provide all willing workers an adequate livelihood through fair employment and to guarantee a reasonably secure future for the working class. He did not believe that a violent revolution would occur in England, partly because he anticipated that even the worst of governments would accept this responsibility, and partly because he had a deep appreciation of the stubborn patience of the English working class. Still, to the extent that revolution is the turbulent manifestation of the divine power's refusal to continue to tolerate a corrupt, false, and stultified society, Carlyle believed that revolution was not only desirable but inevitable in England. If this were indeed God's world, then there was no reason to feel fear, though he felt anger and resentment at corruption, even on the brink of or in the midst of the purging fire. "Twenty choleras and 20 Revolutions" should not "terrify" him. "The crash of the whole Solar and Stellar System could only kill you once" (FK 184–85).

Dickens was more apprehensive. Often in his writings he points with alarm at the appalling condition of the poor: unfed, uncared-for, uneducated, unsanitary, unregarded by society. His opinion of the ruling class is obvious when he describes Mr. Gradgrind in *Hard Times* (written in 1854) as a member of Parliament: "one of the deaf honourable gentlemen, dumb honourable gentlemen, blind honourable gentlemen, lame honourable gentlemen, dead honourable gentlemen, to every other consideration. Else where-fore live we in a Christian land, eighteen hundred and odd years after our Master?" (*HT* i 14).

The ignorance and insensitiveness, if not active indifference, of the middle classes pained Dickens keenly. With Gradgrind's numb, confused daughter, he is not severe, but he is objective:

> For the first time in her life Louisa had come into one of the dwell-ings of the Coketown Hands; for the first time in her life she was face to face with anything like individuality in connexion with them. She knew of their existence by hundreds and by thousands. She knew what results in work a given number of them would produce in a given space of time. She knew them in crowds passing to and from their nests, like ants or beetles. But she knew from her reading infinitely more of the ways of toiling insects than of these toiling men and women.
>
> Something to be worked so much and paid so much, and there ended; something to be infallibly settled by laws of supply and de-mand; something that blundered against those laws, and floundered into difficulty; something that was a little pinched when wheat was dear, and over-ate itself when wheat was cheap; something that in-creased at such a rate of percentage, and yielded such another per-centage of crime, and such another percentage of pauperism; something wholesale, of which vast fortunes were made; *something that occasionally rose like a sea, and did some harm and waste* (chiefly to itself), and fell again; this she knew the Coketown Hands to be. But, she had scarcely thought more of separating them into units, than of separating the sea itself into its component drops. (*HT* ii 6; emphasis added)

It would severely shift the center of gravity of this book to extract many more proofs of Dickens's fears on the subject, but one last sample from *Hard Times* shows them clearly. Here, his wrath is directed at the primitive state of education in his country. Education, he felt, was the necessary saving grace: a solution to street crime, rampant disease, and other scourges of the world he knew, it would undercut the risk that England might have its own revolution.

> Utilitarian economists, skeletons of schoolmasters, Commissioners of Fact, genteel and used-up infidels, gabblers of many little dog's-eared creeds, the poor you will have always with you. Cultivate in them, while there is yet time, the utmost graces of the fancies and affections, to adorn their lives so much in need of ornament; or, in the day of your triumph, when romance is utterly driven out of their souls, and they and a bare existence stand face to face, *Reality will take a wolfish turn, and make an end of you.* (*HT* ii 6; emphasis added)

FROM RIGHT TO LEFT: THE ARC OF CHANGE

Crane Brinton, in *The Anatomy of Revolution*, published in 1938 and revised in 1956, studies four revolutions and develops a convincing set of what he calls "uniformities" common to most if not all. The four are the English Revolution of the seventeenth century, which culminated in the execution of Charles I in 1649 and the ten-year rule of Oliver Cromwell (1599–1658); the American Revolution of 1775–81; the French Revolution; and the Russian Revolution, which began in 1917.

Brinton notes, as his first uniformity, that in each of the societies studied, prior to the definitive outbreak there were economic, or at least financial, difficulties and issues, often concerned with taxation. But the problems tended to be governmental, not society-wide: in none of the four cases had there been pervasive economic want and, in fact, each society had been making good progress in broadening economic activity and raising standards of living overall. Often, the problem was that, as conditions improved, expectations rose even faster, and middle-class resentment of the privileged classes increased faster yet.

In France, for example, the eighteenth century saw substantial increases in population, foreign trade, building, manufacturing, land clearance, and agriculture. The year 1788–89 was a "trough year," but by no means so severe as, for example, the Great Depression year of 1932. But the prosperity was unevenly shared: the middle class of merchants, bankers, landed peasantry, and professionals did relatively very well, but, probably out of resentment of "Monseigneur," it was just these relatively well-off people who in the 1780s were loudest against the government and most reluctant to pay taxes or lend it money. It was not that they were deprived, but they felt frustrated and cramped by the old rules and customs. They had grievances, and they felt wronged.

Another uniformity common to all four societies was that their governments were inept and inefficient. Their institutions had not kept pace with social change and economic improvement. In France, for example, it was very difficult to get action, even if you were the king himself. Once, Louis XV, traveling in the provinces, was received in a town hall with a leaking roof. "Ah, if I were only a minister, I'd have that fixed," he said. Reforms were attempted: the unlucky Charles I made genuine efforts to import some efficient methods which were working in France (as instituted by Cardinal Richelieu). George III and his ministers were trying hard to learn how to administer their colonies. In France and Russia there were attempts to make government more efficient and responsive, many of which were opposed or undercut by those with a stake in the status quo. But the attempts themselves made those who needed them more and more aware of their necessity and more and more outraged when they fell short or were aborted.

A third uniformity in the prologue to and opening stages of revolution was, in every case, ineffectual and irresolute use of force in the maintenance of order. We know something about Lexington and Concord and the Battle of Bunker Hill. We know also about the fall of the Bastille—which behaved more like a house of cards than the virtually impregnable fortress it was. The soft-headedness of King Louis XVI is proverbial, and his soft heart cost the lives of nine hundred Swiss guardsmen because at the storming of the Tuileries in 1792 he would not let them do their job. The Russian czar and his advisors, "in spite of their celebrated Asiatic background, were by the late nineteenth century more than half ashamed to use force, and therefore used it badly," and those on whom coercion was attempted were enraged, not cowed (CB 53).

The upper classes in three of the four societies Brinton examines were feudal in their descent, aristocratic in their manners, and convinced of the divine right of their status. But a uniformity Brinton notices is their divided, confused state, particularly in France, where many members of the upper class espoused the cause of the discontented or repressed classes. In Russia, however, the privileged nobility were hated by the excluded. Brinton speculates that many of its aristocrats were "insufferably haughty, overbearing, dissolute, vain, empty-headed, and the rest, just as if they had come from the pages of *A Tale of Two Cities*" (CB 54).

(It is worth noting that, in contrast to the other three societies, the American ruling class was emerging at the time of our revolution. It was relatively young and relatively able—indeed very able. And in large measure it supported our revolution, which, Brinton believes, was one of the reasons we never had a full-blown Terror.)

The fall of the Bastille is now a mythic event, hardly studied any more for the facts of what happened (which are complex, controversial, and confusing, if they are even remembered). The important thing to Brinton was that Paris from that moment was in the hands of the mob for three days: a mob shouting against the nobility and the court, shouting for the National Assembly. When the city was quiet again the National Assembly "could proceed in the useful assurance that the people were on its side, could feel that it had *carte blanche* to neglect royal protests as it went about its task of remaking France" (CB 75).

In all four revolutions, moderates of various sorts took charge to create the nucleus of new government, once the first violence had spent itself. The role of the moderates is a revolutionary uniformity. "Their sentiments and training impel them to try and put a stop to disorder, to salvage what they can of established routines" (CB 76).

The moderates, once in power, had intractable problems: they had to institute reforms and govern simultaneously. They had to deal with foreign or civil wars, or both. They soon found they were accused of trying to subvert the revolution—to betray it—because of their very moderation. In Russia quickly, in France and in England more slowly, there came a show of force between them and the radicals, and they were beaten. The extremists took over. When she heard that her party, the Girondists, had been defeated, the moderate Madame Roland wrote in her prison diary:

When I was a child of twelve, I wept that I had not been born in Sparta or in Rome; and in the French Revolution I thought I saw the unexpected triumph of principles upon which I had been nourished. Liberty, I said to myself in those days, has two sources: high morality, which makes wise laws, and enlightenment, which teaches us our rights. From now on, there will be no more degrading inequalities, I thought; nothing can now prevent human improvement; the general good will support and guarantee the happiness of the individual. Oh, those shining illusions, those seductive dreams! (MR 49)

The analogous process in America was the milder rivalry between Federalists and Republicans, culminating in Thomas Jefferson's assumption of the presidency in 1800, though there was an earlier stage when moderates and radicals fought over the question of accommodation with England versus revolution, a battle won by the radicals with the signing and promulgation of the Declaration of Independence.

A striking fact about all four revolutions is the way initial success breathes euphoria and optimism. Doubt, debate, and agitation are suspended. The revolution appears already achieved. In England after Parliament's initial successes in wringing concessions from Charles I; in America after Concord and Lexington, "and that greatest of moral victories, Bunker Hill"; in France after the Bastille; and in Russia after the czar's abdication came a moment of joy and hope, the illusion of the union of the Real and the Ideal.

The "honeymoon stage," as Brinton calls it, was most vivid in France, where the revolution broke out in peacetime at the climax of the great intellectual movement called the Enlightenment. For one moment of bliss the ideal future seemed attainable. The English poet, William Wordsworth, went to Paris in 1790 and was thrilled:

France standing on the top of golden hours
And human nature seeming born again.
Bliss was it in that dawn to be alive,
But to be young was very heaven! (The Prelude)

Charles James Fox, a leading Whig politician in England, commented on the Bastille's fall, "How much the greatest event it is that ever happened in the world! and how much the best!" When

America's distinguished journalist Lincoln Steffens went to Russia in 1919, he reported back that he had seen the future, "and it works."

In all the revolutions, there was a tendency for power to go from the conservatives (the "Right," so-called for their location on the floor of the National Assembly) to the moderates (the "Center"), to the radicals or extremists (the "Left"). Power, moving in this way, gets more concentrated as its base narrows (for the defeated group at each stage drops out). This concentration, as it reaches the extreme, eventually results in a backlash. The moment when radicalism took command in France was probably August 10, 1792, with the mob's invasion of the Tuileries and the massacre of the king's guard.

The moderates inevitably fail, in part because they cannot immediately produce the results demanded of them, working with the old institutions they have inherited, in part precisely because they are *moderate* and concerned about human rights, due process, and other concepts which begin to seem inconvenient luxuries when war is on. The Terror was partly explained by the fact that France was threatened from without and needed strong, fanatic discipline, indiscriminate enthusiasm, and "unpondered loyalty," in Brinton's phrase, to fight a war and crush perceived or assumed disloyalty at home.

The extremists were always few in number. The "New Model Army" of Cromwell's day never had more than 40,000 members in a nation of four million or so; the Jacobins at most were half-a-million souls in a nation of twenty million; up until Stalin took over, the Communist party was never more than 1 percent of Russia's one hundred million. Most students of the American Revolution believe it was actively engineered, supported, and fought by no more than 10 percent of the population.

These people, in all four revolutions (though in America far less so) combined very high ideals with "contempt for the inhibitions and principles which serve most other men as ideals." They were "not philosopher-kings but philosopher-killers." They infused a ruthless realism with prophetic fire: "practical men unfettered by common sense, Machiavellians in the service of the Beautiful and the Good." They were men of action, and they got things done, sometimes almost miraculously as in their expulsion of the armies sent against France by its neighbors.

As Brinton puts it, "only a sincere extremist in a revolution can kill men because he loves man, attain peace through violence, and free men by enslaving them. Such contrasts in action would paralyze a conventionally practical leader, but the extremist seems quite undisturbed by it" (CB 159–60). Trollope's brilliant portrait of Robespierre is completely attuned to these ideas (see Chapter 6).

The overthrow of the monarchy on August 10, 1792, was achieved through a collaboration of the Jacobin and other political clubs, local militias from all over France which had assembled in Paris to celebrate "Bastille Day," and the ward organizations which became the Paris Commune. These *sansculotte* elements coalesced again ten months later to support the ouster of the "moderate" Girondins.

"Once the extremists are in power, there is no more finicky regard for the liberties of the individual or for the forms of legality. The extremists, after clamoring for liberty and toleration while they were in opposition, turn very authoritarian when they reach power . . . this seems to be one of the uniformities. . . . Liberty for everyone, liberty full, free, and fair, is of course the ultimate goal. But such liberty at present would mean that men corrupted by the bad old ways would be able to realize their wicked plans, restore the bad old institutions, and frustrate the good men" (CB 164–66). Robespierre himself called the revolutionary government "the despotism of liberty against tyranny." Thucydides's commentary on the behavior of Athenian democracy could have been written about the Jacobins (see page 118).

The Terror governments got the biggest tasks done: England, France, and Russia esaped anarchy and defeated foreign invasion. But the lower-level bureaurats were inexperienced, often petty fanatics, show-offs, posturing patriots, incompetent blowhards. One of the reasons they were so hard to bear was their very inefficiency, arbitrariness, and volatility. The people they ruled lived in a state of suspense and fear, vulnerable to accidents of personality and venality.

The fanaticism, or "religiosity" of extremism inspired men to work hard together for an ideal not anywhere so far achieved. "Religion attempts to close in favor of human hopes the gap between what men are and what men would like to be; at least in its youthful, fresh, and active phase, it will not for a moment admit that such a gap can long exist" (CB 184).

A redistribution of property occurs. In England, the Royalists lost much of their land, and moderate Presbyterians lost their clerical livings. In America, the great Tory estates were broken into many small holdings. In France and Russia, the church lost both land and capital. The winners gained in wealth, but asceticism was a high value for them, whether Calvinist or Communist.

Proselytizing is a feature in revolution. The Puritans, the Jacobins, and the Communists all had supra-national ideas and sought to promulgate their faiths beyond national borders. The most important uniformity of all in the four revolutions is that "as gospels, as forms of religion, they are all universalist in aspiration and nationalist, exclusive, in ultimate fact. They end up with a God meant indeed for all mankind, but brought to mankind, usually a not altogether willing mankind, by a Chosen People" (CB 195). Brinton points out that the four show a progressively increasing hostility to organized Christianity, particularly in its more ecumenical forms. There is "an overwhelming preponderance of emphasis on the individual conscience over against the corporate Church and its traditions; the French and even the American revolutions are full in the tide of eighteenth-century secularism; the Russian Revolution is proudly materialistic" (CB 196).

The crisis stage in the four revolutions entails the interaction of seven important variables:

1. The habit of violence: while the Terror did not formally begin until late 1793, the eruptions of 1789 and the September Massacres in 1792 established the mood.

2. Foreign and civil war: dissenters now seem deserters, traitors.

3. The rawness of new governmental machinery, with mistakes and "jams" leading to impatience and impetuous lashing out.

4. Acute economic crisis, as in the starvation in Paris; failed efforts to improve conditions leading to recriminations, denunciations.

5. Class struggles: polarization and sharpening antagonisms.

6. Stress and strain on a leadership not formed to compromise but to push on to extremes, to heighten already dangerous tensions.

7. Religious absolutism, seeking the Reign of Virtue. "Religious aims and emotions help to differentiate the crises of our revolutions from ordinary military or economic crises, and to give to the Reigns of Terror and Virtue their extraordinary mixture of spiritual fury, of exaltation,

of devotion and self-sacrifice, of cruelty, madness, and high-grade humbug." (CB 202–3).

The last uniformity, of course, is the backlash—the reaction. As with Robespierre, there comes a point when revulsion sets in. Echoes of conscience and practicality reappear. Of course sometimes, with the help of arms from abroad, reaction becomes a principle of a new order, as happened in 1815. Then, the pendulum swung again: after Louis XVIII, the relatively reasonable brother of the late king—under whose reign a Parliamentary system was established once more—died in 1824, the Comte d'Artois, youngest and most reactionary brother, became Charles X. He lasted six years before running for his life in the Revolution of 1830.

The son of Philippe Egalité, Louis Philippe the "Citizen King," was brought to power, but in 1848 his rule ended, and many other thrones were toppled or seriously jeopardized. Ultimately, Louis Napoleon, Bonaparte's nephew, was elected President and then crowned emperor Napoleon III. The Franco-Prussian War finished him in 1870, but during his reign Dickens wrote Sidney Carton's final meditation, and the vision he had of a stable, serene France was, all things considered, not far off the mark—at least compared with 1793.

The ultimate effect of the French Revolution was to complete the work of a long line of monarchs: to make the central power truly *the* power. The old chaos of overlapping jurisdictions, the struggles between monarchical authority and the feudal nobility, were subsumed in an able bureaucracy, an efficient legal system, and an excellent army. With these, Napoleon made an extraordinary first step toward the unification of Europe and set the stage for the increasingly integrated Europe we see stumbling toward us today.

But the nation-state, with all power to a mystical people (*Volk*) as conceived by Abbé Sieyès, proved to be the box of Pandora. Did the fascism of the twentieth century emerge from it?

TOPICS FOR WRITTEN AND ORAL DISCUSSION

1. Recall the courtier's comment after the fall of the Bastille: "Sire, this is not a revolt: it is a revolution." Was this a legitimate remark at the moment it was uttered? Discuss what Liancourt meant.

2. Why do you think the term "Glorious Revolution" was applied to the events in England in 1688?

3. Apply the "uniformities" of revolution to the French, as depicted in Dickens. Does this procedure make Charles Darnay's decision to go to Paris easier to understand and defend? Look closely at the dates in the Chronology.

4. Look over the list of seven variables associated with the crisis of revolution and see what traces of them you can spot in the Chronology at the beginning of Chapter 3. (Some of them will not appear as moments in time or sequence, but there is a good deal of information in the Chronology going beyond that.)

5. Do the events of the French Revolution support the Brinton theory of a step-by-step lurching from right to left?

6. If you have studied the subject, do you think the Russian Revolution supports the Brinton thesis? Can you apply it to events in China after 1945?

SUGGESTED READINGS AND WORKS CITED

CB   Brinton, Crane. *The Anatomy of Revolution*. New York: W. W. Norton, 1938; revised 1956.

———. *A Decade of Revolution: 1789–1799*. New York and London: Harper and Bros., 1934.

HT   Dickens, Charles. *Hard Times for These Times*. London: Bradbury and Evans, 1854.

DD/AN   Durant, Will and Ariel. *The Age of Napoleon*. New York: Simon and Schuster, 1975.

DD/RR   ———. *Rousseau and Revolution*. New York: Simon and Schuster, 1967.

Gurr, Ted Robert. *Why Men Rebel*. Princeton, N.J.: Princeton University Press, 1970.

FK   Kaplan, Fred. *Thomas Carlyle*. Ithaca, N.Y.: Cornell University Press, 1983.

Postgate, Raymond. *Revolution from 1789 to 1906*. New York: Harper and Row, 1920. Reprint 1962.

MR   Roland, Marie-Jeanne. *Memoirs*. Trans. and ed. Evelyn Shuckburgh. Mount Kisco, N.Y.: Moyer Bell, 1990.

Wordsworth, William. *The Prelude: or, Growth of a Poet's Mind*. Oxford: de Selincourt, 1926.

9

Due Process of Law: The Rights of Man

THE MEANING OF DUE PROCESS

Due process refers to the taking of legal action in a way consistent with principles established to enforce and protect *private, individual rights*. To Americans, the idea is derived from the Fifth Amendment to the United States Constitution ("No person shall be deprived of life, liberty, or property, without due process of law"), but it comes originally from the early common law of England and its subsequent constitutional history.

The first concrete written expression of due process seems to have been the 39th article of the Magna Carta (1215). King John was obliged to promise that, "No freeman shall be taken or imprisoned or disseised [stripped of his property or rights of inheritance] or exiled or in any way destroyed . . . except by the legal judgment of his peers or by the law of the land." Later statutes made it clear that "the legal judgment of his peers" and "the law of the land" were substantially the same thing: due process of law.

The Fifth Amendment to the U.S. Constitution refers to the Federal system, and after it was held several times to be inapplicable to actions by the several states, the Fourteenth Amendment was adopted in 1868, after the Civil War, making the states subject to a federally enforceable requirement that their laws and procedures be consistent with the due process mandate.

The Supreme Court of the United States, not without controversy, has taken decisions over the years that have resulted in a sort of classification system where due process is at issue. If a law may reasonably be held to promote the public welfare, and the means it selects seem reasonably related to a legitimate public interest, it will be held to meet the due process standard; but if a law impinges on a fundamental right, such as the right to travel or to vote, it must pass a "compelling interest" test.

In applying the due process standard, the Court has been vigorously criticized from one side or the other. It has been accused of meddling unduly with the states' chosen modes of administering justice; and it has been attacked by those who think it should more rigorously enforce the Bill of Rights across the board. Some justices have thought that the framers of the Constitution intended the states to be governed by the first ten amendments; others have argued that the states should have some latitude, providing they meet a general test of fundamental fairness. These latter seem to have largely prevailed. Today, due process seems to mean those principles of justice which are "so rooted in the traditions and conscience of our people as to be ranked as fundamental." But by usage and tradition, it now seems to be generally accepted that most if not all of the Bill of Rights is included in those fundamental rights.

THE COMMON SENSE OF TOM PAINE

Thomas Paine, the author of *Common Sense*, a little fifty-page booklet, which did as much as anything to inspirit and indeed launch the American Revolution, was born on January 29, 1737 in the town of Thetford, England. His Quaker father was a corset-maker who could not afford much in the way of an education for his son. Paine, who educated himself fiercely, unremittingly, once remarked: "I seldom passed five minutes of my life, however circumstanced, in which I did not acquire some knowledge."

Tom Paine's first nearly forty years were lived in poverty and struggle. He felt rootless, lonely (his first wife died, his second quickly separated), and essentially homeless. He became an internationalist. Though he lived in England all during that time, he came to feel, act, and really be as much a citizen of America and later of revolutionary France as of England: he may have been in fact the first Citizen of the World.

He immigrated to Philadelphia in 1774, was a printer's assistant, then editor of *The Pennsylvania Magazine*, and soon an ardent apostle of independence. *Common Sense*, which he signed, "Written by an Englishman," went through the colonies like wildfire. Published in mid-1776, it sold somewhere between 300,000 and 500,000 copies in a population of 3 million—it would take a sale of over 33 million copies today to match such success—and all these in the first three months. By the time the colonies had achieved their goal of freedom from England, Paine was internationally known. He had become the voice of liberty.

Paine was way ahead of his time. Not only did he demand that monarchy and aristocracy be replaced with a republic, he sought a steeply graduated income tax that would redistribute concentrated wealth and use it to wipe out poverty, educate every child, and make old age economically secure.

He was brilliant, articulate, and intolerant—of superstition, bigotry, and inherited class privilege. His famous work, *The Rights of Man*, written to rebut Edmund Burke's attacks on the French Revolution and published in England in 1790, led to accusations of treason, and he had to flee to France, where in 1792 he was made a citizen and elected to the Convention. He allied himself with the moderates, who lost power and many their lives in the Terror. His citizenship was revoked, and he was cast into prison, to be released in 1795, when he rejoined the Convention after the Terror's passing.

THE RIGHTS OF MAN

In Part the First of *The Rights of Man*, Paine recounts the events that led up to the fall of the Bastille and concludes:

> Occupied with establishing a constitution founded on the Rights of Man and the Authority of the People, the only authority on which Government has a right to exist in any country, the National Assembly felt none of those mean passions which mark the character of impertinent governments, founding themselves on their own authority, or on the absurdity of hereditary succession. One of its first works, instead of vindictive proclamations . . . was to publish a declaration of the Rights of Man, as the basis on which the new constitution was to be built.

The man who first proposed that the Assembly issue the Declaration was Lafayette, France's most visible representative to the American revolutionary army. It may not be so well remembered that he drafted the document under the direct scrutiny of Thomas Jefferson, who was at the time the United States ambassador in Paris. In fact, the Assembly Committee considering it asked Jefferson to advise them, which, given his official capacity, he felt unable to do. But a deputation of assemblymen, republicans and monarchists alike, went to his home on the final day of debate, August 26, 1789, to air in his hearing their differences of opinion concerning the role of the king in the government.

The following Declaration, as adopted by the Assembly and published by Paine in *The Rights of Man*, also presents parallel quotations or paraphrases from the Declaration of Independence and the Constitution of the United States (1787). Our purpose is to highlight certain similarities and differences between the American and French approaches and choices of language. The parallelisms are not always exact and in some cases should be regarded as analogies.

Articles III and VI of the Declaration, which are least like the American approach, are discussed later in this chapter in "The Promise Undermined."

FROM THOMAS PAINE, *THE RIGHTS OF MAN* (1790)
New York: Heritage Press, 1961

Declaration
OF THE RIGHTS OF MAN
AND OF CITIZENS
BY THE
NATIONAL ASSEMBLY OF FRANCE

The Representatives of the people of FRANCE, formed into a NATIONAL ASSEMBLY, considering that ignorance, neglect or contempt of human rights, are the sole causes of public misfortunes and corruptions of Government, have resolved to set forth in a solemn declaration, these natural, imprescriptible, and inalienable rights: that this declaration being constantly present to the minds of the members of the body social, they may be forever kept attentive to their rights and their duties; that the acts of the legislative and executive powers of Government, being capable every moment of being compared with the end of political institutions, may be more respected; and also, that the future claims of the citizens, being directed by simple and incontestable principles, may always tend to the maintenance of the Constitution, and the general happiness.

For these reasons the NATIONAL ASSEMBLY doth recognise and declare, in the presence of the Supreme Being, and with the hope of his blessing and favour, the following *sacred* rights of men and of citizens:

I   Men are born, and always continue, Free and Equal in respect of their Rights. Civil Distinctions, therefore, can be founded only on Public Utility.

We hold these truths to be self-evident: that all men are created Equal. Declaration of Independence, par. 1

II   The end of all Political Associations is the Preservation of the Natural and Imprescriptible Rights of Man; and these Rights are Liberty, Property, Security, and Resistance of Oppression.

All men are endowed by their Creator with certain Unalienable Rights; among these are Life, Liberty and the pursuit of Happiness. Declaration of Independence, par. 1.

III   The Nation is essentially the source of all Sovereignty; nor can any *Individual*, or *any Body of Men*, be entitled to any Authority which is not Expressly Derived from it. [See "The Promise Undermined" on page 181.]

It has become necessary for one people to dissolve the political bands which have connected them with another, and to assume among the powers of the earth, the separate and equal station to which the Laws of Nature and of Nature's God entitle them. Declaration of Independence, prologue.

IV   Political Liberty consists in the Power of doing whatever does not injure another. The exercise of the Natural Rights of every Man, has no other limits than those which are Necessary to secure to every *other* Man the free exercise of the same Rights; and these Limits are Determinable only by the Law.

To secure these rights, governments are instituted among Men, deriving their just powers from the consent of the governed. Declaration of Independence, par. 1.

V   The Law ought to Prohibit only Actions hurtful to Society. What is not Prohibited by the Law should not be hindered; nor should Anyone be Compelled to that which the Law does not Require.

The enumeration in the Constitution of certain rights, shall not be construed to deny or disparage others retained by the people. U.S. Constitution, amend. 9.

The powers not delegated to the United States by the Constitution, nor prohibited by it to the States, are reserved to the States respectively, or to the people. U.S. Constitution, amend. 10.

VI   The Law is an Expression of the Will of the Community. All Citizens have a Right to Concur, either Personally or by their Representatives, in its Formation. It should be the same to all, whether it Protects or Punishes; and all being Equal in its Sight, are Equally eligible to all Honours, Places, and Employments, according to their different Abilities, without any other Distinction than that created by their Virtues and Talents. [See "The Promise Undermined" on page 181.]

All legislative Powers herein granted shall be vested in a Congress of the United States, which shall consist of a Senate and House of Representatives. The House shall be composed of Members chosen by the people of the several States, and the Electors in each State shall have the Qualifications requisite for Electors of the most numerous Branch of the State Legislature. The Senate of the United States shall be composed of two Senators from each State, chosen by the Legislature thereof. U.S. Constitution, art. 1, sec. 1–3.

The Senate of the United States shall be composed of two Senators from each State, elected by the people thereof. U.S. Constitution, amend. 17.

The citizens of each State shall be entitled to all Privileges and Immunities of Citizens in the several States. U.S. Constitution, art. 4, sec. 2.

All persons born or naturalized in the United States, and subject to the jurisdiction thereof, are citizens of the United States and of the State wherein they reside. No State shall make or enforce any law which shall abridge the privileges or immunities of citizens of the United States; nor shall any State deprive any person of life, liberty or property, without due process of law; nor deny to any person within its jurisdiction the equal protection of its laws. U.S. Constitution, amend. 14, sec. 1.

The right of citizens of the United States to vote shall not be denied or abridged by the United States or by any State on account of race, color, or previous condition of servitude. U.S. Constitution, amend. 15, sec. 1.

The right of citizens of the United States to vote shall not be denied or abridged by the United States or by any State on account of sex. U.S. Constitution, amend. 19.

The right of citizens of the United States to vote for President or Vice President or for Senator or Representative in Congress, shall not be denied or abridged by the United States or any State by reason of failure to pay any poll tax or other tax. U.S. Constitution, amend. 24.

The right of citizens of the United States, who are eighteen years of age or older, to vote shall not be denied or abridged by the United States or any state on account of age. U.S. Constitution, amend. 26.

VII No Man should be Accused, Arrested, or Held in Confinement, except in Cases determined by the Law, and according to the Forms which it has prescribed. All who promote, solicit, execute, or cause to be executed, Arbitrary Orders, ought to be Punished, and every Citizen called upon, or apprehended by Virtue of the Law, ought immediately to obey, and renders himself Culpable by Resistance.

The privilege of the Writ of Habeas Corpus shall not be suspended, unless when in Cases of Rebellion or Invasion the public Safety may require it. U.S. Constitution, art. 1, sec. 9.

The right of the people to be secure in their persons, houses, papers, and effects, against unreasonable searches and seizures, shall not be violated, and no Warrants shall issue, but upon probable cause, supported by Oath or affirmation, and particularly describing the place to be searched, and the persons or things to be seized. U.S. Constitution, amend. 4.

No person shall be held to answer for a capital, or otherwise infamous crime, unless on a presentment or indictment of a Grand Jury, nor be deprived of life, liberty, or property, without due process of law. U.S. Constitution, amend. 5.

In all criminal prosecutions, the accused shall enjoy the right to a speedy and public trial, by an impartial jury, and to be informed of the nature and cause of the accusation; to be confronted with the witnesses against him; to have compulsory process for obtaining witnesses in his favor; and to have the Assistance of Counsel for his defence. U.S. Constitution, amend. 6.

VIII   The Law ought to impose no other Penalties but such as are Absolutely and Evidently Necessary; and no one ought to be Punished, but in Virtue of a Law promulgated before the Offence, and Legally Applied.

No Bill of Attainder or ex post facto law shall be passed. U.S. Constitution, art. 1, sec. 9.

IX   Every man being Presumed Innocent till he has been Convicted, whenever his Detention becomes indispensable, all Rigour to him, more than is necessary to Secure his Person, ought to be provided against by the Law.

Excessive bail shall not be required, nor excessive fines imposed, nor cruel and unusual punishments inflicted. U.S. Constitution, amend. 8.

X   No Man ought to be molested on account of his Opinions, not even on account of his *Religious* Opinions, provided his Avowal of them does not disturb the Public Order established by the Law.

XI   The Unrestrained Communication of Thoughts and Opinions being one of the most precious Rights of Man, every Citizen may Speak, Write, and Publish freely, provided he is responsible for the Abuse of this Liberty, in cases determined by the Law.

No religious Test shall ever be required as a Qualification to any Office or public Trust under the United States. U.S. Constitution, art. 6.

Congress shall make no law respecting an establishment of religion, or prohibiting the free exercise thereof; or abridging the freedom of speech, or of the press; or of the right of the people peaceably to assemble and petition the government for a redress of grievances. U.S. Constitution, amend. 1.

XII   A Public Force being Necessary to give Security to the rights of Men and of Citizens, that Force is Instituted for the Benefit of the Community and not for the Particular Benefit of the Persons to whom it is Intrusted.

A well regulated Militia, being necessary to the security of a free State, the right of the people to keep and bear Arms, shall not be infringed. U.S. Constitution, amend. 2.

No Soldier shall, in time of peace, be quartered in any house, without the consent of the Owner, nor in time of war, but in a manner to be prescribed by law. U.S. Constitution, amend. 3.

XIII   A Common Contribution being Necessary for the Support of the Public Force, and for Defraying the Other Expenses of Government, it ought to be divided Equally among the Members of the Community, according to their Abilities.

No Capitation, or other direct, Tax shall be laid, unless in proportion to the Census. U.S. Constitution, art. 1, sec. 9.

The Congress shall have power to lay and collect taxes on incomes, from whatever sources derived, without apportionment among the several States, and without regard to any census or enumeration. U.S. Constitution, amend. 16.

XIV   Every Citizen has a right, either by Himself or his Representative, to a Free Voice in determining the necessity of Public Contributions, the Appropriation of them, and their Amount, Mode of Assessment, and Duration.

The Congress shall have Power to lay and collect Taxes, Duties, Imposts and Excises, to pay the Debts and provide for the common Defence and general Welfare of the United States; but all Duties, Imposts and Excises shall be uniform throughout the United States U.S. Constitution, art. 1, sec. 8.

XV   Every Community has a Right to Demand of all its Agents an Account of their Conduct.

No person holding any Office of Profit or Trust under the United States shall, without the Consent of Congress, accept of any present, Emolument, Office or Title, of any kind whatever, from any King, Prince, or foreign State. U.S. Constitution, art. 1, sec. 9.

XVI   Every Community in which a Separation of Powers and a Security of Rights is not provided for, wants a Constitution.

XVII   The Right to Property being Inviolable and Sacred, no one ought to be Deprived of it, except in Cases of Evident Public Necessity, legally ascertained, and on Condition of a previous Just Indemnity.

No person shall be deprived of property, without due process of law, nor shall private property be taken for public use, without just compensation. U.S. Constitution, amend. 5.

[Paine continues:] The first three articles comprehend in general terms the whole of a Declaration of Rights, all the succeeding articles either originate from them or follow as elucidations. The 4th, 5th, and 6th define more particularly what is only generally expressed in the 1st, 2nd, and 3rd.

The 7th, 8th, 9th, 10th, and 11th articles are declaratory of *principles* upon which laws shall be constructed, conformable to *rights* already declared. But it is questioned by some very good people in France, as well as in other countries, whether the 10th article sufficiently guarantees the right it is intended to accord with; besides which it takes off from the divine dignity of religion, and weakens its operative force upon the mind, to make it a subject of human laws. It then presents itself to man like light intercepted by a cloudy medium, in which the source of it is obscured from his sight, and he sees nothing to reverence in the dusky ray.

The remaining articles, beginning with the twelfth, are substantially contained in the principles of the preceding articles; but in the particular situation in which France then was, having to undo what was wrong, as well as to set up what was right, it was proper to be more particular than what in another condition of things would be necessary.

While the Declaration of Rights was before the National Assembly, some of its members remarked that if a declaration of rights were published it should be accompanied by a Declaration of Duties. The observation discovered a mind that reflected, and it only erred by not reflecting far enough. A Declaration of Rights is, by reciprocity, a Declaration of Duties also. Whatever is my right as a man is also the right of another; and it becomes my duty to guarantee as well as to possess.

The three first articles are the base of Liberty, as well individual as national; nor can any country be called free whose government does not take its beginning from the principles they contain, and continue to preserve them pure; and the whole of the Declaration of Rights is of more value to the world, and will do more good, than all the laws and statutes that have yet been promulgated.

In the declaratory exordium which prefaces the Declaration of Rights we see the solemn and majestic spectacle of a nation opening its commission, under the auspices of its Creator, to establish a Government, a scene so new, and so transcendantly unequalled by anything in the Euro pean world, that the name of a Revolution is diminutive of its character, and it rises into a Regeneration of man. What are the present Governments of Europe but a scene of iniquity and oppression? What is that of England? Do not its own inhabitants say it is a market where every man has his price, and where corruption is common traffic at the expense of a deluded people? No wonder, then, that the French Revolution is traduced. Had it confined itself merely to the destruction of flagrant despotism perhaps Mr Burke and some others had been silent. Their cry now is, "It has gone too far"—that is, it has gone too far for them. It stares corruption in the face, and the venal tribe are all alarmed. Their fear discovers itself in their outrage, and they are but publishing the groans of a wounded vice. But from such opposition the French Revolution, instead of suffering, receives an homage. The more it is struck the more sparks it will emit; and the fear is it will not be struck enough. It has nothing to dread from attacks; truth has given it an establishment, and time will record it with a name as lasting as his own.

Having now traced the progress of the French Revolution through most of its principal stages, from its commencement to the taking of the Bastille, and its establishment by the Declaration of Rights, I will close the subject with the energetic apostrophe of M. de la Fayette—*"May this great monument, raised to Liberty, serve as a lesson to the oppressor, and an example to the oppressed."*

THE PROMISE UNDERMINED

In her excellent article, "The Decline and Fall of the French Revolution" (*New York Review of Books* 37, No. 2, February 15, 1990), Conor Cruise O'Brien notes that the American influence on the Declaration of the Rights of Man was not exclusive. There was another great influence: the *Contrat Social* of Jean-Jacques Rousseau.

The man who injected Rousseau's concept of the "general will" into the Declaration was Emmanuel-Joseph (the Abbé) Sieyès, author of the influential pamphlet *What Is the Third Estate?* (1789): "The nation exists before all, it is the origin of everything. Its will is always legal, it is the law itself." He was critical of the American formulation because he felt it clung to an old image of power and its limitations. For him, the Declaration could not be "a concession, a transaction, a treaty condition, or a contract between two authorities. There is only *one* power, only *one* authority." As Ms. O'Brien puts it: "In its final form the Declaration [of the Rights of Man] embodies a series of rights, American-style, but it goes on to nullify these by two Articles [III and VI] written in an entirely different spirit." "These propositions," Ms. O'Brien goes on, "may appear innocuous on the printed page but, as applied in the course of the Revolution, what they meant was that 'authority emanating expressly from the nation'—or understood so to emanate—was without limit of any kind, and that a person deemed to be in opposition to the general will was an outlaw: neither a citizen nor even a man, and so without rights of any kind. To set yourself outside the nation, and in opposition to the general will was to put yourself outside nature itself." Here was the appalling logic of extermination in the holy name of Revolution.

The law of 22 Prairial (June 10, 1794) made it death to:

1. advocate the monarchy
2. slander the public
3. outrage morality
4. give out false news
5. steal public property
6. profiteer or embezzle
7. impede the transport of food
8. interfere in the prosecution of France's war with its foreign enemies

The law let the courts decide whether an accused should be allowed counsel, what witnesses would be heard and when, and how much evidence to receive. One juryman said, "I am always convinced. In a revolution all who appear before this Tribunal ought to be condemned" (DD/AN 80).

The law was revoked on August 1, 1794, after Robespierre and his allies had been guillotined (July 28). But many argue today that the French Revolution, imbued with the Rousseau–Sieyès idea of a single "general will," was the progenitor of twentieth-century totalitarianism.

THE LETTRE DE CACHET
IN THE EIGHTEENTH CENTURY

A famous, indeed infamous, aristocratic abuse in pre-Revolutionary France was the *lettre de cachet*, by which an aristocrat could incarcerate his son, or an enemy, simply by getting the signature of some political authority. There was no "process" at all, only political influence. Two English observers provide contemporary evidence of this abuse: Helen Maria Williams and Arthur Young.

The book of letters from France published in 1792 in England by Miss Williams (see Chapter 6) contains a description of the use of the *lettre de cachet* just eleven years before the fall of the Bastille. We have presented it essentially as it appears in her book. Monsieur du F— was Augustin François Thomas du Fossé (1750–1833), unlucky son of the Baron du Fossé.

FROM HELEN MARIA WILLIAMS, *LETTERS ON THE FRENCH
REVOLUTION, WRITTEN IN FRANCE, IN THE SUMMER OF 1790,
TO A FRIEND IN ENGLAND*
London: G. G. and J. Robinson, 1792

Letter XVIII

Mons. du F— arrived at his father's chateau in Normandy, in June 1778, and was received by the Baron, and all his family, with the most affectionate cordiality. . . . He had not been many days at the chateau, when he perceived, with surprize and consternation, that his steps were continually watched by two servants armed with *fusées* [rockets; should be *fusils*, flint-lock muskets].

His father now shewed him an *arrêt*, which, on the fourth of June 1776, he had obtained from the parliament of Rouen against his marriage. The Baron then ordered his son to accompany him to his house at Rouen, whither they went, attended by several servants. That evening, when the attendants withdrew after supper, the Baron, entirely throwing off the mask of civility and kindness, which he had worn in such opposition to his nature, reproached his son, in terms of the utmost bitterness, for his past conduct, inveighed against his marriage, and, after having exhausted every expression of rage and resentment, at length suffered him to retire to his own apartment.

There the unhappy Mons. du F—, absorbed in the most gloomy reflections, lamented in vain that fatal credulity which had led him to put himself into the power of his implacable father. At the hour of midnight his meditations were interrupted by the sound of feet approaching his chamber; and in a few moments the door was thrown open, and his father, attended by a servant armed, and two *Cavaliers de Maréchaussée* [policemen], entered the room. Resistance and supplication were alike unavailing . . . he was conducted in the dead of night, July the 7th, 1778, to St. Yon, a convent used as a place of confinement near Rouen, where he was thrown into a dungeon.

Where are the words that can convey an adequate idea of the sufferings of Madame du F— during this period? Three weeks after her husband's departure from England, she heard the general report of the town of Rouen, that the Baron du F— had obtained a letter de cachet against his son, and thrown him into prison. This was all she heard of her husband for the space of two years. Ignorant of the place of his confinement, uncertain if he still lived, perhaps her miseries were even more poignant than his. . . . For herself, she would have welcomed death with thankfulness; but she considered that her child now depended entirely on her labours for support: and this was a motive sufficiently powerful to prompt her to the careful preservation of her own life, though it had long become a burden. The child was three years old when her father left England; recollected him perfectly; and, whenever her mother went to visit her, used to call with eagerness for her papa. The enquiry, in the voice of her child, of "When shall I see my dear, dear papa?" was heard by this unhappy mother with a degree of agony which it were a vain attempt to describe.

Letter XIX

Mons. du F— was repeatedly offered his liberty, but upon conditions which he abhorred. He was required for ever to renounce his wife; who, while she remained with her child in a distant country, was to receive from his father a small pension, as an equivalent for the pangs of disappointed affection, of disgrace and dishonour.

Nor can imagination form an idea of a scene more dreadful than his prison, where he perceived with horror that the greatest number of those prisoners who had been many years in confinement, had an appearance of frenzy in their looks, which shewed that reason had been too weak for the long struggle with calamity, and had at last yielded to despair. In a cell adjoining Mons. du F—'s was an old man who had been confined nearly forty years. His grey beard hung down to his waist, and, during the day, he was chained by his neck to the wall. He was never allowed to leave his cell, and never spoke; but Mons. du F— used to hear the rattling of his chains.

The prisoners, a few excepted, were generally brought from their cells at the hour of noon, and dined together. But this gloomy repast was served in uninterrupted silence. They were not suffered to utter one word, and the penalty of transgressing this rule was a rigorous confinement of several weeks. As soon as this comfortless meal was finished, the prisoners were instantly obliged to return to their dungeons, in which they were locked up till the same hour the following day. Mons. du F—, in his damp and melancholy cell, passed two winters without fire, and suffered so severely from cold that he was obliged to wrap himself up in the few clothes which covered his bed. Nor was he allowed any light.

Mons. du F— remained two years in prison without receiving any intelligence of his wife, on whose account he suffered the most distracting anxiety. He had reason to apprehend that her frame, which had already been enfeebled by her misfortunes, would sink beneath this additional load of misery, and that she would perhaps be rendered unable to procure that little pittance, which might preserve herself and her child from want. [He writes her a letter, which was secretly conveyed out of the prison and reached her in England. It is quoted in full. The wife's reply comes, and he is overjoyed.]

On the 10th of October, 1780, the Baron du F— came to the convent, and ordered the monks to bring his son from his dungeon to the parlour, and leave them together. . . . When the monks withdrew, the Baron begain upbraiding him in the most bitter terms, for his obstinate resistance to his will . . . his son answered, that not merely were his affections interested, but that his honour obliged him to maintain, with inviolable fidelity, a solemn and sacred engagement. The rage of the Baron, at these words, became unbounded. He stamped the ground with his feet; he aimed a stroke at his son, who, taking advantage of this moment of frenzy, determined to attempt his escape. [He throws himself from the roof, falling fifty feet, and is reclaimed by the monks and placed in their infirmary.]

The report that Mons. du F— had been found lying on the road bathed in blood, and had in that condition been dragged to the prison of St. Yon, was soon spread through the town of Rouen. Every one sympathized in the fate of this unfortunate young man, and execrated the tyranny of his unrelenting father. [From his bed, the young man smuggles out another letter to his wife.]

Letter XXI

At length the Parliament of Rouen began to interest itself in the cause of Mons. du F—. The circumstances of his confinement were mentioned in that Assembly, and the President sent his Secretary to Mons. du F—'s prison, who had now quitted his bed, and was able to walk with the assistance of crutches. By the advice of the President, Mons. du F— addressed some letters to the Parliament, representing his situation in the most pathetic terms, and imploring their interference in his behalf.

The Baron du F— perceived that . . . it would be impossible to silence the murmurs of the public, while he remained confined at St. Yon. He determined, therefore, to remove him to some distant prison, where his name and family were unknown; and where, beyond the jurisdiction of the Parliament of Rouen, his groans might rise unpitied and unavenged. [The Baron has his younger son entice the elder into writing a letter requesting removal to another locale but overplays his hand: Mons. du F— tears up the letter.]

Soon after this, Mons. de B—, the ambassador of the tyrant, again returned to his brother with fresh credentials. . . . Upon Mons. du F—'s asserting that he could no longer confide in the promises made him by his family, his brother, in a formal written engagement, to which he signed his name, gave him the most solemn assurance, that this promise should be fulfilled with fidelity. [After taking legal advice, Mons. du F— complies.]

Soon after, an order was sent from Versailles for his release from the prison of St. Yon, and with it a *lettre de cachet*, whereby he was exiled to Beauvais, with a command not to leave that town. Mons. de B—, acting as a *Cavalier de la Marechaussée*, conducted his brother to this place of exile, and there left him. A short time after, Mons. du F— received an intimation . . . that his father was on the point of obtaining another *lettre de cachet*, to remove him from Beauvais, to some prison in the south of France, where he might never more be heard of. [Advised to flee instantly, Mons. du F— does so, having the freedom of Beauvais.]

When they reached Lisle in Flanders, not having a passport, they were obliged to wait from eleven o'clock at night till ten the next morning, before they could obtain permission from the Governor to proceed on their journey. Mons. du F— concluded that he was pursued, and suffered the most dreadful apprehensions of being overtaken. His companion [a Rouen magistrate], with some address, at length obtained a passport, and attended him as far as Ostend. The wind proving contrary, he was detained two days in a state of the most distracting inquietude, and concealed himself on board the vessel in which he had taken his passage for England. At length the wind became favourable; the vessel sailed, and arrived late in the night at Margate. Mons. du F—, when he reached the English shore, knelt down, and, in a transport of joy, kissed the earth of that dear country which had twice proved his asylum.

[He is reunited with his wife; public clamor forces his father to allow him an income; the two live by tutoring students in French.]

FROM ARTHUR YOUNG, *TRAVELS IN FRANCE DURING THE YEARS 1787, 1788, 1789* (1790)
Matilda Betham-Edwards, ed.
4th ed. corr. and rev. London: G. Bell, 1892

Take the road to Lourde, where is a castle on a rock, garrisoned for the mere purpose of keeping state prisoners, sent hither by *lettres de cachet*. Seven or eight are *known* to be here at present [August 11, 1787]; thirty have been here at a time; and many for life—torn by the relentless hand of jealous tyranny from the bosom of domestic comfort; from wives, children, friends, and hurried for crimes unknown to themselves—more probably for virtues—to languish in this detested abode of misery—and die of despair. Oh, liberty! liberty!—and yet this is the mildest government of any considerable country in Europe, our own excepted. The dispensations of providence seem to have permitted the human race to exist only as the prey of tyrants, as it has made pigeons for the prey of hawks (60).

An anecdote, which I have from an authority to be depended on, will explain the profligacy of government, in respect to these arbitrary imprisonments. Lord Albemarle, when ambassador in France, about the year 1753, negotiating the fixing of the limits of the American colonies . . . calling one day on the minister for foreign affairs, was introduced, for a few minutes, into his cabinet, while he finished a short conversation in the apartment in which he usually received those who conferred with him. As his lordship walked backwards and forwards, in a very small room . . . he could not help seeing a paper lying on the table, written in a large legible hand, and containing a list of the prisoners in the Bastile [*sic*], in which the first name was Gordon. When the minister entered, lord Albemarle apologized for his involuntarily remarking the paper; the other replied, that it was not of the least consequence, for they made no secret of the names. Lord A. then said, that he had seen the name of Gordon first in the list, and he begged to know, as in all probability the person of this name was a British subject, on what account he had been put into the Bastile. The minister told him, that he knew nothing of the matter, but would make the proper inquiries. The next time he saw lord Albemarle, he informed him, that, on inquiring into the case of Gordon, he could find no person who could give him the least information; on which he had Gordon himself interrogated, who solemnly affirmed, that he had not the smallest knowledge, or even suspicion, of the cause of his imprisonment, but that he had been confined 30 years; however, added the minister, I ordered him to be immediately released, and he is now at large. Such a case wants no comment (313–14n).

HUMAN RIGHTS ACROSS THE CHANNEL

The Habeas Corpus Act of 1679 in England aimed to end undue pretrial imprisonment, but it was often suspended in times of threat, as it was in 1794 by George III. When in force, it secured to each arrested person a speedy trial or speedy release; but when it was suspended political suspects could be held indefinitely without trial. There was widespread fear of revolution in England, newly deprived of its American colonies and in near panic after the execution of Louis XVI. A land of fifteen million with no standing army, it faced across the Channel a revolutionary France of about twenty-eight million people boasting at the moment a galvanized, successful army. No wonder the English were nervous.

Critics of the British Constitution (however defined) could be exiled for seven years to Australia. Meetings of more than fifty people required governmental license and oversight. A number of prominent radicals were tried for treason, but they were acquitted. But when war came, following Louis XVI's death, English patriotism overwhelmed issues of class and economics. "Revolution subsided into reform, and spread itself out through the nineteenth century" (DD/AN 374).

TOPICS FOR WRITTEN AND ORAL DISCUSSION

1. "Imprescriptible" is a curious word to use to describe rights. Its dictionary meaning suggests that the French thought (in Paine's translation) that the rights of liberty, property, security, and resistance of oppression *could* not be (or perhaps more logically did not *need* to be) ordained or specified: they existed as a matter of Natural Law. The American word "Unalienable" means incapable of being sold, transferred, given up or, perhaps, taken away. We are "endowed by our Creator" with rights we cannot surrender or lose (legally). Is there a difference in these approaches? Do all the rights specified under either approach seem entitled to equal standing?

2. Article III of *The Rights of Man* states that the Nation is the "source of all sovereignty." But Thomas Paine says, "the Authority of the People [is] the only authority on which Government has a right to exist in any country." Nation, Government, People. What are the differences among them? What is the American approach?

3. A Bill of Attainder under English common law was a statute which made certain crimes (treason and outlawry in particular) punishable by forfeiture of lands, inheritances, and civil rights generally. Why do you think the framers of the American Constitution thought it necessary specifically to forbid such laws? In France a declaration that someone was *hors de loi*—outside the law—was dreadful to that individual, because it meant identification was enough for execution: no need for any due process whatever. Discuss the contrast between these two approaches.

4. An ex post facto law made an action previously committed a crime, though it was legal at the time it was performed. What kinds of conditions would make it necessary to forbid such laws explicitly? When might we see such laws enforced?

5. Paine comments that, "in the particular situation in which France then was, having to undo what was wrong, as well as to set up what was right, it was proper to be more particular than what in another condition of things would be necessary." What provisions in the American Constitution seem to be there for a similar reason? Are they irrelevant today or having unintended consequences?

6. What are the elements you would want to feel are present in order to know that due process of law is being adhered to?

7. Considering the state of human rights through nearly all French history up to 1789, does it seem natural that the people overreacted? Did Rousseau and Sieyès themselves overreact?

8. Dickens probably read Helen Maria Williams's letters; they would have been available to him in the British Library. Might the story of the eldest Fossé son have been the source of any plot elements in *A Tale of Two Cities*? What parallels can you see? Could Charles Darnay's uncle have used a *lettre de cachet* against him? Would he have had any motivation to do so?

SUGGESTED READINGS AND WORKS CITED

DD/AN   Durant, Will and Ariel. *The Age of Napoleon*. New York: Simon and Schuster, 1975.

DD/RR   ———. *Rousseau and Revolution*. New York: Simon and Schuster, 1967.

Fast, Howard. *Citizen Tom Paine*. New York: Duell, Sloan and Pearce, 1943.

O'Brien, Conor Cruise. "The Decline and Fall of the French Revolution." *New York Review of Books* 37, no. 2 (February 15, 1990).

Paine, Thomas. *The Rights of Man*. Reprint. New York: Heritage Press, 1961.

HMW   Williams, Helen Maria. *An Eye-Witness Account of the French Revolution*. Ed. by Jack Fruchtman. New York: Peter Lang, 1996.

———. *Helen Williams and the French Revolution*. Edited by Jane Shuter. Austin, Tex.: Raintree Steck-Vaughn, 1996.

———. *Letters on the French Revolution, Written in France, in the Summer of 1790, to a Friend in England*. London: G. G. and J. Robinson, 1792.

Young, Arthur. *Travels in France during the Years 1787, 1788, 1789*. Ed. Matilda Betham-Edwards, 4th ed. corr. and rev. London: G. Bell, 1892.

10

Capital Punishment: Usually Cruel Before the Guillotine

INTRODUCTION

Throughout the generations and well into the time of Charles Dickens, capital punishment was not only frequently used, and for a great many offenses, but was often, if not always, barbaric and inhumane in the way it was imposed and accomplished. This was in part a consequence of the limitations of technology. We do not often stop to think of it today, but hanging a man (or woman) in a relatively quick, surefire way is not an easy business. It requires experience, skill, and close attention. In its glory days, great pride was taken by efficient executioners, who knew exactly where to place the noose's knot on the neck, how to locate and adjust the door of the "drop," and other secrets of the trade.

The breaking of the neck, not strangulation, was the goal: The former was quick and sure, the latter slow and sometimes a failure (and the victim's discomfort in the meanwhile was distressing to the tender-hearted). "Stringing up" a subject was far less likely to produce the wished-for result than "dropping" him through a trapdoor to a sudden, sharp jerking halt. The crowd's difficulty with Foulon (*TTC* ii 22) is a good example of the pitfalls inexperienced executioners could encounter. In Scotland in 1724, a murderess was hanged. In a fierce clash recounted by Hubert Cole, her friends and relations successfully fought off medical students who sought the body (see Chapter 12). This was fortunate, since the woman was found to be still alive when cut down. She "survived for many years in a state of sinful notoriety as 'half-hangit Maggie Dickson' " (HC 94).

In Dickens's *Barnaby Rudge*, Ned Dennis, a professional hangman, is a macabre comic figure. We laugh at his keen professional interest in the minutiae of his craft and his unconscious readiness to study the necks of those he encounters, to determine how readily and deftly he could "work them off" if called upon.

> "Did you ever . . ." whispered Dennis, with a horrible kind of admiration, such as that with which a cannibal might regard his intimate friend, when hungry—"did you ever"—and here he drew still closer to [Gashford's] ear, and fenced his mouth with both his open hands—"see such a throat as his? Do but cast your eye upon it. There's a neck for stretching!" (*BR* 37)

He is proud of his contribution to society:

> "I'm of as genteel a calling, brother, as any man in England—as light a business as any gentleman could desire."
>
> "Was you 'prenticed to it?" asked Mr Tappertit.
>
> "No. Natural genius," said Mr Dennis. "No 'prenticing. It comes by natur. . . . Look at that hand of mine—many and many a job that hand has done, with a neatness and dexterity never known afore. When I look at that hand," said Mr Dennis, shaking it in the air, "and remember the helegant bits of work it has turned off, I feel quite molloncholy to think it should ever grow old and feeble. But such is life."
>
> He heaved a deep sigh as he indulged in these reflections, and putting his fingers with an absent air on Hugh's throat, and particularly under his left ear, as if he were studying the anatomical development of that part of his frame, shook his head in a despondent manner and actually shed tears.
>
> "You're a kind of artist, I suppose—eh!" said Mr Tappertit.
>
> "Yes," rejoined Dennis; "yes—I may call myself a artist—a fancy workman—art improves natur'—that's my motto." (*BR* 39)

THE DICKENS VIEW

Dickens was greatly interested in capital punishment and wrote about it often. He campaigned all his life and with ultimate success to have it removed from public view and conducted behind prison walls. He thought it was dehumanizing in the extreme to the populace, which arrived hours early to take points of best vantage. Those who could afford it bought balcony and window viewing-points for exorbitant sums; entertained themselves with puppet shows, performing bears, tumblers, and jugglers while waiting; and in every possible way turned death in life into a spectacle for amusement and a week's income for pickpockets.

Dickens depicts the English fascination with capital punishment early on in *A Tale of Two Cities*. At Darnay's trial for treason in 1780, his punishment (if found guilty, as all assume he will be) is described "with relish" by an onlooker:

> "[H]e'll be drawn on a hurdle to be half hanged, and then he'll be taken down and sliced before his own face, and then his inside will be taken out and burnt while he looks on, and then his head will be chopped off, and he'll be cut into quarters. That's the sentence."
>
> Everybody present, except the one wigged gentleman who looked at the ceiling, stared at [Darnay]. All the human breath in the place, rolled at him, like a sea, or a wind, or a fire. Eager faces strained round pillars and corners, to get a sight of him; spectators in back rows stood up, not to miss a hair of him; people on the floor of the court, laid their hands on the shoulders of the people before them, to help themselves, at anybody's cost, to a view of him— stood a-tiptoe, got upon ledges, stood upon next to nothing, to see every inch of him.
>
> The sort of interest with which this man was stared and breathed at, was not a sort that elevated humanity. Had he stood in peril of a less horrible sentence—had there been a chance of any one of its savage details being spared—by just so much would he have lost in his fascination. The form that was to be doomed to be so shamefully mangled, was the sight; the immortal creature that was to be so butchered and torn asunder, yielded the sensation. Whatever gloss the various spectators put upon the interest, according to their several arts and powers of self-deceit, the interest was, at the root of it, Ogreish. (*TTC* ii 2)

This extreme form of capital punishment had been mandated by English law for hundreds of years. In *A Child's History of England* (1851–53), Dickens reports that one David of Wales was sentenced to be hanged, drawn, and quartered, and that from that time

(about 1300) this became the established mode of punishing traitors: "a punishment wholly without excuse, as being revolting,
vile, and cruel, after its object is dead; and which has no sense in
it, as its only real degradation (and that nothing can blot out) is
to the country that permits on any consideration such abominable
barbarity" (*CHE* 16).

It had its counterparts when other crimes, considered particularly offensive to the state, were at issue. Here is the appalling
description of a regicide's punishment in France:

> [H]is right hand, armed with the knife, will be burnt off before his
> face . . . into wounds which will be made in his arms, his breast,
> and his legs, there will be poured boiling oil, melted lead, hot resin,
> wax, and sulphur; finally . . . he will be torn limb from limb by four
> strong horses. (*TTC* ii 15)

National methodologies fascinated Dickens. In *American Notes*
(1842), he wrote that in America the technique differed from that
used in England or on the continent:

> The prison-yard in which [the guard] pauses now, has been the
> scene of terrible performances. Into this narrow, grave-like place,
> men are brought out to die. The wretched creature stands beneath
> the gibbet on the ground; the rope about his neck, and when the
> sign is given, a weight at its other end comes running down, and
> swings him up into the air—a corpse. (*AN* 6)

Here the unfortunate does not fall: he flies, one hopes with the
same instant, deathly jerk that resulted from the "drop."

But what about the axe? the sword? the knife? England's early,
great tradition was the headsman: the executioner of Mary, Queen
of Scots; the Earl of Essex; Sir Walter Raleigh. But these were all
aristocrats. Beheading was considered too good for plebeian victims.

A practical consideration when it came to executions was that
there had to be so many of them. There was good reason for Ned
Dennis's pride in his work: it required skill and much experience
to do it well, and he was greatly needed, for capital punishment
was society's knee-jerk response to almost everything.

[T]he forger was put to death; the utterer of a bad note was put to Death; the unlawful opener of a letter was put to Death; the purloiner of forty shillings and sixpence was put to Death; the holder of a horse . . . who made off with it, was put to Death; the coiner of a bad shilling was put to Death; the sounders of three-fourths of the notes in the whole gamut of Crime, were put to Death. (*TTC* ii 1)

England's *Annual Register* for 1781 records executions for stealing 2½ crowns, breaking and entering with intent to steal, robbing a pedlar of some stockings, stealing shoe-buckles, and stealing a tablecloth. In 1800 in England, about two hundred crimes were still punished by death.

DR. GUILLOTIN AND "SAMSON"

As we read of the blood and butchery of September 1792 and the Terror that came later, it is hard to recall that the goals of many revolutionaries in France were idealistic, even altruistic, and usually quite scientific and rationalistic. The French Revolution resulted in many improvements, some of which it is hard to believe Europe could ever have done without. Reform was everywhere, and it came even (and perhaps especially) to executions.

Dr. Joseph Ignace Guillotin (1738–1814), a deputy to the National Assembly, was keenly interested in improving society's habits and attitudes regarding capital punishment. He sponsored several changes in the laws that today seem self-evidently reasonable and just. At his urging, capital crimes were declared to be wholly personal: the families of perpetrators were not to be subject to sanction as such, and wholesale confiscation of their and even the criminal's property was abolished. He persuaded the Assembly to decree that the bodies of the executed were to be delivered to their families upon their request, and if there was none, they were to be buried with no mention of cause of death placed on the burial register.

But Guillotin's major preoccupation was to achieve another innovation. In the words of Henri Sanson, Dr. Guillotin was

disgusted . . . at the sight of the gibbet, which exhibited a corpse for hours before the mob, [and] he determined to substitute for all former modes a punishment by which suffering would be mitigated. He saw no better means for the furtherance of his object than decapitation. It had hitherto been reserved for a privileged class, and, in all respects, it was a more manly and natural way of inflicting death. But then the executioner's sword had often failed to accomplish its work: the hand was apt to tremble, and machinery only could give a guarantee of unswerving precision. (HS 255–56)

The expert was Henri Sanson, the lineal descendant of headsmen who executed every state victim and common criminal in France for nearly two hundred years. For seven generations, from father to son, they hung, beheaded, quartered, and tortured. Henri was dismissed (to his professed relief and gratitude) in 1847. He had only daughters, and so his line came to an end.

In his Memoir he reports three encounters of his grandfather, Charles-Henri Sanson, with Louis XVI. The story seems almost too pat to be credible, but it warrants retelling here, if only for the sartorial details.

On the first occasion, Charles obtained an audience with the king because his creditors were hounding him and he feared prison. The state owed him a great deal of money which, the king said, it could not afford to pay. Sanson records, "Louis wore a lilac coat embroidered with gold, short breeches [*culottes*] and pumps; the blue and red ribbons of the order of Saint-Louis hung across his satin waistcoat. A lace collar and frill was partly covered by a loose cravat, which showed the prominent muscles of his neck. The King was of strong but common build. His hair was powdered and curled, and was tied with a ribbon at the back of his neck." Charles stood in the doorway, transfixed in awe. The king heard him out and gave him a safe-conduct for three months (dated April 19, 1789), ordering that he not be constrained or molested by his creditors or anyone else. The safe-conduct expired five days after the fall of the Bastille, but Henri Sanson tells us no more about it.

The best mode of capital punishment was an issue at that time, and Henri reports that his grandfather sent a memo to the minister of justice detailing some of the problems. It was difficult to decapitate with a sword: the culprit had to be courageous enough to remain without moving, and swords got blunt very quickly. "There can be no doubt," he said, "that when I shall have to deal consecutively with several criminals, the terror excited by the sight of blood must lead to deplorable consequences. The other culprits must lose the firmness which is absolutely needed in such executions" (HS 258). He ended by insisting that a machine was called for: one which would keep the subject's body immovable in a horizontal position. He was the great authority of course, and Dr. Guillotin sought and received his advice.

Sanson studied engravings (one was by Cranach) of machines used in other countries, and he noted in particular the *Mannaïa*, a knife delivery system in use in Genoa. There was a record, too, of a sliding axe used at Toulouse in 1631 to finish the Marshal de Montmorency.

One day, while playing chamber music (Sanson on the violin) with his friend Schmidt, a German engineer and pianist, Sanson confided his problem. "Schmidt hesitated for a moment, and then traced a few rapid lines on a piece of paper, which he handed to my grandfather. *It was the guillotine*" (HS 258).

Dr. Guillotin, when he saw the sketch, rushed to the Assembly. He managed to tickle its funnybone. "He said that the culprit would only feel *a slight freshness on the neck*. The phrase was sufficiently ingenious, but when he added, '*With this machine I chop your head off in a twinkling, and you do not suffer!*' the Assembly gave way to irrepressible laughter" (HS 259–60).

Then came Sanson's second sighting of Louis XVI. Dr. Antoine Louis, the king's physician, was appointed to study the device. Louis, Sanson, and Guillotin were conferring when the king, incognito, looked in. He studied the drawing and said that the knife-blade shown, which was crescent-shaped, would not do for all necks. Charles Sanson *looked at the king and saw that he was right* [emphasis added]. The king, gratified at his agreement, sketched another version with an "oblique line" and recommended experimenting with both. The final recommendation to the Assembly covered both blades, and it was adopted in 1791. The oblique version won out in the last tests.

"Such was the King's second interview with my grandfather," writes Henri Sanson. "Their next official meeting was to take place on January 21 of the following year." We know what happened then: if Henri is to believed, the king went to his reward under the knife he had designed. Let us hope he felt only a freshness on the neck.

Now it is August 1792:

> The hour is now at hand when the history of the scaffold and the history of France are to be blended into one. In a few days the despised headsman shall become the key of the vault of the social edifice which is being constructed. Until then he could answer to those who saluted him with the insulting epithet of *bourreau* [horrid wretch], "Why do you despise me if you do not despise your laws?" The excitement of a nation now gives him the right to exclaim: "It seems as if you had made a revolution only to give me work!" (HS 264)

For nine months after official adoption of the guillotine as the State's instrument of capital vengeance, things were pretty quiet. A few forgers were worked off. But August 10, 1792, when nine hundred Swiss were slaughtered and the King deposed, changed everything. On August 19, Sanson tells that a mob, seeing the machine being convoyed to its usual spot for duty, intervened and forced its diversion to the more public and accessible Place du Carrousel. It was set up, and a young citizen in a red cap demanded that it be used and offered to help. When he picked up a severed head to display it, he had a fit and died of "violent emotion." But the Place du Carrousel was always used thereafter.

At first, the guillotine was not popular:

> For crowds accustomed to the prolonged and emotionally rich ritual of penitential processions, loud public confessions, the climactic jump of the body on the gibbet, the exposure of the hanging remains, even in some rare cases the prolonged ordeal of breaking on the wheel, the *machine* was a distinct disappointment. It was too expeditious. A swish, a thud; sometimes not even a display of the head; the executioner reduced to a low-grade mechanic like some flunkey pulling a bell rope. . . . [Guillotin] had proposed a reform of capital punishment in keeping with the equal status accorded to all citizens. Instead of barbaric practices which degraded the spectators as much as the criminal, a method of surgical instaneity was to be adopted. Not only would decapitation spare the prisoner gratuitous pain, it would offer to common criminals the dignified execution hitherto reserved for the privileged orders. (SS 198)

Both Dickens and Carlyle, probably misled by popular report, seem to have exaggerated the number of people who died under the new machine. Schama gives the results in the last, bloodiest months of the Terror:

Month	Executions	Acquittals
Germinal	155	59
Floréal	354	159
Prairial	509	164
Messidor	796	208
Thermidor 1–9	342	84

The daily averages were Germinal, 5; Prairial, 17; Messidor, 26; Thermidor, 38.

The tragedy for Joseph Ignace Guillotin was that a technological advance conceived for sincerely humanitarian purposes enabled butchers to butcher efficiently without prior training and experience. They did not have to be Ned Dennises when they had the guillotine. The good doctor died knowing that his name was welded forever to the blood and terror of the French Revolution's worst excesses.

The guillotine, like the Xerox 914, had by coming into existence created the demand for it, and just as plain paper copying (which had never seemed needed before) became an instant necessity once it was possible, so the wholesale slaughter of aristocrats and others, innocent and helpless though they were, once it was practicable, became inevitable in the insane, fanatic time of the Terror.

TOPICS FOR WRITTEN AND ORAL DISCUSSION

1. The French Revolution had many consequences, not all of them benign. But a case might be made that one positive result was a more humane form of human execution. The guillotine technology was exported to other countries by Napoléon, and Dickens observed it in use in Italy. Please comment.

2. What do you imagine Louis XVI was thinking as he stepped onto the platform where the invention to which he had contributed awaited him? Given his personality, would he have felt bitterness at the irony which was part of the moment? Or might he have congratulated himself on having contributed to the quickness of his end?

3. With the materials in this chapter, develop an essay on Dickens's general attitude toward capital punishment.

4. Look back at Chapter 1. As a literary device, how would you classify the juxtaposition of a Xerox copier and the guillotine? What reaction do you have?

SUGGESTED READINGS AND WORKS CITED

HC   Cole, Hubert. *Things for the Surgeons: A History of the Resurrection Men*. London: Heinemann, 1964.

AN   Dickens, Charles. *American Notes for General Circulation*. London: Chapman and Hall, 1842.

BR   ———. *Barnaby Rudge: A Tale of the Riots of 'Eighty*. London: Chapman and Hall, 1841.

CHE ———. *A Child's History of England*. London: Chapman and Hall, serial published in *Household Words*, January 1851–December 1853.

HS   Sanson, Henri. *Sept Générations d'Exécuteurs* [Seven Generations of Executioners] (English transl.; selections). 2 vols. in 1. London: Chatto and Windus, 1876.

SS   Schama, Simon. *Citizens: A Chronicle of the French Revolution*. New York: Vintage Books, 1990.

11

Prison Isolation and Its Consequences

INTRODUCTION

Dickens was fascinated by prisons and prisoners. His works are full of specific references and descriptions and of metaphorical treatments of the human condition in terms of constraint and confinement. He became over his lifetime an authority on penology and the effects of different methods of punishment. His powers of observation made him much respected in this field (as in medicine), and his own work provides probably the best obtainable insight into Doctor Manette's condition as it would have been understood in his day.

He was impatient with some prison reform, which he thought softheaded rather than kindhearted, and toward the end of his life he became increasingly conservative in his views. In 1853 he helped write and publish an article, "In and Out of Jail," which said:

> I think it right and necessary that there should be in jails some degraded kind of hard and irksome work, belonging only to jails. What kind of work does the determined thief, or the determined swindler, or the determined vagrant, most abhor? Find me that work; and to it, in preference to any other, I set that man relent-

lessly. Now, I make bold to whisper the inquiry whether the work best answering to this description is not almost invariably found to be useless work? And to such useless work, I plainly say, I desire to set that determined thief, swindler, or vagrant, *for his punishment*. I have not the least hesitation in avowing that it is a satisfaction to me to see that determined thief sweating profusely at the treadmill or the crank, and extremely galled to know that he is doing nothing all the time but undergoing *punishment*. I have a very strong idea that he is sent to prison, rightfully, for that purpose; and I have no idea whatever that he is yet entitled to the privilege of being taught a trade, or that his life out of that place has established his claim within that place to work as men work who are not despoilers of their kind.

This firm, perhaps harsh, view may seem surprising to the many who think of Dickens as a softhearted, even sentimental sort. But a key to understanding the foregoing is to note that, in contrast with the imprisonment inflicted on Doctor Manette (mitigated after years by his obtaining a cobbler's bench), the prison treatment of which Dickens heartily approved involved enforced, repetitive activity as well as human contact.

Miss Pross, unexpectedly insightful, gives Jarvis Lorry her theory as to why Doctor Manette avoids discussing or thinking about his imprisonment and his twilight life as a shoemaker:

> He is afraid of the whole subject. It's plain enough, I should think, why he may be. It's a dreadful remembrance. Besides that, his loss of himself grew out of it. Not knowing how he lost himself, or how he recovered himself, he may never feel certain of not losing himself again. That alone wouldn't make the subject pleasant, I should think. . . . Sometimes, he gets up in the dead of the night, and will be heard, by us overhead there, walking up and down, walking up and down, in his room. Ladybird has learnt to know then that his mind is walking up and down, walking up and down, in his old prison. She hurries to him, and they go on together, walking up and down, walking up and down, until he is composed. But he never says a word of the true reason of his restlessness, to her, and she finds it best not to hint at it to him. In silence they go walking up and down together, walking up and down together, till her love and company have brought him to himself. (*TTC* ii 6)

Dickens's psychological insight is manifest as he writes in "Nine Days" (*TTC* ii 18) of the relapse Doctor Manette experiences when

Charles Darnay tells him his real name, Evrémonde. The insights and the sympathy Dickens brought to bear were rooted in long experience. Indeed, it is not too much to say that, in his time and even now, no greater authority on the psychological effects of prison isolation can be found than Dickens himself.

SOLITARY CONFINEMENT

Nowhere is Dickens's depiction of the inhumane consequences of imprisonment "in solitary" any more graphic than in his *American Notes*, written and published immediately following his visit to the United States in 1842. He visited a great prison outside Philadelphia, "conducted on a plan peculiar to the state of Pennsylvania. The system here, is rigid, strict, and hopeless solitary confinement. I believe it, in its effects, to be cruel and wrong." Here are extracts from the work. (Some passages are italicized, having particular resonance for students of *A Tale of Two Cities*.)

FROM CHARLES DICKENS, *AMERICAN NOTES*
London: Chapman and Hall, 1842

In its intention, I am well convinced that it is kind, humane, and meant for reformation; but I am persuaded that those who devised this system of Prison Discipline, and those benevolent gentlemen who carry it into execution, do not know what it is that they are doing. I believe that very few men are capable of estimating the immense amount of torture and agony which this dreadful punishment, prolonged for years, inflicts upon the sufferers; and in guessing at it myself, and in reasoning from what I have seen written upon their faces, and what to my certain knowledge they feel within, I am only the more convinced that there is a depth of terrible endurance in it which none but the sufferers themselves can fathom, and which no man has a right to inflict upon his fellow-creature.

I hold this slow and daily tampering with the mysteries of the brain, to be immeasurably worse than any torture of the body: and because its ghastly signs and tokens are not so palpable to the eye and sense of touch as scars upon the flesh; because its wounds are not upon the surface, and it extorts few cries that human ears can hear; therefore I the more denounce it, as a secret punishment which slumbering humanity is not roused up to stay.

I was accompanied to this prison by two gentlemen officially connected with its management, and passed the day in going from cell to cell, and talking with the inmates.

Between the body of the prison and the outer wall, there is a spacious garden. Entering it, by a wicket in the massive gate, we pursued the path before us to its other termination, and passed into a large chamber, from which seven long passages radiate.

Standing at the central point, and looking down these dreary passages, the dull repose and quiet that prevails, is awful. Occasionally, there is a drowsy sound from some lone weaver's shuttle, *or shoemaker's last*, but it is stifled by the thick walls and heavy dungeon-door, and only serves to make the general stillness more profound. Over the head and face of every prisoner who comes into this melancholy house, a black hood is drawn; and in this dark shroud, an emblem of the curtain dropped between him and the living world, he is led to the cell from which he never again comes forth, until his whole term of imprisonment has expired. He never hears of wife and children; home or friends; the life or death of any single creature. He sees the prison-officers, but with that exception he never looks upon a human countenance, or hears a human voice. *He is a man buried alive*; to be dug out in the slow round of years; and in the meantime dead to everything but torturing anxieties and horrible despair.

His name and crime, and term of suffering, are unknown, even to the officer who delivers him his daily food. There is a number over his cell-door, and in a book of which the governor of the prison has one copy, and the moral instructor another: this is the index of his history. *Beyond these pages the prison has no record of his existence*: and though he live to be in the same cell ten weary years, he has no means of knowing, down to the very last hour, in what part of the building it is situated; what kind of men there are about him; whether in the long winter nights there are living people near, or he is in some lonely corner of the great jail, with walls, and passages, and iron doors between him and the nearest sharer in its solitary horrors.

Every cell has double doors: the outer one of sturdy oak, the other of grated iron, wherein there is a trap through which his food is handed. He has a Bible, and a slate and pencil, and, under certain restrictions, has sometimes other books, provided for the purpose, and pen and ink and paper. His razor, plate, and can, and basin, hang upon the wall, or shine upon the little shelf. Fresh water is laid on in every cell, and he can draw it at his pleasure. During the day, his bedstead turns up against the wall, and leaves more space for him to work in. *His loom, or bench, or wheel, is there; and there he labours, sleeps and wakes, and counts the seasons as they change, and grows old.*

The first man I saw, was seated at his loom, at work. He had been there six years, and was to remain, I think, three more. He had been convicted as a receiver of stolen goods, but even after his long imprisonment, denied his guilt, and said he had been hardly dealt by. It was his second offence.

He stopped his work when we went in, took off his spectacles, and answered freely to everything that was said to him, but always with a strange kind of pause first, and in a low, thoughtful voice. He wore a paper hat of his own making, and was pleased to have it noticed and commended. He had very ingeniously manufactured a sort of Dutch clock from some disregarded odds and ends; and his vinegar-bottle served for the pendulum. Seeing my interest in this contrivance, he looked up at it with a great deal of pride, and said that he had been thinking of improving it, and that he hoped the hammer and a little piece of broken glass beside it "would play music before long." He had extracted some colours from the yarn with which he worked, and painted a few poor figures on the wall. One, of a female, over the door, he called "The Lady of the Lake."

He smiled as I looked at these contrivances to while away the time; but when I looked from them to him, I saw that his lip trembled, and could have counted the beating of his heart. I forget how it came about, but some allusion was made to his having a wife. He shook his head at the word, turned aside, and covered his face with his hands.

"But you are resigned now!" said one of the gentlemen after a short pause, during which he had resumed his former manner. He answered with a sigh that seemed quite reckless in its hopelessness, "Oh yes, oh yes! I am resigned to it." "And are a better man, you think?" "Well, I hope so: I'm sure I hope I may be." "And time goes pretty quickly?" "Time is very long, gentlemen, within these four walls!"

He gazed about him—Heaven knows how wearily!—as he said these words; and in the act of doing so, fell into a strange stare as if he had forgotten something. A moment afterwards he sighed heavily, put on his spectacles, and went about his work again.

In another cell, there was a German, sentenced to five years' imprisonment for larceny, two of which had just expired. With colours procured in the same manner, he had painted every inch of the walls and ceiling quite beautifully. He had laid out the few feet of ground, behind, with exquisite neatness, and had made a little bed in the centre, that looked by-the-bye like a grave. The taste and ingenuity he had displayed in everything were most extraordinary; and yet a more dejected, heart-broken, wretched creature, it would be difficult to imagine. I never saw such a picture of forlorn affliction and distress of mind. My heart bled for him; and when the tears ran down his cheeks, and he took one of the visitors aside, to ask, with his trembling hands nervously clutching at his coat to detain him, whether there was no hope of his dismal sentence being commuted, the spectacle was really too painful to witness. I never saw or heard of any kind of misery that impressed me more than the wretchedness of this man.

In a third cell, was a tall strong black, a burglar, working at his proper trade of making screws and the like. His time was nearly out. He was not only a very dexterous thief, but was notorious for his boldness and hardihood, and for the number of his previous convictions. He entertained us with a long account of his achievements, which he narrated with such infinite relish, that he actually seemed to lick his lips as he told us racy anecdotes of stolen plate, and of old ladies whom he had watched as they sat at windows in silver spectacles (he had plainly had an eye to their metal even from the other side of the street) and had afterwards robbed. This fellow, upon the slightest encouragement, would have mingled with his professional recollections the most detestable cant; but I am very much mistaken if he could have surpassed the unmitigated hypocrasy [*sic*] with which he declared that he blessed the day on which he came into that prison, and that he never would commit another robbery as long as he lived.

There was one man who was allowed, as an indulgence, to keep rabbits. His room having rather a close smell in consequence, they called to him at the door to come out into the passage. He complied of course, and stood shading his haggard face in the unwonted sunlight of the great window, looking as wan and unearthly as if he had been summoned from the grave. He had a white rabbit in his breast; and when the little creature, getting down upon the ground, stole back into the cell, and he, being dismissed, crept timidly after it, I thought it would have been very hard to say in what respect the man was the nobler animal of the two.

There was an English thief, who had been there but a few days out of seven years: a villainous, low-browed, thin-lipped fellow, with a white face; who had as yet no relish for visitors, and who, but for the additional penalty, would have gladly stabbed me with his shoemaker's knife. There was another German who had entered the jail but yesterday, and who started from his bed when we looked in, and pleaded, in his broken English, very hard for work. There was a poet, who after doing two days' work in every four-and-twenty hours, one for himself and one for the prison, wrote verses about ships (he was by trade a mariner), and "the maddening wine-cup," and his friends at home. There were very many of them. Some reddened at the sight of visitors, and some turned very pale. Some two or three had prisoner nurses with them, for they were very sick; and one, a fat old negro whose leg had been taken off within the jail, had for his attendant a classical scholar and an accomplished surgeon, himself a prisoner likewise. Sitting upon the stairs, engaged in some slight work, was a pretty coloured boy. "Is there no refuge for young criminals in Philadelphia, then?" said I. "Yes, but only for white children." Noble aristocracy of crime!

There was a sailor who had been there upwards of eleven years, and who in a few months' time would be free. Eleven years of solitary confinement!

"I am very glad to hear your time is nearly out." What does he say? Nothing. Why does he stare at his hands, and pick the flesh upon his fingers, and raise his eyes for an instant, every now and then, to those bare walls which have seen his head turn grey? It is a way he has sometimes.

Does he never look men in the face, and *does he always pluck at those hands of his, as though he were bent on parting skin and bone?* It is his humour: nothing more.

It is his humour too, to say that he does not look forward to going out; that he is not glad the time is drawing near; that he did look forward to it once, but that was very long ago; that he has lost all care for everything. It is his humour to be a helpless, crushed, and broken man. And, Heaven be his witness that he has his humour thoroughly gratified!

I asked the governor if he had any person in his charge who was shortly going out. He had one, he said, whose time was up next day; but he had only been a prisoner two years.

Two years! I looked back through two years of my own life—out of jail, prosperous, happy, surrounded by blessings, comforts, good fortune—and thought how wide a gap it was, and *how long those two years passed in solitary captivity would have been.* I have the face of this man, who was going to be released next day, before me now. It is almost more memorable in its happiness than the other faces in their misery. How easy and how natural it was for him to say that the system was a good one; and that the time went "pretty quick—considering;" and that when a man once felt that he had offended the law, and must satisfy it, "he got along, somehow:" and so forth!

"What did he call you back to say to you, in that strange flutter?" I asked of my conductor, when he had locked the door and joined me in the passage.

"Oh! That he was afraid the soles of his boots were not fit for walking, as they were a good deal worn when he came in; and that he would thank me very much to have them mended, ready."

Those boots had been taken off his feet, and put away with the rest of his clothes, two years before!

I took that opportunity of inquiring how they conducted themselves immediately before going out; adding that I presumed they trembled very much.

"Well, it's not so much a trembling," was the answer—"though they do quiver—as *a complete derangement of the nervous system*. They can't sign their names to the book; sometimes can't even hold the pen; look about 'em without appearing to know why, or where they are; and sometimes get up and sit down again, twenty times in a minute. This is when they're in the office, where they are taken with the hood on, as they were brought in. When they get outside the gate, they stop, and look first one way and then the other; not knowing which to take. Sometimes they stagger as if they were drunk, and sometimes are forced to lean against the fence, they're so bad:—but they clear off in course of time."

As I walked among these solitary cells, and looked at the faces of the men within them, I tried to picture to myself the thoughts and feelings natural to their condition. I imagined the hood just taken off, and the scene of their captivity disclosed to them in all its dismal monotony.

At first, the man is stunned. His confinement is a hideous vision; and his old life a reality. He throws himself upon his bed, and lies there abandoned to despair. By degrees the insupportable solitude and barrenness of the place rouses him from this stupor, and when the trap in his grated door is opened, he humble begs and prays for work. *"Give me some work to do, or I shall go raving mad!"*

He has it; and by fits and starts applies himself to labour; but every now and then there comes upon him a burning sense of the years that must be wasted in that stone coffin, and an agony so piercing in the recollection of those who are hidden from his view and knowledge, that he starts from his seat, and striding up and down the narrow room with both hands clasped on his uplifted head, hears spirits tempting him to beat his brains out on the wall.

Again he falls upon his bed, and lies there, moaning. Suddenly he starts up, wondering whether any other man is near; whether there is another cell like that on either side of him: and listens keenly.

There is no sound, but other prisoners may be near for all that. He remembers to have heard once, when he little thought of coming here himself, that the cells were so constructed that the prisoners could not hear each other, though the officers could hear them. Where is the nearest man—upon the right, or on the left? or is there one in both directions? Where is he sitting now—with his face to the light? or is he walking to and fro? How is he dressed? Has he been here long? Is he much worn away? Is he very white and spectre-like? Does *he* think of his neighbour too?

Scarcely venturing to breathe, and listening while he thinks, he conjures up a figure with his back towards him, and imagines it moving about in this next cell. He has no idea of the face, but he is certain of the dark form of a stooping man. In the cell upon the other side, he puts another figure, whose face is hidden from him also. Day after day, and often when he wakes up in the middle of the night, he thinks of these two men until he is almost distracted. He never changes them. There they are always as he first imagined them—an old man on the right; a younger man upon the left—whose hidden features torture him to death, and have a mystery that makes him tremble.

The weary days pass on with solemn pace, like mourners at a funeral; and slowly he begins to feel that the white walls of the cell have something dreadful in them: that their colour is horrible: that their smooth surface chills his blood: that there is one hateful corner which torments him. Every morning when he wakes, he hides his head beneath the coverlet, and shudders to see the ghastly ceiling looking down upon him. The blessed light of day itself peeps in, an ugly phantom face, through the unchangeable crevice which is his prison window.

By slow but sure degrees, the terrors of that hateful corner swell until they beset him at all times; invade his rest, make his dreams hideous, and his nights dreadful. At first, he took a strange dislike to it; feeling as though it gave birth in his brain to something of corresponding shape, which ought not to be there, and racked his head with pains. Then he began to fear it, then to dream of it, and of men whispering its name and pointing to it. Then he could not bear to look at it, nor yet to turn his back upon it. Now, it is every night the lurking-place of a ghost: a shadow:—a silent something, horrible to see, but whether bird, or beast, or muffled human shape, he cannot tell.

When he is in his cell by day, he fears the little yard without. When he is in the yard, he dreads to re-enter the cell. When night comes, there stands the phantom in the corner. If he had the courage to stand in its place, and drive it out (he had once: being desperate), it broods upon his bed. In the twilight, and always at the same hour, a voice calls to him by name; as the darkness thickens his Loom begins to live; and even that, his comfort, is a hideous figure, watching him till daybreak.

Again, by slow degrees, these horrible fancies depart from him one by one: returning sometimes, unexpectedly, but at longer intervals, and in less alarming shapes. He has talked upon religious matter with the gentleman who visits him, and has read his Bible, and has written a prayer upon his slates, and hung it up as a kind of protection, and an assurance of Heavenly companionship. He dreams now, sometimes, of his children or his wife, but is sure that they are dead, or have deserted him. He is easily moved to tears; is gentle, submissive, and broken-spirited. Occasionally, the old agony comes back: a very little thing will revive it; even a familiar sound, or the scent of summer flowers in the air; but it does not last long, now: for the world without has come to be the vision, and this solitary life, the sad reality.

If his term of imprisonment be short—I mean comparatively, for short it cannot be—the last half year is almost worse than all; for then he thinks the prison will take fire and he be burnt in the ruins, or that he is doomed to die within the walls, or that he will be detained on some false charge and sentenced for another term: or that something, no matter what, must happen to prevent his going at large. And this is natural, and impossible to be reasoned against, because after his long separation from human life, and his great suffering, any event will appear to him more probable in the contemplation, than the being restored to liberty and his fellow-creatures.

If his period of confinement has been very long, the prospect of release bewilders and confuses him. His broken heart may flutter for a moment, when he thinks of the world outside, and what it might have been to him in all those lonely years, but that is all. The cell-door has been closed too long on all its hopes and cares. Better to have hanged him in the beginning than bring him to this pass, and send him forth to mingle with his kind, who are his kind no more.

On the haggard face of every man among these prisoners, the same expression sat. I know not what to liken it to. *It had something of that strained attention which we see upon the faces of the blind and deaf, mingled with a kind of horror, as though they had all been secretly terrified.* In every little chamber that I entered, and at every grate through which I looked, I seemed to see the same appalling countenance. It lives in my memory, with the fascination of a remarkable picture. Parade before my eyes, a hundred men, with one among them newly released from this solitary suffering, and I would point him out.

My firm conviction is that, independent of the mental anguish it occasions—an anguish so acute and so tremendous, that all imagination of it must fall far short of the reality—it wears the mind into a morbid state, which renders it unfit for the rough contact and busy action of the world. It is my fixed opinion that those who have undergone this punishment, MUST pass into society again morally unhealthy and diseased. There are many instances on record, of men who have chosen, or have been condemned, to lives of perfect solitude, but I scarcely remember one, even among sages of strong and vigorous intellect, where its effect has not become apparent, in some disordered train of thought, or some gloomy hallucination. What monstrous phantoms, bred of despondency and doubt, and born and reared in solitude, have stalked upon the earth, making creation ugly, and darkening the face of Heaven!

Suicides are rare among these prisoners: are almost, indeed, unknown. But no argument in favour of the system, can reasonably be deduced from this circumstance, although it is very often urged. All men who have made diseases of the mind their study, know perfectly well that such extreme depression and despair as will change the whole character, and beat down all its powers of elasticity and self-resistance, may be at work within a man, and yet stop short of self-destruction. This is a common case.

That it makes the senses dull, and by degrees impairs the bodily faculties, I am quite sure. I remarked to those who were with me in this very establishment at Philadelphia, that the criminals who had been there long, were deaf. They, who were in the habit of seeing these men constantly, were perfectly amazed at the idea, which they regarded as groundless and fanciful. And yet the very first prisoner to whom they appealed—one of their own selection—confirmed my impression (which was unknown to him) instantly, and said, with a genuine air it was impossible to doubt, that he couldn't think how it happened, but he *was* growing very dull of hearing.

That it is a singularly unequal punishment, and affects the worst man least, there is no doubt. In its superior efficiency as a means of reformation, compared with that other code of regulations which allows the prisoners to work in company without communicating together, I have not the smallest faith. All the instances of reformation that were mentioned to me, were of a kind that might have been—and I have no doubt whatever, in my own mind, would have been—equally well brought about by the Silent System. With regard to such men as the negro burglar and the English thief, even the most enthusiastic have scarcely any hope of their conversion.

It seems to me that the objection that nothing wholesome or good has ever had its growth in such unnatural solitude, and that even a dog or any of the more intelligent among beasts, would pine, and mope, and rust away, beneath its influence, would be in itself a sufficient argument against this system. But when we recollect, in addition, how very cruel and severe it is, and that a solitary life is always liable to peculiar and distinct objections of a most deplorable nature, which have arisen here, and call to mind, moreover, that the choice is not between this system, and a bad or ill-considered one, but between it and another which has worked well, and is, in its whole design and practice, excellent; there is surely more than sufficient reason for abandoning a mode of punishment attended by so little hope or promise, and fraught, beyond dispute, with such a host of evils.

Dickens's ideas about solitary confinement and its effects on the mind had a gestation period (seventeen years) almost exactly as long as the incarceration of Doctor Manette.

TOPICS FOR WRITTEN AND ORAL DISCUSSION

1. Go through the long extract from *American Notes* and pick out the italicized phrases. What connections can you make between these various selections and the events of *A Tale of Two Cities?*

2. Once out of prison, Doctor Manette's shoemaking seems depressing and pathetic. Why was it so important to him?

3. The treadmill was what it sounds like: a device on which a prisoner walked. His weight pressed down each stair as he reached it, and the whole revolved around in a vertical plane. Such devices are no longer used in prisons. What do you think about that?

4. Given your choice if you were imprisoned (of course, unjustly, but these things happen), would you prefer isolation or useless work?

SUGGESTED READINGS AND WORKS CITED

Burney, Christopher. *Solitary Confinement*. London: Clarke and Cock-eran, 1952.

AN Dickens, Charles. *American Notes for General Circulation*. London: Chapman and Hall, 1842.

HWC/IJ ———. "In and Out of Jail." *Household Words*. London: Chapman and Hall, 1838.

Jackson, Michael. *Prisoners of Isolation: Solitary Confinement in Canada*. Toronto: University of Toronto Press, 1983.

12

Human Dissection and the "Resurrection Man"

Anatomy: the science of bodily structure, as discovered by dissection; the body of facts and deductions as to the structure of organized beings, animal or vegetable, ascertained by dissection; the doctrine or science of the structure of organized bodies

Autopsy, also called Necropsy, Postmortem, or Postmortem examination: the dissection and examination of a dead body and its organs and structures to determine the cause of death, to observe the effects of disease, and to establish the sequence of changes and thus the evolution and mechanisms of disease processes

Dissection: the methodical cutting-up of an animal or plant for the purpose of displaying the position, structure, and relation of the various internal parts; anatomization

BODY PARTS IN HUMAN HISTORY

The editor's New York State driver's license has the following printed material on the back:

—————— ORGAN DONOR INFORMATION ——————
I HEREBY MAKE AN ANATOMICAL GIFT, TO BE EFFECTIVE UPON MY DEATH,

OF: □ ANY NEEDED ORGAN PARTS □ THE FOLLOWING BODY
PARTS: ————————————————————————————————
————————————————————— □ LIMITATIONS: ——————————

DONOR'S SIGNATURE: —————————————————— DATE: ——————
WITNESS: ————————————— WITNESS: ——————————————

This simple form, though printed so small as to be nearly impossible to fill out and use, represents a state of things very different
from that prevailing in the days of Jeremiah Cruncher. Not only
has medical science greatly advanced, making possible organ trans-
plants inconceivable in Dickens's day, but attitudes and prejudices,
religious and other, toward the dissection and exploitation of human remains have profoundly altered. "The history of tolerance
and popularity of human dissection," says Jack Kevorkian, "closely
parallels the history of evolution of human values, the history of
the conquest of stultified superstition by enlightened reason, the
history of philosophy in the various social and cultural settings of
its tortuous, complex, but progressive course" (JK iii).

For most of human history, human dissection has not been well
regarded because of tribal and national traditions and taboos, religious doctrine, and esthetic considerations. For a long time, also,
men were ignorant of the potential value of such research, and
there was often a general assumption that dissections of animals
provided enough knowledge and insight to go on with. The great
breakthrough was provided by the French Revolution, as will be
seen below.

It can be inferred from the Talmud that rabbis among the ancient
Hebrews dissected animals used in sacrifice, particularly cattle,
sheep, and poultry. But Jewish doctrine explicitly forbade human
dissection as degrading and a desecration to the dead person. Only
the bodies of those somehow dishonored in life were ever available.

The Egyptians, though they had advanced embalming techniques, did not dissect. They decried molestation of corpses, for
they believed the human body survived on some plane in the af-
terlife.

Hippocrates expressed no doctrinal antipathy to human dissection, but there is no evidence that he ever used it. The Greeks
generally had great respect for the dead body: they believed that

Charles Dickens's principal illustrator, Hablôt K. Browne ("Phiz"), did this impression of body snatchers at work for *A Tale of Two Cities*, but the illustration was not used.

the soul wandered by the Styx until its remains had been buried or cremated.

Diogenes (412–323 B.C.E.) thought reverence for human corpses was ridiculous and should be eradicated: once the soul had left the body the remains were trash. Aristotle (384–322 B.C.E.) was less doctrinaire on the split between soul and body, but he did think that the corpse was no longer the human being. The Stoics said death was simply the separation of divine reason from earthly matter. Epicurus (341–270 B.C.E.) thought death was final, total extinction, which made the body simply food for worms. And so there came a shift.

In Ptolemy's Alexandria, after the death of Alexander the Great (356–323 B.C.) there occurred a liberal golden age for human dissection, evidenced by the writings of Pliny, Celsus, Galen, and Tertullian. Galen (129–99) thought human dissection had been practiced by the ancients, who passed their lore down orally from father to son. The first to correlate the patient's symptoms (complaints) and his signs (what could be seen and felt) with what was found upon examining the "affected part of the deceased," he is considered the father of modern medicine.

The philosophers of those days favored the study of anatomy, but dissection was usually thought unnecessary: surface topography, examinations of wounds, and animal analogies were enough. No studies systematizing anatomy have come down to us, perhaps because of the destruction of the great library of Alexandria by the Romans in 48 B.C.E. Thereafter, human dissection was thought unnecessary. It had hit-or-miss status for a thousand stagnant years.

There was one anomaly: under Roman law a woman who had died pregnant could not be buried before the fetus was removed, on the ground that it might be viable. This was the first time any form of postmortem examination was mandated by law. Later Christian doctrine harmonized with this to assure baptism of the fetus. But for religious and sentimental reasons there remained a strong societal aversion to dissection. Rome, in particular, stringently protected the remains and graves of the dead. Cicero once said that the deceased should be considered "deified." Even dead gladiators were inviolate.

Teutonic law made molesting a corpse a criminal act, and the Koran forbade mutilation of corpses.

Innocent III (1198–1216), the most powerful Pope of the Dark

Ages, strongly opposed human dissection, and in 1300 Boniface VIII issued a bull threatening excommunication for dissection or "cooking out" bones (a common practice during the Crusades for bodies being brought home for burial), with a punishment as extreme as burning at the stake. Later, however, forensic postmortems were allowed for the many Popes who had died under suspicious circumstances!

With the arrival of the Renaissance, the pendulum swung again. Frederick II (1194–1250) of Sicily, founder of the Universities of Padua and Naples, decreed in 1238 that every two years the bodies of two executed criminals be delivered to the medical schools for an "Anatomica Publica," which every physician was obliged to attend. It was the first time human dissection was endorsed by the state. The spark spread to France and Spain. In 1314, the French sanctioned examinations in cases of violent death. A school for pathologic anatomy was founded at the monastery at Guadelupe in Spain in 1322.

In 1440, the first teaching dissection was performed in Vienna. A graduate from Padua took a full week for the demonstration. Development in Germany was slow: only in 1485 did the University at Tübingen permit a public dissection—once every three or four years.

Leonardo da Vinci (1462–1519) did pioneer work with a high degree of accuracy. He dissected over thirty corpses, noting "abnormal anatomy," and left over 750 annotated sketches. Michelangelo in 1495 dissected bodies supplied by a local monastery. In 1523, Pope Clement VII explicitly authorized human dissection for teaching purposes.

The sixteenth century was "the century of anatomy." Belgian Andreas Vesalius (1514–64) in *Seven Books on the Structure of the Human Body* (1543) challenged hundreds of Galen's tenets. Hearing of the work, Emperor Charles V asked for guidance from his Theological Council at Salamanca. It ruled favorably, but the Inquisition later sentenced Vesalius to death, commuting their decision to require a pilgrimage to Jerusalem.

Grave robbing was already a common practice. Medical men were desperate for subjects to work on, and there were never enough available through legal means. Vesalius himself had set a precedent by stealing a body from a gibbet outside Louvain. In Padua, Naples, and Salerno, students followed his example.

With the philosophers Spinoza, Descartes, Francis Bacon, and later John Locke, the scientific method arrived. The stranglehold of dogma was broken, and by the seventeenth century studies in anatomy, pathology, and physiology were well established. Human dissection was the essential underpinning.

Forensic anatomy arrived last in England. The great William Harvey (1578–1657) in *The Circulation of the Blood* (1628) remarked: "I venture to say that the examination of a single body of one who has died of tabes or some other disease of long standing or poisonous nature, is of more service to medicine than the dissection of the bodies of ten men who have been hanged" (JK 56).

But the continent led the way. The autopsy came of age with Giovanni Morgagni, the father of modern pathology, who described what could be seen in the body with the naked eye. In *On the Seats and Causes of Diseases as Investigated by Anatomy* (1761), he compared symptoms and observations in some 700 patients with the anatomical findings developed when their dead bodies could be examined. The study of the patient had replaced the study of books.

Rudolf Virchow (1821–1902) of Berlin, who introduced the doctrine of cellular continuity of all life into pathology, commented that "there is in human nature a strong tendency to sink into mysticism rather than to seek the tedious but correct way to orderly thinking" (JK 60). It was indeed a long time before men could overcome this tendency and turn to nature and experimentation for answers to questions on the essence, causes, and mechanisms of a disease.

The French Revolution provided the impetus for that surge. With the death of the old school, there appeared a fresh materialism that embraced the new order of logic and demanded analytical proof to back up ideas. Gone were purely speculative sciences. "*From the ashes of the eighteenth century Frenchmen wrested anatomic and pathologic leadership from Italy and led the medical world into the most glorious century of achievement it has ever known*" (JK 63–64; emphasis added).

Paris was the dynamic center, and in pathology Vienna took the lead. Carol von Rokitansky (1804–78) personally performed 30,000 necropsies from 1827 to 1866 (aided by the fact that the law made relatives' consent unnecessary).

In England, the great figure was Sir Astley Cooper (1768–1841).

He changed human dissection from a slipshod, unscientific affair into a discipline and was a prime consumer of burgled bodies. But England was far behind Europe in human dissection. Part of the reason may have been a lack of resolve among those who needed the improvements being made elsewhere but could not muster the political will and muscle to get change; another part was surely Christian fundamentalism and ignorance. The dissenters were literalists: the human body was sacred because it would rise again on the Last Day.

BODY-SNATCHING IN ENGLAND AND IN DICKENS

A sub-theme in *A Tale of Two Cities* revolves around the industry of "resurrecting" human cadavers from their fresh graves and selling them to medical men and laboratories willing to ask no questions, so they could engage in research on human anatomy through dissection. As we have seen, for most of at least the previous 1,800 years, there had been stringent religious and legal taboos against such activities, partly resulting (predominantly so in England) from a literal Christian belief in the resurrection of the body, which presumably would not be available for the Second Coming and Judgment Day if it had been demolished in a laboratory.

This taboo had first been set aside in Italy in the early thirteenth century. The Enlightenment and the French Revolution completed the shift, and by the early nineteenth century French hospitals routinely engaged in human dissection, as Thomas Carlyle was startled to discover when he visited Paris in 1824.

In 1858, Henry Morley wrote an article that Dickens published in his periodical *Household Words*, entitled "Use and Abuse of the Dead":

Thirty years ago, in England, it is hardly exaggeration to say, that there no more existed honest means of studying the Divine handiwork in our own frame than in the days of Vesalius, three hundred years ago. The necessity of dissection was indeed admitted, but the power to dissect, except by encouragement of desecration, was denied. Churchyards were robbed, sick chambers were robbed; the high price that anatomists were compelled to pay for means of study tempted wretched men to commit murder. . . . In those days the calling of the resurrectionist was followed as an independent business by men who took pride in it, scorned the clumsiness of amateurs, and even resented all intrusion in the churchyards over which they had established claims.

Dickens's resurrection man, Jerry Cruncher, makes a surprisingly adroit defense of his activities to Jarvis Lorry:

> I don't say it is, but even if it wos. And which it is to be took into account that if it wos, it wouldn't, even then, be all o' one side. There'd be two sides to it. There might be medical doctors at the present hour, a picking up their guineas where a honest tradesman don't pick up his fardens [farthings]—fardens! no, nor yet his half fardens—half fardens! no, nor yet his quarter—a banking away like smoke at Tellson's, and a cocking their medical eyes at that tradesman on the sly, a going in and going out to their own carriages— ah! equally like smoke, if not more so. Then, wot with undertakers, and wot with parish clerks, and wot with sextons, and wot with private watchmen (all awaricious and all in it), a man wouldn't get much by it, even if it wos so. And wot little a man did get, would never prosper with him, Mr Lorry. He'd never have no good of it; he'd want all along to be out of the line, if he could see his way out, being once in—even if it wos so. (*TTC* iii 9)

English and Scottish medical students seeking to study anatomy were handicapped by a statute adopted in 1540 under Henry VIII, which granted the Company of Barber Surgeons only four bodies of convicted and executed murderers per year. It was otherwise illegal to obtain corpses for the purposes of dissection. Although many other crimes were punishable by death (see Chapter 10), only convicted murderers knew their bodies would be food for the surgeons.

The stipulation that only the bodies of criminals might be used— and the further stipulation that it should be murderers and not those who committed any of the two hundred other crimes that qualified them for hanging—made dissection appear to be not only a part of the punishment but also a sort of ultimate sanction for the worst of crimes. So great a stigma was attached to it that people who came to witness hanging would find their enjoyment marred by violent fights between servants of the College of Surgeons and relations of the deceased: the latter determined that their departed friend should not be taken away for dissection, preferring—in a question where it would seem that little room for preference existed—that he should receive the alternative punishment of being gutted, dipped in a tar barrel, and hung up in chains. Even among the non-criminal classes, this sense of the shame attached to dissection reinforced their inherent revulsion from it. (HC 8)

Over time, and particularly because of recurrent wars with the French, there came to be a great need for surgeons with skill and knowledge. These men, hearing of developments on the Continent, were restive under the old restrictions. By the early eighteenth century, grave robbing had become common. The term "resurrection" was in use by 1742. There was much resistance to the practice, however. In 1788 the Court of King's Bench ruled that grave robbing was *contra bonos mores*—against good conscience—and made it a misdemeanor.

Nevertheless, by the end of the century, resurrection men were in serious business. Usually, they had been themselves grave diggers or sextons, or, at the other end of the supply chain, had learned the ropes as hospital porters or dissecting-room attendants. They solicited surgeons' orders for the number and type of bodies needed, sometimes demanding a large down payment at the beginning of the "season" (October to May, when the anatomy schools were open) to fund their expenses. They bribed watchmen and sextons, exhumed bodies, delivered them to hospitals and collected payment from dissecting-room superintendents or the surgeons themselves. They used safe houses to store bodies at night (transport was safer during the day). There were side markets for human teeth and hair: fashion demanded wigs of real hair, dentures of real teeth, so these items would be removed before the corpse went to the laboratory.

Relatives of the dead were frantic to protect their loved ones from the desecration of resurrection. They would scatter flowers, shells, pebbles, and other markers on the graves, carefully noting their locations and checking later to be sure there had been no disturbance. The resurrectionists, in turn, would reconnoiter after a funeral, noting grave locations, the markers on site, and any traps (tripwires to spring guns came into use as the abuses grew worse). Considerable ingenuity was used to devise "patent coffins," which, once closed, could not be opened again (from the outside).

At night, the grave robbers would arrive, having bribed watchmen and sextons to look the other way. They would carefully note the location of any markers and then place them to one side. Then, digging easily through the freshly disturbed soil, they would expose the coffin where the head and shoulders lay. With a crowbar or screw tool they pried up the lid till it snapped against the earth, weighing down the rest of the coffin. They would fish out the corpse with ropes around the neck or hooks fixed to the shroud. (They were scrupulous to leave all clothing and other effects in the coffin, for the penalties for theft were much greater than for body snatching.) They would double up the body, rope it, and put it in a sack. The earth from the grave, which had been carefully placed on canvas or sacking, would be tipped back and smoothed over. The markers would be carefully replaced.

Surgeons were hard-pressed to provide bodies for their students or risk losing them to competing medical schools, which were proliferating. Sir Astley Cooper, when facing a difficult procedure, liked to practice on a body first and was one of the resurrectionists' most active customers. As leader of the Anatomical Club, to which all operating surgeons in London belonged, he led the resistance to a strike by the resurrectionists, who wanted to raise their prices. The surgeons won that battle, and prices stabilized at four guineas for an adult, with a half-guinea discount if the body had already been "opened"; a guinea upwards for a "small," reckoned by body length; and a half guinea for a fetus.

There were many bizarre occurrences. In 1801, raiding parish officers found two men and a woman drinking tea, with the corpses of two children reposing at the end of their bench and six bodies in the next room. In 1812 on New Year's Day, resurrectionists dug up three adults and sold them to the same hospitals that had buried them. A coachman once arrived at a doctor's house with a body in a sack. When the customer kicked the bundle to roll it down his basement steps, there was a grunt from the occupant, a fully-clothed young man in a drunken stupor. The doctor feared a burglary "plant." He shouted after the coach: "There's a live man in this sack!" "That's all right, guv'nor," said the coachman. "Just kill him off when you're ready for him."

The populace took a dim view of resurrection men. Once in the 1820s an enraged mob seized a practitioner and nearly buried him alive. Then they rushed to his house, smashed his furniture, seized his wife and children, and dragged them through a stagnant pond.

One of the many horrific aspects of this traffic involved the prisoners on the hulks, the prison ships that figure in Dickens's *Great Expectations*. They were a fine source of income for the doctors charged with the duty of tending them, as Robert Hughes notes:

Even the doctors were on the take . . . when a hulk prisoner died, his corpse would sometimes be sold for £5 or £6 to the dissectors' agents who haunted the docks, instead of being buried on the cemetery mudbank in the Portsmouth estuary known as Rat's Castle. And die they did, in numbers, because *the naval doctors saw no harm in bleeding a sick prisoner a pint too much.* Then the coffin would be rowed to Rat's Castle, where a chaplain intoned his brief exequies over a box full of stones and sand. Thus, few prisoners looked foward to a spell in the hospital hulk. (RH 142; emphasis added)

In 1828, Parliament appointed a select committee to study the stiuation. Its report acknowledged that body snatching had reached epidemic proportions. There was an extraordinary spate of murders by William Burke (at least sixteen by him alone) and William Hare in Edinburgh in the period 1827–29. These men deliberately selected their victims for their postmortem salability to laboratories. The term "Burking" has become part of the English language.

The committee chairman introduced a bill in Parliament in 1829. Bodies in hospitals and workhouses that had not been claimed seventy-two hours after death were to be sold for dissection. It was an offense to move a dead body without a license. Grave robbing was punishable by six months imprisonment for a first offense, two years for a second. The Anatomy Act of 1831 became law, and the "resurrection man" was soon a thing of the past.

Five years later, Charles Dickens began work on *The Posthumous Papers of the Pickwick Club*, which included an early example of his humorous take on medical dissection:

"Nothing like dissecting, to give one an appetite," said Mr Bob Sawyer, looking round the table.

Mr Pickwick slightly shuddered.

"By the bye, Bob," said Mr Allen, "have you finished that leg yet?"

"Nearly," replied Sawyer, helping himself to half a fowl as he spoke. "It's a very muscular one for a child's."

"Is it?" inquired Mr Allen, carelessly.

"Very," said Bob Sawyer, with his mouth full.

"I've put my name down for an arm, at our place," said Mr Allen. "We're clubbing for a subject, and the list is nearly full, only we can't get hold of any fellow that wants a head. I wish you'd take it."

"No," replied Bob Sawyer, "can't afford expensive luxuries."
"Nonsense!" said Allen.

"Can't indeed," rejoined Bob Sawyer. "I wouldn't mind a brain, but I couldn't stand a whole head." (*PP* 30)

VIEW IN EDINBURGH.

TAKEN ON THE SPOT.

Caricature of Dr. Robert Knox, a customer for murdered bodies delivered by Burke and Hare.

TOPICS FOR WRITTEN AND ORAL DISCUSSION

1. Jeremiah Cruncher, the "resurrection man," adds color and humor to *A Tale of Two Cities*, but there is more to it than that. What contribution does his recent experience in his specialty make to the plot at a critical juncture? Explain.

2. Why is Cruncher so offended by the punishment proposed to be inflicted on Darnay if he is found guilty of treason?

3. Have you made any decision about how you would like your body disposed of if you should suffer a premature demise? What factors would bear on your choice?

4. Does it surprise you that England should have been so far behind other countries in the science of dissection? What reasons would you pick out as the most convincing explanations of this?

SUGGESTED READINGS AND WORKS CITED

Bailey, Brian J. *The Resurrection Men: A History of the Trade in Corpses*. London: Madonald, 1991.

HC   Cole, Hubert. *Things for the Surgeons: A History of the Resurrection Men*. London: Heinemann, 1964.

PP   Dickens, Charles. *The Posthumous Papers of the Pickwick Club*. London: Chapman and Hall, 1837.

Fido, Martin. *Bodysnatchers: A History of the Resurrectionists 1742–1832*. London: Weidenfeld and Nicolson, 1988.

RH   Hughes, Robert. *The Fatal Shore*. New York: Alfred A. Knopf, 1986.

JK   Kevorkian, Jack. *The Story of Dissection*. New York: Philosophical Library, 1959.

Lassek, Arthur M. *Human Dissection: Its Drama and Struggle*. Springfield, Ill.: Thomas, 1958.

Marshall, Tim. *Murdering to Dissect: Grave-Robbing, Frankenstein and the Anatomy Literature*. Manchester, N.Y.: Manchester University Press, 1995.

Richardson, Ruth. *Death, Dissection and the Destitute*. London and New York: Routledge and Kegan Paul, 1987.

Glossary

Dickens and Carlyle make a good many references which the readers of their day understood but which may be obscure to readers now. Here are some explanations. Foreign terms and slang are italicized. The terms cited include references in the novel which are not found in this volume.

Æolus Hall. Cave of the Winds. In Greek and Roman mythology, Æolus was the god of the winds, whom Ulysses visited.

Aggerawators. Cockney slang for men's side-curls. Jeremiah Cruncher, using the term in the singular, obviously means that his wife's ostentatious "flopping" to pray on her knees is aggravating his conscience.

Armagnac Massacres. Supporters of Bernard VII, Count of Armagnac in early fifteenth-century civil strife, suffered devastating reprisals for their opposition to John of Burgundy, and his collaboration with the invading English in the early stages of the Hundred Years War.

Ashantee. A region in what is now northern Ghana; the Ashanti were war-like, brutal people who specialized in selling defeated tribesmen into slavery, particularly their southern neighbors, the Fanti. To deal with these incursions, the British Governor of a series of outposts on the coast, Sir Charles McCarthy, led a force into a disaster at Bonsaso in 1824. He was killed, and his skull was later used as a drinking-cup by the Ashanti chieftain. This historical detail may have been in Dickens's mind as a parallel with the days when the heads of the executed were displayed on Temple Bar.

Assignats. The French government, having confiscated substantial amounts of real estate from some aristocrats, but especially from the Catholic Church, issued currency backed by the property. The *assignats* were the paper money of the Revolution.

Barmecide room. In Dickens's favorite childhood reading, the *Arabian Nights*, there is a story of a Prince Barmecide, at whose palace a magnificent feast was laid; but when the covers were taken off the dishes there was nothing on the plates underneath.

Barrier. The word for the gate in one of the several barriers (walls or fences constructed to control traffic and facilitate customs collection) is *barrière*, and Dickens gives us a flavor of French by using a near equivalent in English rather than an idiomatic translation; this device informs the reader that French is being spoken: The Barrière St.-Denis and the Barrière de la Villette guarded the roads between Paris and the northern coastal ports. The original enclosure of Paris by the so-called "Wall of the Farmers-General" occurred under Calonne. In 1783, fifteen miles or so were reconstructed, and the architect Ledoux designed seventeen large toll-houses and thirty others. The barriers were assaulted by the Paris mob in 1789. Collections at the barriers were discontinued in 1792, and the gates fell into disuse, though most were not torn down until 1860. Four still exist: d'Enfer, de Vincennes, de la Villette and de Monceau.

Bartholomew Butchery. The Massacre of St. Bartholomew, August 24, 1572 (the eve of the saint's day), when French Protestants, particularly their leadership, which was in Paris for a royal wedding, were hunted down and killed on orders of King Charles IX at his mother's initial instigation, on pretext of a Protestant plot against the crown. Three thousand people died in Paris alone.

Bedlam. The common name applied to the Bethlehem Hospital for the insane.

Bed-winch. A crank, lever, or pulley used in raising or adjusting a bed-frame, as Procrustes might have done.

Beelzebub. "Lord of the flies," or (in Matthew 12:24), the prince of the devils. In Milton's *Paradise Lost*, Beelzebub is one of the fallen angels, next to Satan in power.

Blood-money. Blood money was paid as a reward for or an inducement to commit murder.

Bull's eye of the Court. The *Salle de l'Oeuil de Boeuf* was the antechamber to the State Apartments in the king's palace at Versailles, where the central administrative functions of France were conducted. Here, courtiers vied for visibility to the king in the daily royal *levée*. The room had a prominent oval window, from which the whole suite took the name of the "Bull's Eye."

Calendar of the Revolution. The calendar in revolutionary France consisted of twelve thirty-day months (three ten-day weeks in each), and five festival days. The revolution was considered to have begun September 21, 1792, at the autumnal equinox, so the first three months are autumnal: *Vendémiaire* (vintage), *Brumaire* (fog), *Frimaire* (frost); then the winter three: *Nivôse, Pluviôse, Ventôse* (snow, rain, and wind); the spring: *Germinal, Floréal, Prairial* (bud, flower, meadow); and summer: *Messidor, Thermidor, Fructidor* (reap, heat, fruit).

Capet Veto. Capet was the family name of Louis XVI. The phrase refers to his power (at the outset of the Convention) to veto its decrees.

Carmagnole, la. A popular Revolutionary dance or jig, and also a short woolen jacket worn by immigrant laborers from Italy, accompanied by a blue, white, and red cummerbund and a red hat. Carmagnola is a town in the Piedmont region of northern Italy.

Chaldean. Dickens uses the word to refer to a language spoken by an ancient Semitic people that ruled for a time in Babylonia.

Champ-de-Mars. The parade ground in Paris where troops were mustered and large rallies of the populace took place.

Chimera. In Greek mythology, a fire-breathing monster, with the head of a lion, the body of a goat, and the tail of a dragon.

Ci-devant. Formerly, a short-hand term for the deposed, unfrocked, or expelled; a disenfranchised, dispropertied aristocrat.

Cimmerian. A reference to a mythical people whose land Homer described as being in perpetual mist and darkness; dark, gloomy.

Citoyen, Citoyenne. The terms for male and female citizens in revolutionary France. This came to be the mode of salutation to a fellow, friend, or stranger.

Clerkenwell. A borough in north London.

Cock-Lane ghost. This famous hoax was perpetrated in 1762 by William Parsons, who lived at 33 Cock Lane in the Smithfield district of London. He owed money to a man named Kent. He said the knocking sounds he could hear were made by "Fanny," who had been murdered by Kent, her brother-in-law, but after a year of wonderment and investigation, in which the famous Dr. Samuel Johnson participated, Parsons's daughter was exposed as the "rapper," using a board she concealed in her bed. Parsons went to the pillory, and interest in Spiritualism was dealt a blow.

Convulsionists. A fanatical religious sect in France, who believed their ills would be cured if they went into a trance at the tomb of François de

Paris, a Jansenist buried at Saint-Médard, near Paris. Their "convulsions," which became known in the 1730s, were like those of the dervishes and the Shakers and were held to be evidence of Divine possession.

Cordeliers. Members of one of the moderate leftist political clubs active in the Convention, including Hébert (known as *Père Duchesne* for his journalist's nom-de-plume); most were arrested March 15, 1794 and guillotined.

Debtors' prison. Well into Dickens's day, debtors who could not pay their obligations were sent to special prisons, to remain there until their debts were forgiven or discharged: they sometimes died there.

Dover mail. The coach carrying mail and passengers to the Dover–Calais packet, or ferry; in 1775 and for decades after, long-distance mail delivery was by special fast stage-coach, so-called because at intervals (stages) along the road there were wayside inns where ostlers (grooms) would rush fresh horses into service as passengers had refreshment.

Drag. A shoe brake used on coaches when descending a steep grade.

Dragoon march. A forced pace.

Drawer. A waiter, who typically drew wine or beer from the cask. The term fell out of use during the nineteenth century.

Epos. A primitive epic poem, handed down by word of mouth over long periods of time.

Fabled rustic. In popular legend, he succeeded in raising the Devil and then fled him in terror.

Farmer-general. The *fermier-général* bought for a fixed amount the right to be a tax collector, and enriched himself greatly, if he could, by keeping the balance of what he collected. He served a useful function in financing the government by making advances against expected collections. The farmers-general took in about one-third of the government's revenues, from indirect taxes primarily on salt (*gabelle*) and tobacco and were naturally hated by the poor who had to pay these imposts.

Fata Morgana. A seductive mirage or illusion, "fata" is the Italian word for "fairy," and commonly refers to a vision seen at sea from the shore. Morgan le Fay ("Morgana the Fairy") was King Arthur's wicked sister who employed arts of illusion and deception in trying to bring about his death.

Feuillants. Members (allegedly, and some actually, Royalist) of one of the relatively conservative "constitutional" political clubs active on the right in the Convention.

Fermier général. *See* Farmer-general.

Finger-post. A directional sign at a crossroads, shaped to resemble an arm with a hand at the end, a finger pointing.

Flambeau. A torch.

Furies. In classical mythology and the plays of Euripedes, three female spirits, Alecto, Megæra, and Tisiphone, with snaky hair. They avenged unpunished crimes.

Gabelle. The "salt tax" was actually a law requiring the purchase of a fixed amount of salt annually at a price set by the government. It gave its name to Darnay's faithful family retainer, whose plight nearly cost Darnay his life.

Girondists. A constitutional faction in the Convention, led by Brissot and Vergniaud. Eventually overwhelmed by the Jacobin extremists, most of its members were guillotined.

Gorgon. In classical mythology, any of three terrible sisters with snakes for hair, the sight of whom would turn the beholder into stone. Their names were Stheno, Euryale, and Medusa, the last slain by Perseus who dealt with her by looking at her reflection in his shield.

Hangman. In 1775 in England, several hundred offenses, including minor thievery, were punishable by death, and Dickens enumerates some in *A Tale of Two Cities* in the first chapter of Book ii.

Harlequin. In French and Italian comedy and English pantomime, this stock character wore gay, spangled tights of many colors.

Hilary term. A term, running from January 11 through 31, when the law courts at Westminster were in session.

Into the Gazette. Going into bankruptcy. The *London Gazette* was and is the publication in which bankruptcies are announced.

Jack-boot. A heavy, sturdy boot reaching above the knee.

Jacobins. Members of the relatively extremist political clubs active on the Left in the Convention; led by Danton, Marat, and Robespierre.

"Jacques." This code name was based on a peasant uprising in northern France in 1357–58, which began in the countryside around Beauvais. The rebels called themselves *Jacquerie* after "Jacques Bonhomme"—a name applied to a serf. The revolt was put down with great cruelty and massacre by the local nobles and their private armies, led by the Duke of Orléans and others.

Jalousie-blinds. A window-shade of sloping, overlapping horizontal slats, used to keep out the sun while letting in light and air, akin to Venetian blinds.

Jansenist. A follower of Cornelius Jansen (1585–1638), a Roman Catholic archbishop of Ypres, in Flanders, who denied free will and believed in irresistible grace.

Jezebel. The wife of Ahab (1 Kings 16, 21), she was noted for flamboyance and treachery; she instigated a murder so that her husband might have a vineyard he craved.

Kennel. The gutter that ran down the center of most urban streets to carry off waste and filth; a source of stench and disease in poor neighborhoods.

"King with a large jaw." The English king George III, who reigned from 1760–1820. His "plain" queen was Charlotte Sophia of Mecklenburg-Strelitz, to whom he was devoted.

Laudanum. A liquid opiate or tranquilizing drug. Tincture of opium was frequently used for medicinal purposes in Dickens's time.

Law Terms. The courts at Westminster were open, until the Judicature Act of 1873, only during the four "terms": *Michaelmas* in November; *Hilary* in January, *Easter* from late April to early May, and *Trinity*, which ran from late May to June, with a long break (Long Vacation) between the end of Trinity and the commencement of Michaelmas.

Lettre de cachet. The infamous device used by the privileged in France; "filling up blank forms for the consignment of any one to the oblivion of a prison for any length of time" as the Evrémondes did to Doctor Manette in 1755, and which was declared unlawful by the Paris Parliament on May 3, 1788. In its extreme abuse, letters were sold, with blanks to be filled in with names afterward by the purchaser, who could thus take private revenge on an enemy.

Life Guards. A mounted military corps attached to the Royal Household, responsible for the monarch's safety.

Loadstone rock. The inexorably magnetic, deadly rock in a tale from the *Arabian Nights*.

Loaves and fishes. The reference is to the famous Biblical story of Jesus Christ's miraculous feeding of the multitude who had come to hear him.

Long Vacation. The long break between court sittings in Trinity term, which ended in June, and the reopening of the courts for Michaelmas term in November.

Lucifer. The Devil, or fallen angel, in Milton's *Paradise Lost*.

Mammon. The principle of worldliness and self-aggrandizement: No man can serve two masters. . . . You cannot serve God and mammon (Matthew 6:24, Luke 16:13).

Mangle. A mechanical device with rollers set close together to squeeze water out of laundry after washing.

Megæra. *See* Furies.

MENE, MENE. the first words of the famous "writing on the wall": *mene, mene, tekel upharsin* (translated from the Aramaic: numbered, numbered, weighed and divided), which the Biblical Daniel interpreted to mean that God had weighed Belshazzar and his kingdom, found them wanting, and would destroy them (Daniel 5:25).

Michaelmas. A term in November when the Westminster law courts were in session.

Miserere. From the *Agnus Dei* portion of the Catholic Mass, "have mercy." "*Agnus Dei, qui tollis peccata mundi, miserere nobis*: Lamb of God, who takest away the sins of the world, have mercy upon us."

Moloch. Originally a Canaanite idol to whom children were sacrificed as burnt offerings (Leviticus 18:21 and 2 Kings 23:10); hence an object or deity to whom horrible sacrifices are made. In John Milton's *Paradise Lost*, one of the chief fallen angels.

Montagnards. The elite component of the Jacobins, "the Mountain," so-called because they sat at the top of the steeply raked benches in the hall of the Convention.

Newgate. The English prison outside of which public hangings took place after 1783.

Nonjurant priest. A Catholic priest who refused to take the oath of loyalty to the Revolution, adhering instead to his primary fealty to the Pope.

Noun-substantive. A group of words which in syntax function as a noun.

North Tower. There were in fact two "north towers": the Tour du Puits (shafts or pits) and the Tour du Coin (corner), which were the most secure of the eight towers in the Bastille.

Old Bailey. Criminals were commonly tried in the Old Bailey Court, always referred to by the name of the street it was on (it is now called the Central Criminal Court), and there was a prison there as well.

Orcus. In Roman mythology, the Lower World, otherwise Hades or Hell.

Pallet-bed. A platform bed, with a straw mattress and no springs.

Parlement. one of thirteen courts of law which heard cases on appeal and a variety of special cases, such as sedition, forgery, and document tampering. Parlement also had administrative responsibilities and could set prices in times of emergency and regulate markets. The Paris Parlement had a kind of veto since it had to "register" decrees of the crown before they were enforceable; parlement members were nobility, ranging in number from fifty to one hundred thirty.

Perspective-glass. A telescope.

Pillory. A device, sometimes called the "stocks," with holes for the head and hands, where prisoners would be exposed to public ridicule, showers of refuse, or even stoning. It had a flavor of democracy to it, in that public opinion importantly determined the severity of the punishment, "of which," says Dickens, "no one could foresee the extent."

The Plain. As distinguished from the Mountain, the independent Assemblymen whose seats were lower down, near the debating floor of the chamber.

Poet on a stool. Dante Alighieri, who "mused in the sight of men."

Posting-house. A wayside inn serving stage-coaches passing through.

Pythia. In ancient Greece, the high priestess of Apollo at Delphi, who was believed to be in communion with the god Apollo and to voice his oracles. "Pythian," as Carlyle uses it, would mean "oracular," or uncannily in communion with the beyond.

Ranelagh. An upscale amusement resort in London, east of Chelsea Hospital, with extensive gardens and a great rotunda built in 1742 but torn down in 1804.

Rossignol. Literally "nightingale"; in the context of Maton's prison memoir it meant one who comes to take a prisoner to be executed.

Royal George Hotel. This fictional hostelry may have been modeled on the Ship, a hotel in Dover that was torn down in the 1860s when the railway line was extended.

St Dunstan's side. The church of St Dunstan's-in-the-West was near the Temple Bar.

St Giles. A slum district frequented by criminals, usually avoided by the police in 1775.

Sansculottism. The extremist Revolution ("without trousers"). The *sans-culottes* were the laboring and small merchant classes who wore ankle-length pantaloons instead of the knee breeches (*culottes*) and silk stockings of the upper classes.

Sardanapalus. A seventh century Assyrian king, also known as Assurbanipal and noted for luxurious display.

Scavenger. A collector of rubbish, dirt, and garbage from streets and alleys.

Sessions. Courts of law.

Sicilian Vespers. A massacre of some 2,000 French people that began at evening service (vespers) on Easter Monday, 1282, in Palermo, Sicily. It initiated the Sicilian revolt against the oppressive polices of the Angevin (French) king of Naples-Sicily. The subject of an early Verdi opera.

Skid the wheel. Setting a brake, or "drag," to prevent a coach's wheels from spinning too rapidly; forestalling a runaway on a downhill slope.

Snuff. A preparation of powdered tobacco consumed by sniffing, or by being applied to the gums with a snuff-stick. If fiery enough, inhaling snuff caused a convulsive sneeze, which was considered a pleasurably cathartic experience.

Mrs Southcott. Joanna Southcott (1750–1814) was a farmer's daughter and religious fanatic who gained a substantial following among the credulous with her doggerel prophecies and supernatural claims.

State-projector. A government official in pre-Revolutionary France.

Stuart. "[T]he merry Stuart who sold" England was Charles II, who, it was claimed, accepted a pension from the king of France after his restoration to the throne in 1660.

Stylites. Saint Simeon Stylites (387–459) was the earliest of the Christian ascetic "pillar saints" who lived the last thirty years of his life on top of a column about seventy-feet high near Antioch and preached to the crowds below. His many imitators were called Stylites.

Tartarus. In Greek mythology, the infernal abyss below even Hades, where Zeus hurled the rebel Titans; or simply Hell.

Tartuffe. The hero of a play of the same name by Molière, Tartuffe is the quintessence of hypocrisy who, feigning piety, gains access to the household of the credulous Orgon and tries to seduce his wife. Failing, he attempts to ruin the family. The name is sometimes spelled *Tartufe*.

Tellson's Bank. Dickens makes an inside joke when Lorry says, "We are quite a French House, as well as an English one," because he took the name from Théllusson's Bank in Paris, where Jacques Necker made his fortune before becoming France's finance minister.

The Temple. The common name for an area of law inns, attorney's chambers, quiet squares, and various nooks and crannies, extending, in Dickens's day, from Fleet Street to the Thames.

Temple Bar. A London landmark dividing the Strand from Fleet Street on which, in the good old days, the heads of the executed would be displayed.

Tergiversation. A twisting, evasive action, usually verbal.

Tocsin. An alarm bell.

Tophet. An Old Testament Hell, where human sacrifices by fire were made.

Turnham Green. A district in West London.

Tyburn. A place of public execution used until 1783, named for the stream (now called the Westbourne) which ran from Hampstead along what is now the Edgware Road and into the Thames. The site of the gallows was near the present Marble Arch. The triangular gallows on three legs, affectionately known as the "Tyburn Tree," was often used in executions of "traitors," often Roman Catholics who had violated the stringent laws against the practice of their religion.

Ultima ratio. The last reasoning (of kings), that is to say, artillery or other military force.

Vauxhall Gardens. A famous open-air recreation spot on the Surrey side of the Vauxhall Bridge; the gardens were closed in 1859.

Izaak Walton. A fisherman (1593–1683), author of *The Compleat Angler*.

War of the pygmies and cranes. In classical myth first told in the *Iliad*, a beautiful young girl, Oenoe, born among the Pygmies, was too proud for her own good and angered the goddess Hera. When Oenoe had a son, the pygmies brought gifts, but Hera transformed her into a stork (or crane), and when she tried to take her son the pygmies did not recognize her and drove her off, setting off ongoing enmity between their species.

Wise Arabian stories. The *Second Calender's Story* in the *Arabian Nights* includes the tale of a man enchanted into the form of an ape, and restored to his former shape.

Bibliography

The abbreviation that appears to the left of a title indicates that the work is quoted in this volume. Other works listed are suggested for further reading. The works listed under "Bibliography and Reference" point to many more references to the topics indicated.

WORKS BY CHARLES DICKENS

AN   *American Notes for General Circulation*. London, 1842.

BR   *Barnaby Rudge: A Tale of the Riots of 'Eighty*. London, 1841.

CHE   *A Child's History of England*. London, 1851–53.

CS/HT   *The Holly-Tree*. London, 1855.

DS   *Dombey and Son*. London, 1847.

HT   *Hard Times for These Times*. London, 1854.

HWC/IJ   "In and Out of Jail." *Household Words*. London, 1838.

PI   *Pictures from Italy*. London, 1842.

PP   *The Posthumous Papers of the Pickwick Club*. London, 1837.

TTC   *A Tale of Two Cities*. London, 1859.

BIOGRAPHY

Ackroyd, Peter. *Dickens*. New York: HarperCollins, 1990.

EJ   Johnson, Edgar. *Charles Dickens: His Tragedy and Triumph*. 2 vols. New York: Simon and Schuster, 1952.

Kaplan, Fred. *Dickens: A Biography*. Berkeley: University of California Press, 1983.

NOVELS BY OTHERS

France, Anatole. *The Gods Are Athirst*. Alfred Allinson, trans. London: John Lane, 1913.
Trollope, Anthony. *The Vendée*. 3 vols. London: Henry Colburn, 1850.

BIBLIOGRAPHY AND REFERENCE

Glancy, Ruth F. *A Tale of Two Cities: An Annotated Bibliography*. New York: Garland, 1993.
Johnson, Douglas, ed. *French Society and the Revolution*. Cambridge: Cambridge University Press, 1976.
Scott, Samuel F., and Rothaus, Barry. *Historical Dictionary of the French Revolution, 1789–1799*. 2 vols. Westport, Conn.: Greenwood Press, 1985.

THOMAS CARLYLE

Carlyle, Thomas. *The French Revolution*. New York: George Macy, 1956. Annotated edition: New York: Macmillan & Co. Ltd., 1921–1925.
FK   Kaplan, Fred. *Thomas Carlyle*. Berkeley and Los Angeles: University of California Press, 1993.

THE FRENCH REVOLUTION

Doyle, William. *The Origins of the French Revolution*. New York and London: Oxford University Press, 1981.
DD/AN   Durant, Will and Ariel. *The Age of Napoleon*. New York: Simon and Schuster, 1975.
DD/RR   ———. *Rousseau and Revolution*. New York: Simon and Schuster, 1967.
Lefebvre, Georges. *The Coming of the French Revolution*. Translated by R. R. Palmer. Princeton, N.J.: Princeton University Press, 1947.
SS   Schama, Simon. *Citizens: A Chronicle of the French Revolution*. New York: Vintage Books, 1990.
Soboul, Albert. *The French Revolution*. Translated by Alan Forrest and Colin Jones. New York: New Left Books, 1974.
HMW   Williams, Helen Maria. *An Eye-Witness Acount of the French Revolution*. Edited by Jack Fruchtman. New York: Peter Lang, 1996.

————. *Helen Williams and the French Revolution*. Edited by Jane Shuter. Austin, Tex.: Raintree Steck-Vaughn, 1996.

————. *Letters on the French Revolution, Written in France, in the Summer of 1790, to a Friend in England*. London: G. G. and J. Robinson, 1792.

Yalom, Marilyn. *Blood Sisters: The French Revolution in Women's Memory*. New York: Basic Books, 1933.

THE MOB AND THE TERROR

SL   Loomis, Stanley. *Paris in the Terror: June 1793–July 1794*. Philadelphia: Lippincott, 1964.

Peltier, Jean-Gabriel. *Dernier Tableau de Paris, ou Récit Historique de la Révolution du 10 Août*. London: By the author, 1792–93.

Rudé, George. *The Crowd in the French Revolution*. London and New York: Oxford University Press, 1967.

————. *Paris and London in the Eighteenth Century: Studies in Popular Protest*. London: Collins, 1970.

Soboul, Albert. *The Parisian Sans-Culottes and the French Revolution, 1793–4*. Translated by Gwynne Lewis. Oxford: Clarendon Press, 1964.

THE PRISONS

OB   Blanc, Olivier. *Last Letters: Prisons and Prisoners of the French Revolution, 1793–1794*. Translated by Alan Sheridan. London: Andre Deutsch, 1987.

Dauban, Charles-Aimé. *Les Prisons de Paris sous la Révolution*. Paris: H. Plon, 1870.

Jourgniac Saint-Méard, François de, et al. *Mémoires sur les Journées de Septembre 1792*. Paris: Firmin-Didot Frères, 1858.

MR   Roland, Marie-Jeanne. *Memoirs*. Translated and edited by Evelyn Shuckburgh. Mount Kisco, N.Y.: Moyer Bell, 1990.

REVOLUTION GENERALLY

Brinton, Crane. *A Decade of Revolution: 1789–1799*. New York and London: Harper and Bros., 1934.

CB   ————. *The Anatomy of Revolution*. New York: W. W. Norton, 1938.

Gurr, Ted Robert. *Why Men Rebel*. Princeton, N.J.: Princeton University Press, 1970.

Postgate, Raymond. *Revolution from 1789 to 1906*. New York: Harper and Row, 1920 [reprinted 1962].

DUE PROCESS

Fast, Howard. *Citizen Tom Paine*. New York: Duell, Sloan and Pearce, 1943.
O'Brien, Conor Cruise. "The Decline and Fall of the French Revolution." *New York Review of Books* 37, no. 2 (February 15, 1990).
Paine, Thomas. *Rights of Man*. New York: Heritage Press, 1961.

CAPITAL PUNISHMENT

HS Sanson, Henri. *Sept Générations d'Exécuteurs*. (English translation; selections). 2 vols. in 1. London. Chatto and Windus, 1876.

SOLITARY CONFINEMENT

Burney, Christopher. *Solitary Confinement*. London. Clarke and Cockeran, 1952.
Jackson, Michael. *Prisoners of Isolation: Solitary Confinement in Canada*. Toronto: University of Toronto Press, 1983.
Smith, George W. *A Defense of Solitary Confinement*. 1833.

DISSECTION AND "RESURRECTION"

Bailey, Brian J. *The Resurrection Men: A History of the Trade in Corpses*. London: Madonald, 1991.

Index

Numbers in italic refer to illustrations.

About the Author

GEORGE NEWLIN is the compiler and editor of the three-volume *Everyone in Dickens* (Greenwood Press, 1995) and of *Every Thing in Dickens* (Greenwood Press, 1996). He is now preparing a student casebook in the Literature in Context series on *Great Expectations*. His next major anthological work will be a multivolume series on Anthony Trollope. George Newlin has spent his professional career combining activities in law and finance with volunteer service in the arts and serious avocational musical performance. In 1988 he began developing his concept for a new kind of literary anthology, beginning with the works of Charles Dickens.

The Greenwood Press "Literature in Context" Series

Understanding *To Kill a Mockingbird*: A Student Casebook to Issues, Sources, and Historical Documents
Claudia Durst Johnson

Understanding *The Scarlet Letter*: A Student Casebook to Issues, Sources, and Historical Documents
Claudia Durst Johnson

Understanding *Adventures of Huckleberry Finn*: A Student Casebook to Issues, Sources, and Historical Documents
Claudia Durst Johnson

Understanding *Macbeth*: A Student Casebook to Issues, Sources, and Historical Documents
Faith Nostbakken

Understanding *Of Mice and Men, The Red Pony*, and *The Pearl*: A Student Casebook to Issues, Sources, and Historical Documents
Claudia Durst Johnson

Understanding Anne Frank's *The Diary of a Young Girl*: A Student Casebook to Issues, Sources, and Historical Documents
Hedda Rosner Kopf

Understanding *Pride and Prejudice*: A Student Casebook to Issues, Sources, and Historical Documents
Debra Teachman

Understanding *The Red Badge of Courage*: A Student Casebook to Issues, Sources, and Historical Documents
Claudia Durst Johnson

Understanding Richard Wright's *Black Boy*: A Student Casebook to Issues, Sources, and Historical Documents
Robert Felgar

Understanding *I Know Why the Caged Bird Sings*: A Student Casebook to Issues, Sources, and Historical Documents
Joanne Megna-Wallace

Understanding *The Crucible*: A Student Casebook to Issues, Sources, and Historical Documents
Claudia Durst Johnson and Vernon E. Johnson